Pattern Recognition by Humans and Machines

Volume 2

Visual Perception

This is a volume in
ACADEMIC PRESS
SERIES IN COGNITION AND PERCEPTION
A Series of Monographs and Treatises

Pattern Recognition by Humans and Machines

Volume 2

Visual Perception

Edited by

EILEEN C. SCHWAB

AT&T Information Systems
Indianapolis, Indiana

HOWARD C. NUSBAUM

Speech Research Laboratory
Indiana University
Bloomington, Indiana

1986

ACADEMIC PRESS, INC.
Harcourt Brace Jovanovich, Publishers
Orlando   San Diego   New York   Austin
Boston   London   Sydney   Tokyo   Toronto

ACADEMIC PRESS, INC.
Orlando, Florida 32887

United Kingdom Edition published by
ACADEMIC PRESS INC. (LONDON) LTD.
24–28 Oval Road, London NW1 7DX

LIBRARY OF CONGRESS CATALOGING-IN-PUBLICATION DATA

Main entry under title:

Pattern recognition by humans and machines.

(Academic Press series in cognition and
perception)
    Includes index.
    Contents: v. 1. Speech perception — v. 2 Visual.
perception.
    1. Pattern perception.   2. Pattern recognition
systems.   I. Schwab, Eileen C.   II. Nusbaum, Howard C.
III. Series.
BF311.B316   1986   001.53'4   85-20110
ISBN 0–12–631402–0 (v. 2: hardcover) (alk. paper)
ISBN 0–12–631404–7 (v. 2: paperback) (alk. paper)

PRINTED IN THE UNITED STATES OF AMERICA

86 87 88 89   9 8 7 6 5 4 3 2 1

Contents

BF3.11
P316
1986
v.2
OPTO

Preface

The basic problem of understanding how humans perceive information in the constant bombardment of sensory flux is, without question, one of the most difficult problems facing cognitive science. However, understanding perception is critical to developing a complete theoretical account of human information processing because perception serves to interface the physical world with the mental world. The patterns of energy impinging on sensory receptors must be transformed into representations that are canonical with the structural and dynamic properties of the physical world. At the same time, these representations must be compatible with the cognitive processes that mediate perception, comprehension, and memory. Theories of perception, therefore, need to take into account the physics of light and sound, the structure of objects and language, the neurophysiology of the sensory system, the limitations and capabilities of attention, learning, and memory, and the computational constraints of parallel and serial processing.

Perception will not be understood solely through better or more complete descriptions of the physical stimulus or the neural code that is used to represent the product of sensory transduction. Recognition simply does not occur in the sense organs. Similarly, new algorithms for pattern matching, or theories of memory or attention, or even new basic theories of computation will not, by themselves, solve the problem. Instead, the solution to understanding human perceptual information processing will depend on an interdisciplinary approach that integrates scientific knowledge about cognitive psychology, computation, physics, mathematics, and linguistics.

With this approach in mind, we decided to bring together some of the essential and yet diverse aspects of research on perception. Previous treatments of this subject have tended to consider perception from the

ix

perspective of cognitive psychology alone, or artificial intelligence alone, or some perspective in isolation, but there have been few attempts to integrate work on human perception together with discussions of the basic computational issues surrounding the modeling of perceptual processes. Within the limitation of two volumes, it is impossible to deal with all of the interrelated and interdisciplinary issues that must be considered in the study of perception. Therefore, we chose to focus on several basic problems of pattern recognition in speech perception and visual form perception. Our aim in editing this book, then, was to assemble a set of chapters that would consider perception from the perspectives of cognitive psychology, artificial intelligence, and brain theory.

Certainly at a relatively abstract theoretical level, pattern recognition is, in its essence, quite similar for speech perception and scene perception. There are two theoretically distinguishable parts to the problem of pattern recognition: First, how does the perceptual system segment meaningful forms from the impinging array of sensory input? Second, how are these forms then recognized as linguistic or physical objects? It is our belief that in spite of the apparent differences in the processing and representation of information in speech and vision, there are many similar computational issues that arise across these modalities as well. Some of these cross-modality similarities may be captured in basic questions such as: What are perceptual features, and how are these features organized? What constitutes a perceptual unit, and how are these units segmented and identified? What is the role of attention in perception? How do knowledge and expectation affect the perceptual processing of sensory input? And what is the nature of the mechanisms and representations used in perception? It is this set of fundamental questions that we have chosen to cover in these two volumes.

In considering the theme of perception across the domains of speech and visual form, some questions are quite apparent: Why compare speech perception and visual form perception? Why not compare the perception of spoken and written language, or general audition with vision? The reason is that our intention in editing these volumes was to focus specifically on the perception of meaningful sensory forms in different modalities. Previous books on spoken and written language have emphasized the role of linguistics in perception and thus are concerned with the role of meaning in perception. However, the problems of pattern segmentation and recognition for spoken and written language are not directly comparable; printed words are clearly segmented on the page by orthographic convention, while there are no clear linguistic segmentation boundaries in spoken language. Similarly, with respect to the issues that arise in books comparing the perception of arbitrary patterns in audition and vision, the emphasis is generally more on the psychophysical problems of transduction, coding, and detection than on the cognitive psychology of segmentation and recognition.

These chapters have been organized into two volumes—one focusing on speech perception and the other focusing on visual form perception. It is important to note that within each volume the theoretical issues touched on by the chapters are all quite distinct, while between volumes there are a number of similarities in the issues that are discussed. In Volume 1, some of the basic theoretical questions in speech perception are considered, including the perception of acoustic–phonetic structure and words, the role of attention in speech perception, and models of word and phoneme perception. In Volume 2, several fundamental questions concerning visual form perception are considered, including the perception of features and patterns, the role of eye movements in pattern processing, and models of segmentation and pattern recognition.

These volumes would certainly not have developed without the cooperation and contribution of the authors. In addition, we are grateful to a number of colleagues for their assistance. We would like to thank David Pisoni and Barry Lively for their active support and encouragement of our work on this project. We would also like to acknowledge Stephen Grossberg for his constant stimulation to bring this project to fruition despite several problems and setbacks. Finally, we conceived of this book while we were graduate students at the State University of New York at Buffalo, and it developed as a direct consequence of numerous discussions and arguments about perception with our colleagues and professors there. We thank Steve Greenspan, Jim Sawusch, Irv Biederman, Jim Pomerantz, Erwin Segal, Naomi Weisstein, and Mary Williams for providing the scientific climate from which this book could develop.

Contents of Volume 1

Speech Perception

CHAPTER 1

Visual Form Perception: An Overview*

James R. Pomerantz

*Department of Psychology, State University of
New York at Buffalo, Amherst, New York 14226*

I. INTRODUCTION

The last person to attempt a thorough survey of the literature on form perception concluded that "because the concept of visual form will crumble of its own weight, it will not be possible to write a volume quite like the present one in the future" (Zusne, 1970, p. x). Nevertheless, the topic of visual form perception is still alive and well. In 1983 alone, at least two major books appeared that were devoted principally to this topic (Rock, 1983; Uttal, 1983).

Some of the grounds for Zusne's pessimism, however, remain valid, and true to his prediction, no one has attempted to repeat his undertaking. Form perception is not a unitary psychological process, and it is not likely to be explained in a single, unified theory. Instead, form perception embraces a host of subproblems that are at least partly independent of one another. Perhaps for this reason, form perception has never evolved into as well defined a research area as, say, speech perception, the topic of the companion volume to this book. There is little agreement on precisely what is meant by a form or on where the boundaries lie between form perception, on one hand, and the areas of contour, texture, figure, and object perception on the other.

I.A. Why Form Perception Is A Difficult Problem

Various authors have attempted to bring order to this sprawling field by proposing a standard taxonomy of key terms so that those working in the

---

* Portions of this chapter were presented at the 25th annual meeting of the Psychonomic Society in San Antonio, Texas, November 1984. The final draft of this chapter was completed in December 1984.

1

field could at least speak a common language (e.g., Garner, 1978; Uttal, 1981). As commendable as they may be, such calls for the standardization of nomenclature rarely succeed. Perhaps this will change, but in the past, even more modest attempts to reach agreement on definitions (e.g., Hochberg's 1978 distinction between a shape and a form) have not been widely accepted. I have no reason to believe that I will be any more successful than my predecessors in proposing definitions for terms like shape, form, and object, but because I am discussing them here, I must define the terms that I use.

The problem of defining a form is not likely to disappear until we understand the psychology of form perception, since a form, as I am using the term, is a psychological entity. A physical object has the same characteristics and structure regardless of how (or whether) it is perceived. However, a camouflaged object presented against its background does not constitute a form unless perceivers see it as such. The same holds true for constellations of stars in the night sky or faces in the clouds. Thus I use the term "form" analogously to the term "color" (as opposed to "wavelength"), which is also dependent on an observer.

Psychologists interested in perceptual organization have repeatedly posed the question, What constitutes a stimulus, or pattern? When, for example, is a succession of discrete stimuli to be regarded as a single stimulus? Determining the proper unit of analysis for multidimensional or hierarchically structured stimuli is precisely the problem of form perception, because forms are multidimensional, hierarchical structures. Any viable definition of form must be sought in the empirical data of human perceptual performance. Although the details become complex, we wish to be able to say that a given region of the visual field corresponds to a perceived form if subjects' responses indicate that the region is functioning as a single unit, independent of other regions in the visual field. Subjects' responses should include (or at least be consistent with) their phenomenological descriptions, but the responses must be based first and foremost on objective performance measures of perception.

I.B. Definitions

To start our definition of form, consider the visual field as two-dimensional and static (we ignore depth and motion in this treatment). Human perception divides (or parses) this field into regions, called *shapes*, separated by boundaries, called *contours*. Perceived shapes and contours often correspond to physical shapes and contours, but given the myriad nonlinearities and other distortions of human perception, these correspondences cannot be taken for granted. In Figure 1.1, both shapes (the

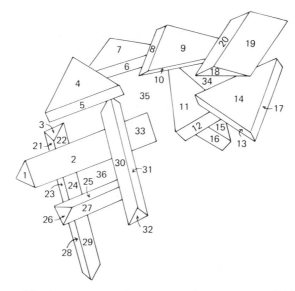

Figure 1.1　A scene comprising contours, shapes, parts, and objects.

assorted polygons) and contours (the black lines) are readily apparent. In addition, human observers perceive *objects* in this scene, such as pyramids, prisms, and the like. Again, these perceptual objects are not necessarily equivalent to physical objects. Thus within this one image we have contours, shapes, and objects, listed in order from the most local to the most global. At a still higher level, which we cannot explore here, humans perceive *relationships* among the objects in the scene, such as one object occluding or resting on another. A more detailed representation of this scene would include color and texture information, which is useful for detecting contours and objects.

The term "part" can be used to refer to almost any spatial component of an object, including shapes, contours, or combinations of these. Although any group of contours or shapes could be proposed as a part, only certain of these components function in an interrelated fashion, and so only a few have any psychological reality. A major problem in perception is to develop procedures that distinguish actual, functional parts from purely nominal parts that lack psychological reality.

Where does form fit into this hierarchy of contour, shape, part, and object? Historically, it has been used at all of these levels to describe three-dimensional volumes, two-dimensional bounded shapes (or the projected shapes of three-dimensional bodies), and unclosed contours (such as the letters M, S, T, and so forth), which do not circumscribe bounded

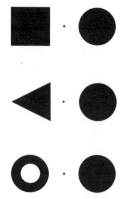

Figure 1.2   Stimuli used by Chen (1982) to examine effects of topological equivalence.

regions but are nevertheless referred to as forms. In my opinion, this multiplicity of meaning has been an obstacle to progress in the field; the notion of form is far too broad and cumbersome to be useful. (Perhaps this is why Zusne predicted that the concept would crumble of its own weight.) It is little wonder that so few facts have been established about form perception when the concept itself encompasses such a wide mix of problems.

I.C. Identifying the Effective Variables of Form

Even if we restrict ourselves to shape perception (i.e., the perception of two-dimensional regions bounded by contours), there are so many variables in the distal stimulus that it is difficult to determine which affect human visual perception or have any psychological reality. For example, consider Chen's (1982) work on the representation of topological properties in visual perception. I select this study mainly because of its potentially sizable impact on our understanding of shape perception, and not because it is any more problematic than most studies dealing with form. Chen argues that two visual stimuli that are topologically different, such as a disk and an annulus, are more discriminable in a near-threshold, "same–different" task than are other pairs of forms that are topologically equivalent, such as a disk and a square or a disk and a triangle (see Figure 1.2). From these results and others, Chen concludes that the visual system is tuned to topological invariants and that many of the global, Gestalt-type phenomena in shape perception may be explained in this manner.

Although Chen's argument could turn out to be correct, more work is needed to establish that the effective dimension for discrimination is indeed the presence of topological differences rather than some other variable that happens to covary with topology. For example, the stimulus pairs in Figure 1.2 also differ in total area (amount of black), total intensity or luminous flux, and total perimeter (Rubin & Kanwisher, 1985). It would appear that Chen's results can be explained adequately by any of these, since the most discriminable pair (disk vs. annulus) also shows the greatest differences in area, intensity, and perimeter. Teasing apart all of these variables (and any others that may be present as well) would require much additional work. For example, in general, the larger the stimulus, the greater its total luminance. Such confounding could be eliminated by adjusting the intensity of the larger stimulus downward so that total luminance would be equated, but then differences in average luminance will be created. Similar difficulties arise in attempting to unconfound area and perimeter.

Even with a fairly restricted set of simple, black-and-white, textureless, two-dimensional, regular shapes, it is not easy to establish which variables of the distal stimulus affect perception. What is more, it seems certain that different variables selectively affect different levels or subprocesses within perception. For example, as the work of Julesz (1981) has shown, a variable such as element orientation may affect texture perception much more than it does form perception. Similarly, Beck (1972) has shown that differences in line orientation (e.g., upright vs. tilted T) are often more salient perceptually than differences in line arrangement (T vs. L), but this is true only under conditions of texture perception with distributed attention. When these forms are perceived in isolation, with focused attention, an L appears to be more different from an upright T than does a tilted T. Once again, these complexities make it easy to understand why there are so few established laws of form perception.

Zusne's (1970) review of the form perception literature contains a lengthy chapter on the "variables of the distal stimulus." Essentially, the approach calls for measuring virtually every objective dimension or feature of the physical stimulus in an attempt to determine which are the best predictors of how forms are detected, discriminated, or recognized. At the risk of oversimplification, and of doing some injustice to certain promising findings, the contributions of this approach have been minimal. Armed with tape measure or even polar planimeters, one may approach a shape and compute its area, perimeter, ratio of perimeter squared to area, its compactness, jaggedness, symmetry, orientation, complexity, and dozens of other variables that can be operationalized and still fail to uncover useful clues about how the form is perceived. This failure is not due to any lack of effort or imagination; rather, it stands as a testimonial to the complexity of the problem.

As our measurements become more sophisticated, this picture may brighten. For example, Uttal (1975, 1983) has successfully pursued the notion that autocorrelation-based measures may be useful in predicting the detectability of visual forms. In his experiments, Uttal presented dot patterns embedded in noise (random dots) and measured the detectability of these patterns (i.e., an observer's ability to discriminate the signal-plus-noise combination from noise alone). He also computed a statistic ("figure of merit") based on the autocorrelation function for these patterns that agrees with the psychophysical data. His results indicate, among other things, that the collinearity of dots increases detectability but that figural goodness does not, a pair of findings that agrees with other data on texture and shape discrimination (Checkosky & Whitlock, 1973; Julesz, 1981; Pomerantz, 1977).

This kind of development is certainly encouraging, but we are still a long way from understanding the variables that underlie our capacity to perceive shapes. As the Gestalt psychologists demonstrated so compellingly years ago, shapes have some elusive emergent features that are not easily measured and that disappear when the shape is analyzed into its constituent parts. Later years have seen a resurgence of interest in the basic phenomena of Gestalt psychology, such as grouping, figure–ground segregation, and the effect of context on perception. We now examine some of these developments and see what progress has occurred in our understanding of the Gestalt principles of perceptual organization.

I.D. The Gestalt Laws

The Gestalt laws of perceptual organization are often referred to as if they were a clearly enumerated set of principles which, although still open to empirical falsification, were largely agreed upon as valid descriptions of perceptual tendencies. Few have ever taken them seriously as laws; "principles" is a more accurate term. However, it is less widely realized that the laws themselves, considered as a set, are distinctly disorganized. Depending on which authors are read, there is considerable variation in the names the laws are given, their description, how they are grouped, and how many of them there are.

More alarming is the vagueness of some of the laws. As Garner (1981) remarks, "Gestalt psychologists undertook simply to catalog phenomena that were more or less holistic but ceased utterly to be analytic about their phenomena." Further, some presentations of the Gestalt laws distinguish between laws of figure–ground segregation and laws of grouping, whereas others do not. Counts of the number of different laws run from a high of 114 (Helson, 1933) to a low of just 1 in treatments in which the principle of Prägnanz (or the minimum principle) is put forth as a single, all-encompassing law (Hochberg, 1978; Pomerantz & Kubovy, 1986).

The individual laws, which are apparently widely accepted by both psychologists in general and specialists in the field of perception, do not attempt to explain the phenomena but only to describe what is perceived. In some cases, phenomenal demonstration is the only means of validating the laws, because they are not sufficiently operationalized to test objectively. The difficulty comes largely from the lack of unambiguous definitions for terms such as "grouping," "figure–ground," and "figural goodness."

Setting these problems aside for the moment, the Gestalt explanation of form perception is usually articulated as follows: Parts become "glued" together to create a cohesive, whole form if they meet the criteria of similarity, proximity, good continuation, symmetry, and so forth as stipulated by the laws of organization. The parts will be so organized if they can be fit into a good figure, presumably even if it requires some distortion (nonveridicality) to accomplish that fit (Pomerantz & Kubovy, 1986). Once so organized, perception of the whole becomes primary; parts can be attended to as parts only through secondary acts of scrutiny that require effort and practice. This whole process is orchestrated through the automatic operation of autochthonous fields of electrical currents in the brain. Although the particular neurophysiology proposed by Köhler (1920) has been shown to be untenable, the idea is still adhered to by some that Gestalt effects work through a mechanism that is automatic. This mechanism works in parallel over the perceptual field, being largely "wired in" from birth and so not educated through experience. Neisser's (1967) preattentive process can be interpreted to perform this function.

I.E. Preview of Conclusions

This is a large set of claims—too large for a detailed, point-by-point critique. Therefore, I have selected some of the most important propositions to discuss how they can be operationalized and to see what evidence has accumulated about them. Based on this evidence, I draw the following conclusions:

1. Grouping of parts into whole forms (i.e., "configuration") can be demonstrated using performance in selective and divided attention tasks as diagnostic tools. A set of parts can be said to configure (group into a whole form) if responses that are logically contingent on all of the parts

can be made as (or more) quickly and accurately as those contingent on just one (or some) of the parts. As we shall see, however, care must be exercised in interpreting results from these tasks, because they are not foolproof indicators of configuration. In particular, this method can fail to detect configuration under certain circumstances that will be explained later.

2. When parts configure into wholes (as defined above), there is usually some specifiable emergent feature involved—that is, a feature that is dependent on the identity and arrangement of the parts but not identifiable with any single part. Possible examples of emergent features would be closure or symmetry. An emergent feature is defined as a property that, in addition to the above, is at least as salient perceptually as any of the parts from which it emerges.

3. There is little evidence for the existence of any perceptual glue that binds together the parts of a whole. Often, emergent features are the first properties of forms to capture the perceiver's attention. Sometimes this attention to emergent features makes it appear as though the parts are inaccessible or glued together, but the available evidence appears to indicate otherwise. Outside of the hidden figures phenomenon (Gottschaldt, 1926), there is little evidence that membership in a whole makes a part more difficult to perceive. The forest does not appear to hide its trees, although it may alter their appearance or interpretation.

Certain of these conclusions are in the spirit of the original Gestalt claims, whereas others represent a departure. In either case, neo-Gestalt psychology, as this contemporary enterprise might be called, is becoming more analytic (in Garner's terms) and can now state more precisely what it means to perceive a whole form. I now go through some of the claims that have been made about configuration and provide evidence that justifies the conclusions just presented.

II. MEASURES OF GROUPING AND CONFIGURATION

Wertheimer (1923) demonstrated several principles of grouping by means of gridlike arrangements of circles or dots (first introduced by Schumann, 1900), which can be seen as organized into rows or columns, or, with lesser frequency, diagonals. Unfortunately, the fact that nearly everyone perceives these alternative groupings made it possible to forestall for years defining what grouping really means. After all, few will demand a definition for a phenomenon so obvious that all can experience it.

Coren and Girgus (1980) have tested the notion that elements belonging to the same perceptual group appear nearer together than they actually are (or nearer together than elements in different groups). Their data indicate a small but significant effect in this direction. Had their experiment turned out otherwise, however, it would not be difficult to imagine how the then vague notion of grouping might have been saved from disconfirmation: Grouped items do not have to appear to be closer together; they simply have to appear to "belong" together. Thus we would have traded the problem of defining grouping for the problem of defining belonging.

II.A. Grouping and Attention

Following notions introduced by Shepard (1964), Lockhead (1966), Garner (1970), Kahneman (1973), and others, it eventually became clear that a perceptual group or unit refers to a unit of attention or information processing. If two units "belong" to the same group, this means that observers are capable of attending and responding to that group *as a group*. Such a premise leads to the first claim about grouping that I wish to evaluate: Tasks requiring divided attention to the several parts of a group should be no more difficult (and should perhaps be less difficult) than tasks allowing attention to just a single part, because from the perceiver's perspective, the group is a single entity and not an amalgam of parts.

A second claim is that selective attention to parts within a group should be difficult or even impossible. This assumption is equivalent to the notion that parts are not perceptually available, or that a forest hides its trees. The elements of a group are bound together by a glue that prevents perceptual "bigamy," whereby an element is married to more than one group simultaneously. As we shall see, these two claims are separate propositions that must be evaluated independently. As the preview of my conclusions indicated, the evidence for the first claim is strong. The second claim also seems strong upon initial examination of the evidence, but when this claim is analyzed more closely, it weakens considerably.

II.B. An Illustration: Parenthesis Patterns

Results suggesting easy divided attention across grouped parts and difficult selective attention to parts within groups may be illustrated with the patterns in Figure 1.3A. These patterns were used as stimuli in a speeded classification experiment (Pomerantz & Schwaitzberg, 1975) that had three main conditions (described below). In all conditions, stimuli were presented one at a time and a two-choice, speeded response was required.

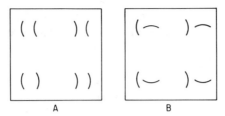

Figure 1.3   (A) The "normally oriented" parenthesis stimuli used by Pomerantz and Garner (1973). (B) "Misoriented" parentheses, in which the right parenthesis has been rotated 90°.

II.B.1. Tasks

First, in the *divided* attention condition, subjects were required to make one response whenever either of the two patterns, ((or)), appeared and the other response to either of the patterns () or)(. This task requires that both the left and the right parenthesis of each pair be attended to; otherwise, performance would fall to chance levels.

Second, in one of two *selective* attention tasks used, one response was made to the patterns ((and (); the other response was made to)(and)). Clearly, the orientation of the left parenthesis is critical here; selectively attending to it would suffice for successful performance. In a second selective attention condition, the right parenthesis is relevant. Note that in Figure 1.3 and in subsequent displays of stimulus sets, the divided attention task requires one response to be made to either of the two patterns in the cells on the positive diagonal of the two-by-two matrix, while the other response is to be made to either of the two patterns on the negative diagonal. In the two selective attention tasks, by contrast, responses are assigned by rows and by columns, respectively.

Third, in the *control* conditions, subjects merely discriminated between pairs of patterns that differed in only the left or the right parenthesis, but not both. For example, in one of the four possible control tasks, one response was to be made to the pattern ((and the other response to (). Clearly, the right parenthesis is relevant in this case. In another control task, subjects discriminated)(from ((; here, the left parenthesis is relevant. In Figure 1.3 and in subsequent displays of stimulus sets, the control tasks require subjects to discriminate between two stimuli that form a single side of the two-by-two matrix.

There are two additional tasks that have been studied with these stimuli but that were not part of the Pomerantz and Schwaitzberg (1975) experiment. These are the conditions with correlated dimensions and with no context, which are used to test for redundancy gains and for configural

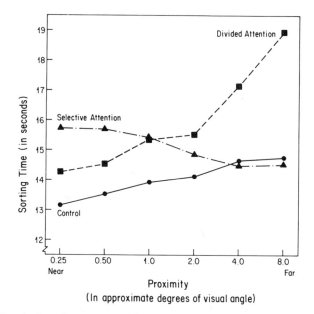

Figure 1.4   Results from Pomerantz and Schwaitzberg's (1975) experiment. As the elements are moved apart, selective attention becomes easier, whereas divided attention becomes harder.

superiority effects, respectively. The diagnostic utility of these effects will be assessed later.

The major stimulus variable in this experiment was the interelement spacing, or proximity. When the two parentheses are close together, they look as though they form a unitary pattern, but as the distance between them increases, the grouping appears to weaken, in accordance with the law of proximity.

II.B.2. Results: Divided Attention

As the data in Figure 1.4 indicate, the findings were as follows. Performance on the divided attention task was superior to that on the selective attention tasks when the parentheses were closely spaced. It would seem impossible to explain these data if subjects were responding to individual parts as such, because one would then have to claim that two parts could be processed more quickly than one. As the parentheses were moved apart, this trend reversed, indicating that grouping was indeed weakening and that subjects were processing the pattern as two separate elements. (In fact, it may have been simple visual acuity limitations that forced this change, because at wide separations both parentheses may not have been clearly visible simultaneously.)

These data support the first claim presented earlier about grouping. Whenever two parts can be processed jointly as quickly and accurately as they can be processed selectively, they can be considered members of the same group. In fact, I have offered this outcome previously as an operational definition of grouping (Pomerantz, 1981).

II.B.3. Results: Selective Attention

The data from the control conditions appear to support the second claim about grouping—namely, that selective attention to individual parts within a group should be difficult or impossible. Figure 1.4 shows that when the parentheses were closely spaced, performance on the selective attention conditions was worse than that on the control conditions. As the parentheses were moved apart, the two conditions converged. The logic behind this comparison is that both the selective attention and the control tasks can be successfully performed by attending to just one part. The only difference between the two tasks concerns whether the irrelevant part varies or stays constant in the stimulus sequence. Any difference in performance between the control and selective attention conditions implies that the irrelevant part is being attended to, despite its lack of relevance.

To summarize, both major claims about grouping have received support from the experiments with parentheses. Thus, the outcomes observed in the selective and divided attention tasks appear to provide an operational definition of grouping.

II.C. Parts That Appear Not to Group

Both of the claims about grouping receive further support from experiments using stimuli that do not appear phenomenally to group. For example, the grouping that exists between the parentheses can be weakened by rotating one of the elements 90° (as in Figure 1.3B). Perhaps this is because symmetry, good continuation, or closure is lost by this change. When these "misoriented" parentheses are tested in the same kind of experiment described for the normally oriented parenthesis pair in Figure 1.3A, the results differ sharply. First, divided attention becomes extremely difficult—much harder than selective attention. This is what would be expected if the two parts no longer form a group. Second, the selective attention task becomes just as easy as the control task, indicating again that subjects are perceiving just one part at a time. Stated

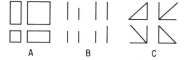

Figure 1.5   Some additional stimulus sets showing configuration and emergent features.

differently, the misoriented parentheses behave like widely separated, normally oriented parentheses.

II.D. Other Configural Stimulus Sets

Still further support is found when other kinds of patterns beyond parenthesis pairs are considered. For example, the three stimulus sets shown in Figure 1.5 have been constructed in the same manner as the parentheses—that is, through the use of two orthogonal, dichotomous dimensions. Although not all of these sets have been tested under all conditions, they all appear to behave much as the parentheses do.

III. EMERGENT FEATURES AND TASK PERFORMANCE

So far, it might seem as though it were a straightforward matter to define grouping theoretically and to diagnose it experimentally. It appears sufficient to generate sets of stimuli consisting of orthogonal sets of dichotomous dimensions or parts and run them through a battery of tasks to determine if the parts group. Matters are not that cut and dried, however. The emergent features associated with grouping and configuration result from idiosyncratic and unpredictable interactions of parts, and as a result they can produce unusual effects that can easily be misinterpreted. Let us examine some additional stimuli and see how their emergent features behave.

Figure 1.6 shows stimulus sets, generated with the same two-by-two, orthogonal design, which appear to contain strong emergent features. Figure 1.6a is the same as Figure 1.5C. The dimensions along which the stimuli vary are: (1) the orientation of the diagonal line, which has either a positive or negative slope and (2) the location of the vertical line, which is positioned on either the left or right side of the figure. This combination of parts creates emergent features corresponding to arrow and triangle forms (see Pomerantz, Sager, & Stoever, 1977). These stimuli have been tested using the full battery of tasks described earlier, and they behave almost exactly like the parentheses in Figure 1.3A. The divided attention task reduces to a simple arrow-versus-triangle discrimination and is easier to

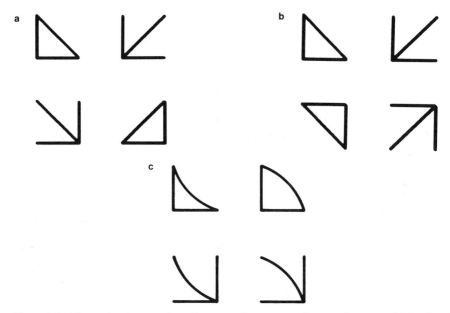

Figure 1.6   Three stimulus sets that all possess the emergent feature of arrow and triangle. The diagnostics described in the text detect the emergent feature only in ( ).

perform than either of the two selective attention tasks, which are of comparable difficulty. The control tasks are also easier than the selective attention tasks, indicating that selective attention is not taking place.

III.A. Mapping of Emergent Features to Response Categories

Figure 1.6b shows a slightly different stimulus set. The only change is that the position of the horizontal line varies between the upper and lower sides of the figure; its variation is correlated perfectly with that of the vertical line. Again, the result is the creation of the emergent features of arrows and triangles, but with one major difference: The arrow–triangle difference is now correlated with the orientation of the diagonal line segment. As a result, the selective attention task in which the diagonal line was relevant can now be performed using the more salient arrow–triangle distinction, since the two are perfectly confounded. However, the divided attention task now becomes quite difficult, so this set of stimulus patterns will not be diagnosed as showing grouped parts by the criteria we have been using. The simple pattern of easy divided attention and difficult selective attention that we found in Figure 1.6a vanishes in 1.6b. Now the selective attention and control tasks are equally easy and divided attention is much harder. The point is that although Figure 1.6a and both contain emergent features (in fact, the same emergent features), the way these emergent features are distributed among the four alternative stimuli is quite different in the two cases, and this has a major impact on performance in the various tasks.

Figure 1.6c shows yet another variation on this theme. As in 1.6a, one dimension is the location of the vertical line, which is positioned on either the left or right side of the figure. The second dimension is the direction of curvature of a diagonal line that has a negative slope and is bowed either upward or downward. Again, we see the same emergent features of arrows and triangles arising from these parts. Now, however, the arrow–triangle distinction is correlated with the position of the vertical line. Once more we will find poor performance on the divided attention task, so again these stimuli do not meet our diagnostic criteria for grouping, even though they clearly group and produce the same emergent features as Figure 1.6a.

These examples show that in certain cases, parts may combine to create emergent features that, despite their existence, may not be sufficient to pass the two main diagnostic criteria for grouping that we have been examining: (1) divided attention superior to selective attention, and (2) selective attention worse than control conditions. Emergent features are a necessary but not sufficient condition for the diagnostics to work; it is also necessary that the emergent features be paired in a certain way with the other features or parts in the set being tested. If a particular emergent feature, such as the presence or absence of symmetry, closure, or good continuation, is correlated with the status of some local part, it is impossible to tell which is being attended to, the emergent feature or the part. This, of course, is the same ubiquitous problem in form perception research that I mentioned earlier: Forms differ in numerous complex and often confounded ways, which makes it difficult to discover the effective variables of the distal stimulus that control perception.

III.B. Parentheses Reconsidered

In light of Figure 1.6, let us reexamine the parentheses in Figure 1.3A to see why (when closely spaced) they led to better divided than selective attention. It appears that the emergent features of these stimuli happen to be distributed so as to favor the divided attention condition. The distinguishing emergent features that make the divided attention task so easy may be the vertical symmetry of () and)(, as opposed to the parallelism of)) and ((. Thus a simple strategy in the divided attention task would be to make one response to the symmetrical patterns and the other to the asymmetrical (or, equivalently, to make one response for the stimuli whose elements are parallel and the other response otherwise). This strategy of attending solely to emergent features could be used equally well in the control conditions. However, this strategy is not viable for the selective attention tasks only, because in each case one symmetrical and one asymmetrical (or one parallel and one nonparallel) stimulus is assigned to each response. Accordingly, the selective attention task cannot be performed as well as the divided attention task.

In this case, poor performance in the selective attention task may be attributable not to any failure of selective attention to individual elements (the second of the two major claims described earlier), but rather to the absence of a salient emergent feature that can be used in performing the task. That is, there may be no perceptual glue that prevents selective attention to parts of unitary configurations; the parts may be just as accessible as the wholes. The difficulty with processing parts in the selective attention tasks is that the feature distinguishing a left from a right parenthesis is not as discriminable as the emergent features distinguishing parenthesis pairs in the control tasks. This line of reasoning will be resumed in Section IV on perceptual glue.

Let us also reconsider the stimuli of Figure 1.3B. These misoriented parenthesis pairs appear neither to group nor to contain any emergent features. With them, divided attention is difficult and selective attention is easy. However, it is possible that they do group and produce emergent features but that all four stimuli possess the *same* emergent feature. Although it is not clear what that feature might be, the point is that an emergent feature (or any type of feature) is of no use in a discrimination task unless it differentiates among the stimuli to be discriminated and is mapped into a suitable fashion onto the required response categories. If these misoriented parenthesis pairs do have a perceivable emergent feature, but one that does not assist in performing any of the tasks, then subjects will be forced to discriminate between the stimuli on the basis of their parts (i.e., the individual parentheses). Figure 1.7 shows a variant on the misoriented parentheses in which the same context—two dots and a surrounding circle—has been added to each stimulus. The familiar configurations that emerge make it clear that the misoriented parentheses are capable of participating in a configuration. However, if the emergent features are the same for all of the stimuli, as they are here, the subject cannot use them in performing the assigned tasks and so their existence will not show up on task performance.

My conclusion is that although the diagnostic tools of selective and divided attention tasks are sometimes capable of detecting grouping and

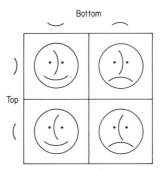

Figure 1.7   A slight modification of the misoriented parentheses, in which the stimuli have been rotated 90 degrees, enclosed within a circle, and have had two dots added.

emergent features, and although they are not likely to indicate grouping when it does not exist, these tools can fail to detect grouping if the emergent features contained in the stimuli either are correlated with one of the simple parts of the stimulus set or fail to be correlated with the diagonals of the set and so cannot be exploited in the divided attention task. I now look at some more perceptual tasks that might serve as diagnostics of emergent features.

III.C. Redundancy Gains and Losses

Another potential diagnostic for grouping and emergent features is performance on tasks in which two correlated features or parts are available to the subject, either one of which is sufficient for performing the task. In terms of the two-by-two matrix of stimuli, these tasks involve discriminating one pattern from the one diagonally opposite it. There are two such tasks, one for the positive and one for the negative diagonal. With the parentheses of Figure 1.3A, these tasks are ((vs.)), and () vs.)(.

With dimensions characterized as *separable* (Garner & Felfoldy, 1970), performance on these conditions is no better (nor worse) than on the control conditions. That is, the redundancy provided by the second, correlated dimension is of no value, because with separable parts, the subject attends to only one part at a time anyway. Examples of pairs of separable dimensions would be color and form or the misoriented parenthesis pairs of Figure 1.3B. With *integral* dimensions, such as the brightness and saturation of color chips, redundancy gains do emerge. These stimuli are perceived not dimensionally but in terms of their overall similarity, and an additional, redundant dimension makes two stimuli more discriminable (Garner, 1974).

With *configural* dimensions, such as normally oriented parentheses, redundancy gains have not been found (Pomerantz & Garner, 1973). In fact, this is one way in which configural dimensions have been operationally defined and differentiated from integral dimensions. In general, configural stimuli that differ in two parts are no more (nor less) perceptually distinct than those that differ in only one part. However, this conclusion was based mainly on the parenthesis stimuli. As we saw with the divided attention task, performance depends on how emergent features happen to be distributed over the stimuli in the set. With the parentheses in Figure 1.3A, the () vs.)(task is performed better than any of the control tasks, whereas the ((vs.)) task is performed more poorly than any of the controls. Averaging over these two tasks with correlated dimensions, they are no faster than the four control conditions, and so no net redundancy gain emerges. What appears to be controlling performance are the individual emergent features of the stimuli. The best patterns in the Gestalt sense, () and)(, are the easiest to discriminate, while the poorer or less symmetric patterns, ((and)), are harder to discriminate. Again, it is the configural aspect of the stimuli that is crucial.

Given the idiosyncratic manner in which emergent features arise in patterns created from parts, it would be unwise to assume that the absence of redundancy gains is a ubiquitous, defining characteristic of configural stimuli. With the arrow and triangle stimuli of Figure 1.6a, we actually find a redundancy loss, because the diagonally related stimulus pairs are the only pairs that are not differentiated by the distinctive arrow–triangle emergent feature. In Figure 1.6b, however, the diagonally related patterns are so differentiated, and so, not surprisingly, the tasks with correlated dimensions show performance equivalent to that on control tasks, which can also be performed using the arrow–triangle emergent feature—that is, neither a redundancy gain nor loss is observed. Given these results, it appears unlikely that redundancy gains or losses will prove to be a useful diagnostic for emergent features. It does not matter whether the parts of these stimuli are redundant or correlated when subjects are not attending to the parts; any redundancy gains or losses that appear under such circumstances should be interpreted as stemming not from the redundancy of parts but rather from the idiosyncratic mapping of emergent features onto response categories.

III.D. Configural Superiority Effects

So far I have examined whether performance in four types of tasks (selective attention, divided attention, correlated dimensions, and control tasks) can serve as effective diagnostics for grouping and emergent fea-

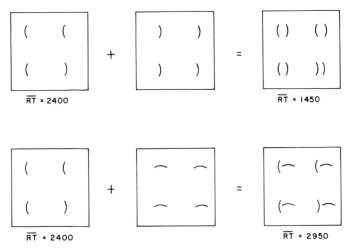

Figure 1.8   Configural superiority effects of the direction of curvature from Pomerantz et al. (1977). With parentheses, adding an identical contextual element to each stimulus can either facilitate reaction time performance (top) or impair it (bottom).

tures. In all four tasks, all of the parts, relevant or not, are presented with each stimulus. Let us now consider a fifth and final task, one that merely deletes the irrelevant part and so presents the relevant one in isolation. This *no context* task is most similar to the previously described control task, in which the irrelevant part is present but not varying. In the case of parentheses, this task would entail a discrimination of) vs. (. By comparing performance on this task with that on the others, we can look in a new way for evidence of emergent features. The logic here is that in each of the four other tasks, all parts are physically present in each stimulus, and any emergent features stemming from those parts will thus be present. Only in the no context task are parts (and therefore their emergent features) actually removed.

Some of these tasks have been examined with the parenthesis and the arrow–triangle stimuli in the configural superiority effect experiments of Pomerantz, Sager, and Stoever (1977). The main finding, shown in Figures 1.8 and 1.9, was that under some circumstances, deleting an uninformative part of a pattern caused a major decline in discrimination performance in a task requiring subjects to locate the disparate stimulus in an array. This result suggests that by deleting a part, a salient emergent feature was also lost. Thus, discriminating) from (was much more difficult than discriminating () from ((, even though the deleted parenthesis was the same for both patterns. With the misoriented parenthesis pairs,

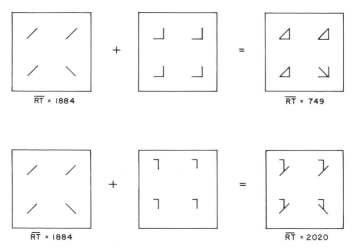

Figure 1.9   More configural superiority effects of positive vs. negative diagonals from Pomerantz et al. (1977). Adding an identical context to each stimulus can either facilitate reaction time performance by creating arrows and triangles (top) or impair it by creating stimuli that do not differ with respect to a salient emergent feature (bottom).

however, deleting one parenthesis caused no harm; in fact, performance improved slightly.

From these results it would appear that we have another independent diagnostic for emergent features—the existence of a configural superiority effect in which parts may be discriminated more rapidly when they are embedded in a noninformative configural context. However, this diagnostic suffers from the same shortcoming that we saw with the selective and divided attention tasks—it may sometimes fail to detect an emergent feature that is present. The reasoning is the same as before: For a positive result with this diagnostic, there must first be emergent features present, but those emergent features must also assist in performing the required discrimination. Again, the misoriented parentheses may in fact produce an emergent feature, but this feature would be the same for all four patterns and so would be of no use to the subject perceiving it.

IV. PERCEPTUAL GLUE

I have argued that a form is a collection of parts that possess emergent features whose presence can sometimes be detected by performance in discrimination tasks. Another characteristic often attributed to forms is that their parts cohere to form a unit, or that there is some sort of metaphorical glue in the perceptual process that bonds the parts of a configuration. For example, Boring's (1942, p. 253) fifth law of form states: "A strong form coheres and resists disintegration by analysis into parts or by fusion with another form."

IV.A. Explaining "Failures" of Selective Attention

Perceptual glue would serve the useful function of assuring the proper grouping of parts to wholes such that (1) the assorted parts of a whole would stick together rather than being scattered into other potential configurations; and (2) any one part could not belong to more than one whole. Glue would also explain the finding that wholes resist perceptual analysis into parts, because attending to a component part of a whole would require extracting that part from the whole to which it is bound. Rather, it is claimed, a whole makes its parts inaccessible (i.e., the forest hides its trees).

Thus perceptual glue provides an explanation for the failures of selective attention that we have seen with the parentheses and with the arrow and triangle stimuli: The glue prevents parts from being extracted individually. Similarly, selective attention succeeds with the misoriented parentheses of Figure 1.3B because the parts therein are not glued together.

IV.B. Evidence against Glue

Let us examine the glue explanation more closely. It is clear that we do not selectively attend to individual parentheses in normally oriented pairs. However, the fact that we do not selectively attend does not imply that we *cannot* selectively attend, nor that doing so would exact some cost for ungluing a whole configuration to free its component parts. Recall from Section III,B that the apparent failures of selective attention might be explained fully without appealing to glue. Subjects may be attending to salient emergent features in the control conditions because those tasks always involve discrimination between two stimuli that always differ with respect to an emergent feature. In the selective attention conditions, emergent features are less useful because they are not mapped uniquely onto response categories (e.g., one arrow and one triangle are mapped onto each of the two responses). Therefore, subjects may opt to attend to parts in the selective attention tasks. Thus, the apparent failure of selective attention (worse performance in the selective attention than in the control tasks) is no failure at all; rather, subjects are attending to emergent features in the control tasks and to parts in the selective attention tasks, and the parts happen to be less salient than the emergent features and so lead to poorer performance. This emergent feature explanation is

22   James R. Pomerantz

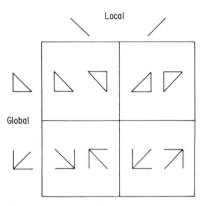

Figure 1.10 Stimuli used by Pomerantz (1983). Selective attention to either the local part (the orientation of the diagonal) or the global shape (arrow vs. triangle) was possible without interference from variation on the irrelevant dimension.

quite different from the glue explanation, because the latter explains the performance difference in terms of the cost of ungluing a perceptual whole.

IV.B.1. Successful Selective Attention

There is further evidence that the component line segments of the arrow and triangle stimuli are not glued together. Recall that with the stimuli in Figure 1.6b, selective attention was easy; performance in the selective attention and the control tasks was approximately equal. A similar result was reported by Pomerantz (1983) using the stimuli in Figure 1.10. In both of these cases, subjects could decide on the position or orientation of a line segment and effectively ignore irrelevant variations of the other line segments or of the global shape. This finding strongly argues against the notion of any perceptual glue.

IV.B.2. Stroop Interference

A second source of evidence against perceptual glue comes from some preliminary data from experiments with normally oriented parentheses, as in Figure 1.3A. In the data reviewed so far, selective attention has been assessed by determining whether *variation* of the irrelevant part interferes with performance. An alternative procedure is to determine whether the *identity* of the irrelevant part matters or, more specifically, whether interference results if the irrelevant part calls for a different response than the relevant part. In previous work (Pomerantz, 1983), I have called these two effects Garner and Stroop interference, respectively—the reference being to W. R. Garner and J. R. Stroop, whose names are closely associated with these effects.

If subjects were instructed to respond to the left part of the stimulus () but could not ignore the right part because of glue, we might expect impaired performance compared with the stimulus ((, where both parts call for the same response. Instead, we usually find improved performance; that is, performance is better with the stimuli () and)(than with ((and)). This result indicates that subjects are processing emergent features of whole configurations and so do better with more symmetric figures. Subjects are apparently not processing each parenthesis pair as two separate parts that happen to be adjacent. However, mild Stroop interference does begin to appear in the selective attention tasks, but not in the control tasks, when the stimuli are presented directly to the fovea. Although these data are only suggestive at this time, they support the notion presented earlier that when it is to subjects' advantage to attend selectively, they can do so; and when they do attend selectively, the parentheses behave more as separate and competing parts than as partners in a unitary configuration. Again, it appears to be the subjects' strategy for the task rather than perceptual glue that is responsible for the absence of selective attention.

IV.B.3. Treisman's Results

Treisman and Paterson (1984) have reported some remarkable experiments that shed new light on the existence of perceptual glue and on the status of emergent features. The feature integration theory of Treisman and Gelade (1980) distinguishes primitive, separable features that are perceived more or less automatically from derived combinations of features that are perceived only through focused attention. If emergent features act more like primitive than derived features, this would provide further independent evidence that emergent features possess a demonstrable psychological reality.

Treisman's work has shown that pairs of separable features, such as color and form, display several diagnostic characteristics, two of which are critical here. First, targets defined in terms of color or shape alone tend to "pop out" from displays without serial search—for example, a red object in a field of blue objects pops out. The same holds true for locating a square in a field of circles. By contrast, conjunctions of separable dimensions do not show this characteristic; searching for a red square in a field of red circles and blue squares is a slow, serial process. In present terms, this is because color and form do not interact to create any

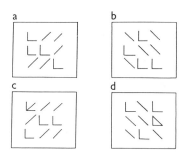

Figure 1.11 Four displays used by Treisman and Paterson (1984) to test for illusory conjunctions and emergent features of form.

emergent features that could be searched for. Therefore, a subject has to search for the conjunction of a particular color and shape. If color and form did create emergent features, and if emergent features had the same primitive status as the features from which they emerge, they would presumably pop out too. If combinations of parts of forms should pop out, that would indicate the presence of emergent features. Thus, we have another diagnostic for emergent features—fast, parallel search. Rapid perceptual segregation of texture fields at boundaries defined by conjunctions of parts would provide additional supportive evidence.

Treisman's second main criterion for diagnosing primitive, separable features involves *illusory conjunctions*. She argues that attention is required to conjoin separable features into unitary objects. Without attention, features are perceived but not pinned down to any specific object in a specific location. Instead, these features are free to float, and in the process they may pair off incorrectly and create illusory conjunctions.

In Treisman and Paterson's (1984) Experiment I, subjects were presented with displays containing right angles (L's) and diagonal lines. The task was to detect the triangle or arrow that was physically present on some trials (see Figure 1.11). If a subject were to report an arrow when none was present, this could indicate that an illusory conjunction had occurred. Of course, this report could be merely an incorrect guess, because sometimes subjects reported an arrow when the diagonal lines in the display were not in the proper orientation to form an arrow but could form only a triangle. For this reason, Treisman and Paterson estimated illusory conjunction rates for arrows by subtracting false alarm rates for arrows when they were inconsistent with the diagonals in the array from false alarm rates when they were consistent. The illusory conjunction rate for triangles was computed similarly.

One main result was a moderately frequent occurrence of illusory arrows. This outcome suggests that arrows are in fact secondary, or derived, patterns that can be composed simply from L's and diagonal line segments. However, the illusory conjunction rate for triangles was far lower than for arrows and in fact was close to zero. This result suggests that a triangle is more than a secondary conjunction of L's and diagonals. Instead, it may be a primary unit containing at least one primitive emergent feature, such as closure. If only the parts are present in the stimulus, and not the emergent feature, no illusory triangle will be seen. This fact provides new and converging evidence for the direct detection of emergent features, a position I have advocated based on entirely different evidence (Pomerantz, 1978, 1981).

Another experiment in this series showed that illusory triangles could be perceived in displays that contained, in addition to the properly oriented L's and diagonals, another figure possessing the feature of closure (namely, a circle). This striking result suggests that closure may be a feature with the same primary status as an oriented line segment or vertex. If so, this experiment demonstrates a three-way illusory conjunction between a line segment, an L vertex, and closure to create the perception of a triangle.

A final experiment from Treisman and Paterson (1984) examined the conditions under which a line segment could "float" and conjoin with an S figure to form an illusory dollar sign ($). Specifically, they asked whether a line that was already a part of an arrow or triangle configuration would be as available to contribute to an illusory dollar sign as an isolated, unattached line. The answer was affirmative. I concur with the authors' conclusion: The component line segments of arrows and triangles do not seem to be at all "sticky."

To perceive a triangle wholistically does not mean that its parts cannot be discerned, or even that selective attention is required to extract its parts. Instead, when we perceive a whole, or Gestalt, we see the parts *plus* any emergent features the pattern contains. There seems to be little need to postulate any perceptual glue to explain the results before us.

V. THE CREATION AND DESTRUCTION OF EMERGENT FEATURES

V.A. Some New Stimulus Sets

Let us look at two more sets of stimuli to see if our understanding of emergent features allows us to predict how they will be perceived. The stimuli in Figure 1.12a are just like the original parentheses except that an

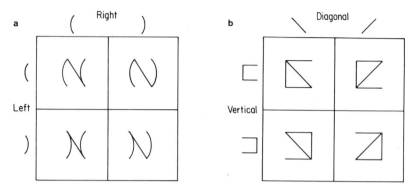

Figure 1.12   Two new stimulus sets tested by the author and Edward Pristach: (a) This set is the same as the original parentheses, with the addition of the same diagonal line to each stimulus. (b) The set is the same as the original arrow and triangle set, with the addition of the same horizontal line to the top of each stimulus.

identical diagonal line segment has been added to each stimulus. This addition alters the appearance of the stimuli radically. Their similarity to each other is increased; they all look like N's whose component segments possess some incidental, nondefining curvature. This metamorphosis appears comparable to that with the misoriented parentheses in Figure 1.3B. In both cases, the parts might produce emergent features that are the same for all stimuli and so are of no use to the subject. Following this reasoning would lead to the prediction that these N's will behave like the misoriented parentheses.

On the other hand, if there is no perceptual glue, subjects might be able to delete the diagonal line selectively from the parentheses in their perceptual processing and so recover the original parenthesis patterns. This process would lead to the prediction that the Ns should behave like the original parentheses in Figure 1.3A.

The results from an ongoing series of experiments my laboratory, conducted with Edward Pristach, fall midway between these predictions. In contrast to the results with the misoriented parentheses, the selective attention task is still quite difficult; variation on the irrelevant part affects performance, which indicates that it is being attended to. In contrast to the results with the normally oriented parentheses, on the other hand, the divided attention task with the N's is also difficult—more difficult, in fact, than the selective attention task.

These results show clearly that the addition of the diagonal line did not destroy the grouping of parentheses it connected; the effect was not like that produced by rotating one parenthesis 90 degrees. This result is consistent with subjects' ignoring the diagonal altogether. However, the data also show that the diagonal could not be ignored completely, because its presence hurt performance on the divided attention task. Perhaps, after all, some glue did keep the diagonal from being stripped away from the parentheses. Alternatively, there may be no glue; subjects may simply find it difficult to attend to two parts and ignore what falls between them. If attention is like a searchbeam, as is often claimed, the beam may be topologically constrained such that it cannot exclude any point that lies between other attended points.

The stimuli in Figure 1.12b provide a test of the searchbeam hypothesis. These stimuli are identical to the arrows and triangles of Figure 1.6a, except that the same horizontal line has been added at the top of each figure. As with the N's, the added line affects the appearance of the stimuli greatly. The figures look more alike, which is not surprising when we consider that they are now mere rotations and reflections of one another. Again, we have two predictions. The added line could destroy the emergent features of arrows and triangles and so lead the subject to process the parts separately. Alternatively, if the line segments were not glued together, and if the upper horizontal line of each figure could be ignored, we would have triangles and arrows once again and would expect comparable performance. Because the horizontal line to be ignored does not fall between the remaining lines that define the arrows and triangles, it could be excluded by the searchbeam.

This time the results were not mixed: Performance was almost indistinguishable from that found with ordinary arrows and triangles. This outcome suggests that the searchbeam explanation for the results with the N-like parentheses is correct. More important, however, these results suggest that a line segment can be filtered from these patterns so that they will function as ordinary arrows and triangles—further evidence against perceptual glue. (It should be noted that the added horizontal line cannot be ignored in experiments involving texture segregation or the search for a target element through a field of many nontargets. Again, this fact may be attributable to the inability of a searchbeam to exclude a part from more than one stimulus simultaneously. All of the experiments just described involve presenting just one stimulus at a time.)

In some ways the patterns in Figure 1.12 are like the well-known embedded figures displays (Gottschaldt, 1926) in which the addition of some context renders a figure undetectable. Indeed, embedded figures could be used as evidence for perceptual glue and for the forest hiding the trees, but I believe that this case is weak. Virtually all effective demonstrations of embedded figures involve eliminating line terminators by continuing the lines smoothly beyond their usual endpoints. When a familiar figure is placed into some context and vanishes, the likely reason is that the embedding process destroyed one set of features while it created another set.

V.B. The Discovery of Emergent Features

We have now seen several stimulus sets in which emergent features are apparent, as well as several methods of diagnosing their presence. Although, considered individually, each of these methods has face validity, their combined use provides strong converging operations. There is plenty of work still to be done, however, for we have seen that these diagnostics sometimes fail to detect the presence of emergent features.

A related problem is that none of these methods helps us go about discovering new emergent features. That process remains mainly an art. I suppose it would be possible to devise an algorithm for generating combinatorial, part-based stimulus sets which could then be tested mechanically with all of the available diagnostics, but this brute force process would be inefficient, costly, and probably error prone. For the time being, at least, phenomenology will continue to be the source of hypotheses about emergent features.

VI. SUMMARY

This chapter has reviewed some of the literature on objective, performance-based measures of the process by which parts group into perceptual wholes. This literature makes it clear that under such circumstances, subjects divert their attention away from individual components; it is less clear why they do so or in what direction they turn their attention. The findings reviewed here suggest that the grouping of parts into wholes does not make the parts imperceptible or inaccessible; the evidence for a perceptual glue binding parts together is thin. Rather, when parts configure into wholes, new, emergent features arise that are available alongside the parts but that are more salient perceptually and will therefore be attended to instead of parts when it is advantageous to do so. A number of diagnostics exist for detecting emergent features, but these do not always succeed, because they depend not only on the presence of emergent features but also on those features being useful to subjects in the tasks they must perform. Although the diagnostics can reveal the existence of emergent features, they do not help guide the search for new ones.

ACKNOWLEDGMENTS

I thank I. Biederman, E. Schwab, and H. Nusbaum for their comments on a draft of this chapter. I also thank Edward Pristach, who is collaborating with me on an ongoing series of experiments, some of whose preliminary results are presented in this chapter.

REFERENCES

Beck, J. (1972). Similarity grouping and peripheral discriminability under uncertainty. *American Journal of Psychology, 85*, 1–20.

Boring, E. G. (1942). *Sensation and perception in the history of experimental psychology.* New York: Appleton-Century-Crofts.

Checkosky, S. F., & Whitlock, D. (1973). Effects of pattern goodness on recognition time in a memory search task. *Journal of Experimental Psychology, 100*, 341–348.

Chen, L. (1982). Topological structure in visual perception. *Science, 218*, 699–700.

Coren, S., & Girgus, J. S. (1980). Principles of perceptual organization and spatial distortion: The Gestalt illusions. *Journal of Experimental Psychology: Human Perception and Performance, 6*, 404–412.

Garner, W. R. (1970). The stimulus in information processing. *American Psychologist, 25*, 350–358.

Garner, W. R. (1974). *The processing of information and structure.* Hillsdale, NJ: Erlbaum.

Garner, W. R. (1978). Selective attention to attributes and to stimuli. *Journal of Experimental Psychology: General, 107*, 287–308.

Garner, W. R. (1981). The analysis of unanalyzed perceptions. In M. Kubovy & J. R. Pomerantz (Eds.), *Perceptual organization.* Hillsdale, NJ: Erlbaum.

Garner, W. R., & Felfoldy, G. L. (1970). Integrality of stimulus dimensions in various types of information processing. *Cognitive Psychology, 1*, 225–241.

Gottschaldt, K. (1926). Uber den Einfluss der Erfahrung auf die Wahrnehmung von Figuren. *Psychologische Forschung, 8*, 261–317 [translated in W. D. Ellis (Ed.) (1950), *A sourcebook of Gestalt psychology.* New York: Humanities Press].

Helson, H. (1933). The fundamental propositions of Gestalt psychology. *Psychological Review, 40*, 13–32.

Hochberg, J. E. (1978). *Perception.* Englewood Cliffs, NJ: Prentice-Hall.

Julesz, B. (1981). Figure and ground perception in briefly presented isodipole textures. In M. Kubovy & J. R. Pomerantz (Eds.), *Perceptual organization.* Hillsdale, NJ: Erlbaum.

Kahneman, D. (1973). *Attention and effort.* Englewood Cliffs, NJ: Prentice-Hall.

Köhler, W. (1920). *Die physischen Gestalten in Ruhe und im stationären Zustand.* Braunschweig: Vieweg.

Lockhead, G. R. (1966). Effects of dimensional redundancy on visual discrimination. *Journal of Experimental Psychology, 72*, 95–104.

Neisser, U. (1967). *Cognitive psychology.* New York: Appleton-Century-Crofts.

Pomerantz, J. R. (1977). Pattern goodness and speed of encoding. *Memory & Cognition, 5*, 235–241.

Pomerantz, J. R. (1978). Are complex visual features derived from simple ones? In E. L. J. Leeuwenberg & H. F. J. M. Buffart (Eds.), *Formal theories of visual perception.* Chichester, England: Wiley.

Pomerantz, J. R. (1981). Perceptual organization in information processing. In M. Kubovy & J. R. Pomerantz (Eds.), *Perceptual organization.* Hillsdale, NJ: Erlbaum.

Pomerantz, J. R. (1983). Global and local precedence: Selective attention in form and motion perception. *Journal of Experimental Psychology: General,* **112,** 516–540.

Pomerantz, J. R., & Garner, W. R. (1973). Stimulus configuration in selective attention tasks. *Perception & Psychophysics,* **14,** 565–569.

Pomerantz, J. R., & Kubovy, M. (1986). Theoretical approaches to perceptual organization. In K. Boff, L. Kaufman & J. Thomas (Eds.), *Handbook of perception and human performance.* New York: Wiley (in press).

Pomerantz, J. R., Sager, L. C., & Stoever, R. J. (1977). Perception of wholes and of their component parts: Some configural superiority effects. *Journal of Experimental Psychology: Human Perception and Performance,* **3,** 422–435.

Pomerantz, J. R., & Schwaitzberg, S. D. (1975). Grouping by proximity: Selective attention measures. *Perception & Psychophysics,* **18,** 355–361.

Rock, I. (1983). *The logic of perception.* Cambridge, MA: MIT Press.

Rubin, J. M., & Kanwisher, N. (1985). Topological perception: Holes in an experiment. *Perception & Psychophysics,* **37,** 179–180.

Schumann, F. (1900). Beitraege zur analyse der Gesichtswahrnehmungen, I. *Zeitschrift für Psychologie,* **23,** 1–32.

Shepard, R. N. (1964). Attention and the metric structure of stimulus space. *Journal of Mathematical Psychology,* **1,** 54–87.

Treisman, A., & Gelade, G. (1980). A feature-integration theory of attention. *Cognitive Psychology,* **12,** 97–136.

Treisman, A., & Paterson, R. (1984). Emergent features, attention and object perception. *Journal of Experimental Psychology: Human Perception and Performance,* **10,** 12–31.

Uttal, W. R. (1975). *An autocorrelation theory of form detection.* Hillsdale, NJ: Erlbaum.

Uttal, W. R. (1981). *A taxonomy of visual processes.* Hillsdale, NJ: Erlbaum.

Uttal, W. R. (1983). *Visual form detection in 3-dimensional space.* Hillsdale, NJ: Erlbaum.

Wertheimer, M. (1923). Untersuchungen zur Lehre von der Gestalt, II. *Psychologische Forschung,* **4,** 301–350 [translated in part in W. D. Ellis (Ed.) (1950), *A sourcebook of Gestalt psychology.* New York: Humanities Press.

Zusne, L. (1970). *Visual perception of form.* New York: Academic Press.

CHAPTER 2

Figure–Ground Organization and the Spatial and Temporal Responses of the Visual System

Naomi Weisstein* and Eva Wong†

*Department of Psychology, State University of
New York at Buffalo, Amherst, New York 14226,
and †Department of Psychology, University of Denver,
Denver, Colorado 80208

I. INTRODUCTION

How we perceive objects as entities separated from their backgrounds is a fascinating question. We need to be able to distinguish objects from their backgrounds before we can reach, touch, avoid, or approach things in the world. Thus the segregation of the visual world into objects or figures and backgrounds is fundamental in a plan of action directed at the environment.

The earliest attempts at studying figure and ground perception were carried out by the Gestalt theorists. They recognized the fundamental division of the perceptual world into figure and ground and devoted considerable efforts to its investigation. Rubin (1921/1958) was the first to make extensive observations on figure and ground. His investigations consisted primarily of detailed phenomenological descriptions of visual impressions of figures and backgrounds. He noted that grounds give the impression that they stand behind figures, and that contours which are shared boundaries between figure and background "belong" to the figure. In other words, a figure seems to be defined and given its shape by the surrounding contour, but ground appears as a formless region.

Using ambiguous pictures whose regions fluctuate between figure and ground, Rubin also made the observation that regions seen as figures have different characteristics than regions seen as ground. For example, a field perceived as a figure is a "richer, more differentiated structure than the same field experienced as ground." Figures were also seen to have different colorations than ground. A black region seen as a figure seems to appear darker than when it is seen as background.

Apart from making phenomenological observations, Rubin also noted stimulus conditions affecting whether a region would be perceived as figure or ground. Small surrounded areas were more readily seen as figures, while larger surrounding regions were more likely to be seen as ground. This effect was termed the "principle of surroundedness" in figure–ground organization.

Rubin's work provided much of the foundation which has allowed others to explore further the stimulus as well as the perceptual properties of figure and ground. Koffka (1935) comments that figures are "more strongly structured, more impressive." Other Gestalt-oriented investigators have looked at the stimulus organizations favoring figure perception and have found that size, hue, contrast, region orientation, and symmetry are prominent factors. Graham (1929) showed that the brighter region was more dominant as a figure than the darker region, although Goldhammer (1934) found the reverse. Subsequently, Harrower (1936) showed that it was the brightness difference rather than the absolute brightness that determined whether a region was predominantly seen as a figure. He found that while a white region was dominant as a figure when it was on a dark grey surrounding background, the same was true for a black region on a light grey field. Oyama and Sasamoto (1957) and Oyama (1960) confirmed this finding but also found that black-colored areas were less likely to be seen as figures.

The relative size of regions also affects whether an area will appear predominantly as a figure. Other factors being constant, smaller areas tend to be perceived more often as figures. This effect was initially observed by Rubin and later confirmed by the findings of Graham (1929), Goldhammer (1934), Oyama and Torii (1955), Künnapas (1957), and Oyama (1960).

Yet another factor of stimulus arrangement is the orientation of regions. Areas oriented horizontally and vertically are more likely to be seen as figures than areas oriented obliquely. This effect was demonstrated by Künnapas (1957) and Oyama (1960). Using a stimulus consisting of a circle divided into six and eight sectors, they found that sectors oriented horizontally and vertically were more dominant as figures. Hue seems to be an ambiguous factor. Harrower (1936) found no influence of color on figural dominance, while Oyama (1960) found that red regions tended to be seen as figures more than blue regions. Symmetry also favors figural dominance, in that symmetrically bounded regions are more likely to be perceived as figures (Bahnsen, 1928).

Not only do stimulus arrangements affect figure–ground organization, but the perceptual properties of figure and ground have also been found to be quite different. Koffka (1935) reported perceptual changes associated with figure–ground reversals in which there were no changes in the physical stimulation, yet regions appeared to "lose color in their transition from figure to ground." This effect of color changes associated with figure–ground reversals was also observed by Frank (1923), using afterimages. Frank found that when the after-image appeared as a figure, it looked more colored than when it was seen as ground. Coren (1969) noted that this was a situation in which the magnitude of contrast changed even though the physical color and luminance remained constant. Perceived figure and ground affected the magnitude of simultaneous color contrast with no correlative changes in physical stimulation.

Using reversible figures, Coren (1969) was able to show that an area was perceived to be brighter when it was seen as a figure than when it was seen as ground. In other words, the amount of contrast was greater for a region when it was perceived as a figure than when it was perceived as ground. Festinger, Coren, and Rivers (1970) attribute this enhanced brightness of the figure to attentional factors. They propose that brightness perception is arrived at by averaging over the entire visual field, with any difference in luminance across regions being positioned around the mean. Because figural areas are attended to and weighted more than ground regions, these regions are given a higher value and thus appear brighter.

Another set of perceptual properties associated with figure and ground is that a figure is often seen as standing in front of a background. As mentioned earlier, this phenomenal impression was first noticed by Rubin (1921). Until now, however, this perceived depth separation between figure and ground has not been well understood. Some theoretical speculations associated with this apparent depth separation of figure and ground in flat pictorial conditions have been made, notably by Hochberg (1971). He noted that when we look at real objects in the world, fixating on the figure or object of interest, the background behind the figure falls on disparate retinal locations. Thus, the fixated figure is sharp, while points on the ground are blurred. Expectancies founded on experience with a three-dimensional world are built up, and as a result, the visual system expects points enclosed within a figural area to be sharp and focused and points lying in ground regions to be blurred and distant. Once these expectancies and "mental schema" are established, even two-dimensional pictures exhibit the perceptual property of figures standing in front of a background.

Julesz (1971) has related the role of visual processing of binocular disparity, motion, and brightness to figure–ground perception. Clusters of dots moving in the same direction were readily segregated from a field of stationary dots. If dots in both areas moved, the faster-moving area was seen more prominently as a figure. In addition, if the slower-moving dots became hidden when they moved into the faster-moving cluster, the powerful depth cue of interposition could make the faster-moving cluster appear in depth in front of the slower-moving background. This finding was recently confirmed independently by Allman, Campbell, and McGuinness (1979) and by Frost and Nakayama (1983). If the disparity were manipulated so that a textured area was seen as a "hole" moving behind a surrounding field, disparity dominates over the Gestalt principle of surroundedness, and the surrounding field, which appeared nearer, could be seen as a figure. In fact, when motion and disparity information combine so that the region behind the surround is also static, the smaller surrounded area is never seen as a figure. These demonstrations show that the early visual processes of stereopsis and motion extraction can also be powerful determinants of figure–ground segregation.

That different stimulus arrangements, perceptual properties, and visual impressions are associated with figure and ground have led some investigators to speculate that figure and ground may involve two different functions in the visual system. The Gestalt theorists were the first to emphasize the functional difference between figure and ground. Their usage of concepts of field forces and energy distribution to articulate the dichotomy of figure and ground was motivated by the assumption of isomorphism (i.e., the parallelism of the structure of perceptual and brain events). They deduced that since figures are more solid and "thinglike" than ground, figures should be held together by stronger forces than ground, and the density of energy distribution should be greater for figures than for ground.

Köhler's (1946) "brain-field" organization theory of figure–ground perception has been seriously challenged by Hochberg (1981), who has demonstrated that the shape of a figure can be perceived under conditions in which parts of the figure are presented to an observer at the same retinal area. Under these circumstances, it is impossible to invoke the kind of isomorphism of overall stimulus configuration and brain–event organization to account for figure–ground perception. Hochberg also points out that since we scan the world with head and eye movements, it is unlikely that the shape of a figure or object can be given in just one fixation. Thus, the perception of a figure is built up from parts given in successive presentations at the same retinal (most likely foveal) location.

Although the Gestaltists' specific theories of figure–ground perception have not stood the test of experimental evidence, the researchers' recognition of the fundamental dichotomy of figure and ground remains an important motivation in the study of the organization of the visual world.

The study of figure–ground perception has since shifted its focus to the effects of figure–ground contexts on perceptual response. Targets are detected, discriminated, and resolved better in figural regions than in ground regions. For example, contour discontinuity is detected more accurately when the contour is part of a figure than when it is part of the ground (Weitzman, 1963b). Figural after-effects—prolonged viewing of a figure, causing a test contour placed adjacent to it to appear displaced away from its actual position—are greater for contours seen as part of a figure than for contours seen as part of a background (Weitzman, 1963a). Sudden displacements of targets during saccadic eye movements are also more detectable for figures than for backgrounds (Bridgeman, 1981). The facilitation of discrimination and the detection of contour and displacements has been attributed to attention drawn toward a figure (Bridgeman, 1981). That figures are attended to more than ground was first proposed by Weaver in 1928. He used introspective and phenomenological observations to arrive at the conclusion, "Figure is in general also the portion of experience which stands forth as attentively clear, while the groundal field occupies a subordinate position in clearness" (p. 74).

Another approach to the differential effects of figure and ground on the discrimination and detection of targets is to hypothesize that figure and ground perception involve different perceptual functions. This approach maintains the fundamental dichotomy of figure and ground but emphasizes *how* figure and ground are analyzed by the visual system and which information processing characteristics are involved. One of the aims of this approach is to focus on the operations concerned in the gathering of information and the execution of a task directed toward a goal.

Julesz (1978) has proposed that figure and ground perception may serve two different purposes in visual information processing. The analysis of a figure may be specialized in the scrutiny of details and vernier signal processing, while the analysis of ground may be specialized in the processing of background textures and surface structures of the visual field. Ground analysis can also be seen as a kind of "early warning system," a quick scan of the visual field that determines whether an area will require a finer resolution of details. There is evidence that the resolution of details and the extraction of sharp edges require high spatial frequency information (Carpenter & Ganz, 1972; Henning, Hertz, & Broadbent, 1975; but see Westheimer & McKee, 1980, for the case of stereo-hyperacuity in which the presence of low spatial frequencies is necessary for this type of acuity to occur). Therefore, it is reasonable to hypothesize an association of high spatial frequency information processing with figure analysis. On the other hand, if ground analysis serves as an early warning system, one would expect ground to be analyzed earlier than figure in the time course of visual processing. This contention has been tested by Calis and Leeuwenberg (1981).

Calis and Leeuwenberg used an "interference" technique in which the first of a pair of stimuli can be distorted by the presentation of the second at varying stimulus onset asynchronies (SOAs). When the first stimulus formed the ground of an object, maximal distortion of the ground occurred at shorter SOAs than when the first stimulus formed a figure. This finding suggests that the processing of ground occurs earlier than the processing of figure. It also gives further substantiation to the idea that information concerning ground is extracted before information about figures, making ground analysis useful as an early warning system.

If figure analysis is involved in detailed, point-by-point scrutiny and proceeds slower and/or later than ground analysis (Calis & Leeuwenberg, 1981; Julesz, 1978), and if high spatial frequency is required for the resolution of details (Carpenter & Ganz, 1972; Julesz, 1971; Marr & Poggio, 1979), then it is possible that figure analysis and high spatial frequency processing are associated. If ground analysis is involved in the extraction of global textures and proceeds faster and occurs earlier than figure analysis (Calis & Leeuwenberg, 1981; Julesz, 1978), and if low spatial frequencies provide information about global background textures and surfaces (Broadbent, 1977; Julesz, 1978; Marr & Poggio, 1979), then it is possible that ground analysis and low spatial frequency processing are related. This conjecture is supported by psychophysical evidence concerning the speed of processing of low and high spatial frequencies. The visual system's response is faster for low spatial and high temporal frequencies, as reflected in shorter latency (Breitmeyer, 1975; Lupp, Hauske, & Wolf, 1976; Vassilev & Mitov, 1976), faster rise time (Robson, 1966; Van Nes, Koenderink, & Bouman, 1967; Watanabe, Mori, Negata, & Hiwatashi, 1968; Watson & Nachmias, 1977), and shorter temporal integration times (Breitmeyer & Ganz, 1977; Hood, 1973; Nachmias, 1967; Tolhurst, 1975). It was this idea of the association of figure–ground perception and the spatial and temporal response of the visual system that formed the background of the research described here.

II. HOW PERCEIVED FIGURE–GROUND AFFECTS THE SPATIAL, TEMPORAL, AND ORIENTATION RESPONSES OF THE VISUAL SYSTEM

II.A. Figure–Ground and Tilt Discrimination

The starting point of our research on figure–ground was our discovery that a region of the visual field perceived as a figure can substantially aid

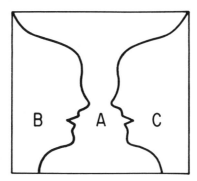

Figure 2.1   Rubin's faces–vase reversible picture. This was the stimulus used in our experiments on the effect of figure–ground organization on the detection and discrimination of sharp and blurred targets. Targets were flashed in locations A, B, and C.

the tilt discrimination of line segments (Wong & Weisstein, 1982). We took an outline drawing of Rubin's faces–vase reversible figure and presented targets within the three regions of the picture (Figure 2.1).

The advantage of using reversible figures like this one is that although a given region may fluctuate between figure and ground, the physical aspects of the stimulus remain constant. When one sees two faces, the central region becomes background, but when a vase is seen, the same central area becomes a figure. This effect gave us the opportunity to look at the purely perceptual effect of figure and ground on discriminating tilted lines. In our initial experiment, the tilted line segments were presented either at tilt threshold but above luminance threshold (Figure 2.2) or at luminance threshold but above tilt threshold (Figure 2.3). In one block of trials, observers were instructed to initiate a trial when they perceived a vase; in another block of trials, they were to initiate a trial when they saw two faces. In any trial, the target was tilted either left or right, and the observer's task was to indicate the presented target's direction of tilt.

In all trials, the observer fixated a dim point located in the center of the display. The target lines were flashed randomly for 20 msec in one of the three locations (A, B, C in Figure 2.1). Four viewing conditions were generated: at-fixation viewing of target on figure; off-fixation viewing of target on figure; at-fixation viewing of target on ground; and off fixation viewing of target on ground. We found that when the target lines were imaged on the figure, they were discriminated three times better than

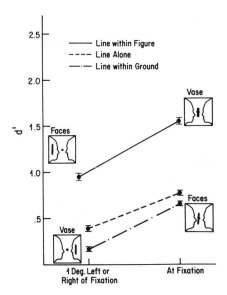

Figure 2.2 The discrimination of tilted lines in figure, ground, and contextless regions when the targets are at tilt threshold but above luminance threshold. Accuracy was measured in terms of d′.

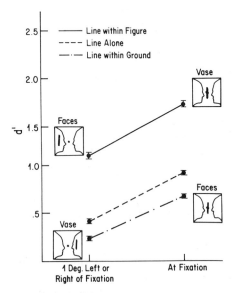

Figure 2.3 The discrimination of tilted lines in figure, ground, and contextless regions when the targets are at luminance threshold but above tilt threshold. Accuracy was measured in terms of d′.

when they were imaged on the ground and two times better than when they were presented without any context.

This result was obtained regardless of whether the targets were at tilt threshold but above luminance threshold or at luminance threshold but above tilt threshold. Thus targets were discriminated with higher accuracy when they were in figural regions than when they were in ground regions. We then wondered whether this facilatative effect of figure on tilt discrimination was generalizable to suprathreshold conditions in which the target line was above both the tilt and luminance thresholds. Using the same design as before, we obtained results showing that the enhancement of discrimination performance by a figure did extend to suprathreshold conditions (Wong & Weisstein, 1984a). However, if we compare this amount of enhancement with that in the threshold conditions, we see that it is less (see Figure 2.4). The probable cause is that at suprathreshold levels, the signal was already high to begin with, and any facilitation by a figure can only raise the signal strength to a maximum level and no more. Thus, the increment of accuracy in performance would not be as great as when the signal was just barely at threshold.

II.B. Figure–Ground and the Detection of Sharp and Blurred Targets

Earlier we introduced the idea that figure and ground perception involved different processing functions. While figure analysis is concerned with detailed, point-by-point analysis and resolution and might be associated with high spatial frequency processing, ground analysis is concerned with the extraction of global background and surface textures which possibly involve using information from the low spatial frequencies. This approach to figure and ground leads to the prediction that we should observe figure facilitation under some stimulus and task conditions and ground facilitation under some stimulus and task conditions and ground facilitation under others.

A task that requires detail resolution of the visual region will be performed better when the stimulus is imaged in the figure, since figure analysis is specialized in the extraction of details. Thus, tasks like the detection of contour discontinuity, the detection of small steps of retinal displacements during eye movements, and the discrimination of lines whose tilt is barely visible will be facilitated in figural regions. However, if a task does not require detail scrutiny and merely demands the detection of whether a threshold stimulus is present or not, the most sensitive process will mediate the detection. Thus, if ground analysis involves low spatial frequency processing and figure analysis involves high spatial fre-

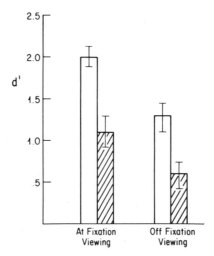

Figure 2.4   The discrimination of tilted lines in figure and ground regions when the targets are above both tilt and luminance thresholds. Accuracy was measured in terms of d'. □, Target against figure;▨, target against ground.

quency processing, it is possible that, depending on which spatial frequencies are presented in a target, one or the other process might dominate and differentially aid perceptual performance. In other words, this deduction leads to the prediction that at thresholds, sharp targets (with high spatial frequency components present) will be detected better in figure regions, while blurred targets (with only the low spatial frequency components present) will be detected better in ground areas.

The experiment that we designed to test this hypothesis was based on the design of earlier experiments, but now the task was detecting the presence of a sharp or blurred line rather than discriminating the orientation of targets (Wong & Weisstein, 1983). The figure–ground context was again an outline of Rubin's faces–vase picture. The target was a vertical line segment presented first at threshold and randomly at the three locations shown in Figure 2.1. In one section of the experiment, the target was a sharp line; in another section, the line was blurred so that no energy was present in the spectrum above 16.67 cycles per degree. The results of this experiment were unambiguous in showing that while sharp targets were detected better in the figure, blurred targets were detected better in ground (see Figure 2.5). Thus, a direct association of spatial frequency and figure and ground was established.

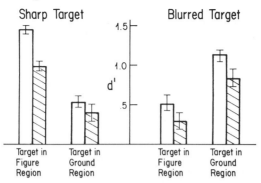

Figure 2.5 The detection of sharp and blurred targets in figure and ground regions. Accuracy was measured in terms of d'. □, On-fixation viewing; ▨, off-fixation viewing.

II.C. Figure–Ground and the Discrimination of Blurred Targets

If high spatial frequencies are involved in the extraction of details, and if figure analysis is more sensitive to high than low spatial frequencies, then we would expect that removing the high spatial frequencies from a stimulus should destroy or attenuate the facilitatory effect of a figure on the performance of tasks which require detail resolution. But will ground have any effect on the discrimination of low spatial frequency targets? Ground has been shown to facilitate the detection of blurred targets (Wong & Weisstein, 1983), but the question remains as to whether it will facilitate the discrimination of blurred targets.

An approach that emphasizes the interaction of processing functions of figure and ground, stimulus constraints, and task requirements will predict that ground should not facilitate perceptual performance if the task demands a function for which ground analysis is not specialized. In this case, although ground analysis is most sensitive to the low spatial frequencies, the information made available through the processing of backgrounds is not useful in the extraction of edges and other minute local details. Therefore, a task that calls for the discrimination of blurred lines with small tilt angles will not be facilitated when the lines fall on regions perceived as ground.

The experiment with which we tested this hypothesis was similar to those described earlier, except that here the task of the observer was to make orientation discriminations of tilted blurred lines (Wong & Weisstein, 1984b). The targets were presented above luminance threshold but at respective tilt thresholds for the sharp and blurred targets (blurring removed the contrast response for spatial frequencies above 15 cycles per degree). The results are clear-cut. When the target was a sharp line segment, we replicated the finding that tilted lines are discriminated better when they are flashed in figural regions than when they are flashed in ground regions (see Figure 2.6).

When the target lines were blurred, neither figure nor ground facilitated perceptual performance. In fact, for blurred targets there was no difference in discriminability for targets flashed against the figure and targets flashed against the ground. Moreover, the discriminability of a blurred target was no different from that of a sharp target imaged on ground. Thus, removal of the high spatial frequencies from a stimulus destroyed any facilitatory effect of the figure on the resolution of small tilt differences. This result is consistent with the idea that figure analysis, being specialized in detail resolution, is most sensitive to the high spatial frequencies, since this information is necessary for the point-by-point analysis of a perceptual region. This result also reaffirms the importance of the complex interaction of figure–ground context, stimulus constraints and task requirements, and demands that future explorations of the effects of figure and ground on perceptual performance take these variables into consideration.

II.D. Figure-Ground and the Bandwidth of Orientation Channels

Figures have been found to facilitate the discriminability of sharp tilted lines but not blurred ones. What type of underlying process might be responsible for this enhancement? There is much psychophysical evidence suggesting that the visual system picks up information using mechanisms akin to channels in a receiving system. This idea that the visual system contains "channels" has proven useful in conceptualizing how certain information in the visual world is picked up and used. Indeed, most models of sensory processing of visual information are tuned-channel models. These models propose that information is processed by channels tuned to a certain orientation, spatial, and temporal frequency. They also assume that visual channels have a certain bandwidth, and that signals that are less than one bandwidth apart are processed in the same pathway.

The likelihood of signal confusion in discriminability is higher for stimuli that are less than one bandwidth apart than for those which are more than one bandwidth apart. In the context of our study on the discrimination of tilted targets in figure and ground, the discrimination would be better for targets that are more than (or at least) one bandwidth apart than for targets which are less than one bandwidth apart. Given the differences

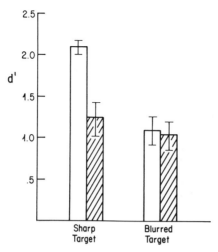

Figure 2.6   The discrimination of sharp and blurred targets in figure and ground regions. Accuracy was measured in terms of d'. □, Target against figure; ▨, target against ground.

we found in the accuracies of tilt discrimination in figure and ground areas, we might ask whether such differences are related to the bandwidth behavior of the orientation channels in figure and ground regions.

The tuning and bandwidth of orientation channels have been examined by several psychophysical methods. These include orientation-specific masking (Campbell & Kulikowski, 1966; Phillips & Wilson, 1984; Wilson, McFarlane, & Phillips, 1983), subthreshold summation (Kulikowski, Abadi, & King-Smith, 1973), adaptation (Blakemore & Campbell, 1969; Blakemore & Nachmias, 1971), and the comparison of discrimination and detection performance at threshold—also known as the discrimination/detection ratio (Thomas & Gille, 1979; Thomas, Gille, & Barker, 1983). Using this ratio, we examined the bandwidth of orientation channels with tilted lines flashed in figure and ground regions. This method of bandwidth measurement compares the probability of discrimination (or identification) accuracy with the probability of detection at a number of detection levels. Plotting discrimination against detection across detection probabilities of .5 to 1.0 in .1 steps, we can generate a regression line in which the slope is the ratio of discrimination to detection.

Some assumptions have to be made concerning the number and distribution of channels. First, we have to assume that all of the channels have symmetrical cosine sensitivity functions. Second, the channels must have equal bandwidth and peak sensitivity. Third, the sensitivity peaks of the channels must be at uniform intervals on the orientation dimension. There is one more characteristic of channels which has to be considered if methods other than the discrimination/detection ratio are used. This is the notion of channel spacing. The discrimination/detection ratio is almost independent of channel spacing for orientation differences in stimulus pairs up to 10 degrees (Thomas & Gille, 1979). Therefore, the assumption of channel spacing does not have to be made if one uses the discrimination/detection method in estimating bandwidth.

In a typical discrimination/detection experiment, a single trial consists of two stimulus presentation intervals. The stimulus is presented randomly from trial to trial in one of the two intervals, and the task of the observer is to judge which interval the stimulus appeared in. This is the detection measure. Next, the observer has to identify which of a given pair of stimuli has been presented. This constitutes the discrimination measure. Since the stimulus setting also varies from trial to trial, relationships of discrimination and detection are generated at various detection probabilities. From these relationships the discrimination/detection ratio emerges. By plotting discrimination against detection at each detection probability, a regression line can be fitted to the data points. This is the discrimination (identification)/detection (I/D) slope. The greater the slope, the better the discriminability of a pair of stimuli.

When we examined the bandwidth of orientation channels in figure and ground using the discrimination/detection ratio, we found that the slopes of the same pair of stimuli of a given orientation difference were very different depending on whether the stimuli were presented in figure or ground areas. The most striking result was the big difference in I/D slopes for stimuli in figure and ground contexts. Whereas the slopes in the ground contexts never exceeded .3, the slopes in the figural contexts approached unity.

The discrimination/detection ratio is an indicator of whether a pair of stimuli are at least one bandwidth apart. We assumed that the visual system picks up orientation information through tuned channels. Consider the case in which a pair of stimuli activate two sets of channels (in other words, the difference between the stimuli is greater than the bandwidth of the channel). In this situation, the stimuli should be discriminated as accurately as they are detected, since the two signals are processed through two separate pathways. Confusion errors should be minimal. If the stimulus is detected, it will also be discriminated or identified. Here the discrimination/detection ratio (the I/D slope) should approach unity. However, if the stimulus pair are less than one bandwidth apart, they will not be processed through different pathways and the identification errors should be higher. Although the stimuli could be detected with accuracy, they could not be discriminated reliably. This dis-

Table 2.1
Identification/Detection (I/D) Slopes of Targets
Presented Alone and in Figure and Ground
Contexts[a]

Orientation differences in degrees	Figure	Ground	Line alone
3.2	.51	.24	.43
4.9	.86	.22	.33
9.8	1.0	.27	.33
13.0	.91	.46	.54
19.5	.98	.46	.79
25.8	.98	.78	.96
31.8	.95	.94	.94

[a] The slopes are calculated from the discrimination/detection ratios.

crepancy of discrimination and detection would yield a low discrimination/detection ratio, since the stimuli are less than one bandwidth apart.

In our experiment, in which the I/D slopes for tilted lines were presented in figure and ground regions, we found that while the I/D slope measured in figure areas approached 1.0 for both stimulus pairs, the I/D slope obtained in the ground regions did not exceed .3. The stimuli were at least one bandwidth apart in figure regions, while the same pairs of tilted lines were less than one bandwidth apart in ground regions. The orientation differences at which the I/D slope becomes unity is the lower limit for the channel bandwidth. From our data, at an orientation difference of 3.2°, the I/D slope is .51 for targets flashed in figure regions, .24 for targets flashed in ground regions, and .43 for targets flashed in the absence of any context. At this orientation difference, stimuli are less than one bandwidth apart in all context conditions. At an orientation difference of 4.9°, the I/D slope is 0.86 for targets in the figure, 0.22 for targets in the ground, and 0.33 for targets in the absence of context.

Table 2.1 shows the I/D slopes for the various orientation differences used in the experiment for one observer. At an orientation difference of 9.8°, the I/D slope for targets presented in figure regions approached unity. However, for targets presented in ground regions and in the absence of context, the I/D slopes were still substantially below 1.0. These data show that when stimuli are at least one bandwidth apart in figure regions, these same tilted line segments are less than one bandwidth apart in ground regions.

It is not until an orientation difference of 25.8° that the I/D slope for targets in contextless fields approximates 1.0. For ground regions, the orientation difference where the I/D slope approaches 1.0 is at least 31.8°. These differences in I/D slopes for targets presented in figure and ground regions are consistent with the finding that the discrimination of sharp tilted lines is better in figural regions, since stimuli which are 4.9° apart in orientation are being processed through different pathways in figure but not ground regions. Thus, the likelihood of confusion in discriminability in figure regions is less than in ground regions.

II.E. Metacontrast Masking of Targets by Figure and Ground

We turn now to the temporal aspects of figure and ground effects on target identification. Metacontrast masking has been used to study the speed and timing of mask and target (Breitmeyer & Ganz, 1976; Weisstein, Ozog, & Szoc, 1975). Consider a theory of metacontrast which postulates that the fast and slow components of a signal are associated with a response to a stimulus, and that metacontrast masking is the interruption of the slow response to the target by the fast response (Breitmeyer & Ganz, 1976; Weisstein et al., 1975). The faster the speed of processing of the mask, the longer the SOA (stimulus onset asynchrony) must be in order for the responses to the mask and the target overlap to produce masking effects.

Williams and Weisstein (1981) have successfully applied the metacontrast paradigm in the study of the time course of the object-superiority effect—the finding that a target line is identified more accurately when it is presented in an objectlike context than in a context of unconnected lines (Weisstein & Harris, 1974). Williams and Weisstein (1981) found that masks consisting of patterns which are more three-dimensional and objectlike must be presented with longer SOAs than masks consisting of unconnected lines before a masking effect can be observed. This finding indicates that the fast component of the objectlike mask must be faster than that of the non-objectlike mask. In addition, its SOA must be longer in order for the mask and target signals to coincide to produce masking.

Using metacontrast masking, we studied the time course of figure and ground with reference to the SOAs required to mask targets when the mask was a figure and when it was ground. In a typical metacontrast masking experiment, a target is presented for a brief period followed by the masking stimulus at various intervals. In our experiment the target

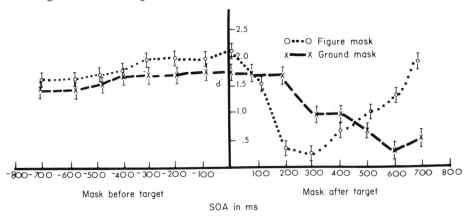

Figure 2.7   Metacontrast masking function of tilted lines by figure and ground mask.

was a line tilted 45° left or right of the vertical. The mask was the Rubin faces–vase outline picture. The target was flashed for 50 msec, and the masking stimulus was presented at various SOAs for 50 msec before and after the target. The target was tilted left or right randomly, and the observer's task was to identify the orientation direction of the target and to report whether he or she saw faces or a vase in that particular trial. Targets were always presented in the central region of the picture. Figure 2.7 shows the results obtained from one observer.

When the mask preceded the target by a large interval, no effect of the mask on the target was seen, regardless of whether the mask was seen as figure or ground. When the mask preceded the target by a short interval (300 msec to 0 msec), an enhancement of the target's discriminability was observed if the masking area was perceived as a figure. When the mask was perceived as ground, the presentation of mask and target at zero asynchrony resulted in the degradation of discrimination performance. This condition was precisely that in which we first discovered the facilitatory effect of figures on tilt discrimination (Wong & Weisstein, 1982).

When the mask appeared after the target (the metacontrast or backward masking condition), degradation of the target was observed. This occurred regardless of whether the masking stimulus was seen as figure or ground. However, as Figure 2.7 shows, the masking functions were very different for a "figure mask" than for a "ground mask." When the masking area was seen as ground, the degradation of the target occurred at much longer SOAs than when the masking region was seen as a figure. The maximum masking of the figure occurred at an SOA of 300 msec. By the 700-msec SOA, the masking effect of the figure had disappeared, while the masking effect of the ground region was still strong. The maximum masking effect of ground occurred around 600 msec, some 300 msec after the maxima for the figure mask. These metacontrast masking functions reveal further information about how perceptual organization affects the discrimination of tilted lines. In a masking condition, both mask and target appear for brief periods. Unlike the designs of the experiments discussed earlier, this design does not allow the observer to focus on a particular perceptual organization and be alerted to certain stimulus aspects. This is especially true in backward masking situations, in which the mask is presented after the target.

In view of the metacontrast theories discussed earlier (Breitmeyer & Ganz, 1976; Weisstein et al., 1975), the metacontrast functions we have obtained, here inform us about the timecourse of figure and ground processing in the same way they revealed the time course of the object-superiority effect (Williams & Weisstein, 1981). If longer SOAs are associated with the ground mask and shorter SOAs with the figure mask, then the speed of ground processing (at least for the fast component) must be faster than that of figure processing. This conclusion agrees with those of Calis and Leeuwenberg (1981): Backgrounds are processed faster than figures. The metacontrast results, together with the data establishing an association of low spatial frequencies with ground processing, support the idea that figures and ground have different functional and processing requirements. The functional differences are associated with the particular types of tasks that the visual system is required to perform: detail resolution in figure analysis and global background information extraction in ground processing.

III. HOW SPATIAL AND TEMPORAL RESPONSES OF THE VISUAL SYSTEM AFFECT FIGURE–GROUND ORGANIZATION

We have seen that a number of factors affect whether a region of the visual field is seen as a figure or as background. Stimulus variables such as symmetry, horizontal–vertical alignment, contrast difference, and location in depth plane all contribute to figure–ground organization. We turn now to how sensory processes may contribute to figure–ground perception. Earlier we introduced and discussed our findings concerning how figure and ground organization can affect the spatial, temporal, and orientation responses of the visual system. We now look at how temporal responses of the visual system, such as flicker, can affect figure–ground perception.

III.A. Flickering Areas of the Visual Field

It is known that motion, occlusion, and motion sheering off edges can produce strong effects of region segregation in depth, as well as determine which region will be seen as a figure (see Section II). We have found that flicker can induce depth in areas of the visual field such that flickering regions are perceived to be localized in a depth plane behind nonflickering regions (Wong & Weisstein, 1986). Since the average temporal luminance of the flickering and nonflickering regions is the same, this flicker-induced depth effect cannot be attributed to luminance differences between the flickering and nonflickering areas. At first glance, this phenomenon of flicker-induced depth seems to be related to the kinds of depth and regional segregation produced by the differential velocity of moving fields, since both flicker and motion involve temporal changes. For example, Regan and Beverely (1984) report that motion contrast defines boundaries and segregates regions more efficiently than luminance contrast. However, a closer examination of our phenomenon reveals that it may involve different processes than segregation by motion. Depth produced by areas moving at different velocities is probably related to the depth signaled by motion parallax. Faster-moving areas are localized nearer than slower-moving areas; stationary areas are localized farthest away. In our flicker-induced depth segregation, it is the nonflickering (or static) areas that are seen in front. Moreover, the amount of depth segregation perceived is dependent on the temporal frequency or flicker rate.

Using square–wave flicker, we examined the amount of depth segregation at a number of temporal frequencies. Depth segregation by flicker is greatest between 6 and 8 Hz. As the temporal frequency goes up or down, depth disappears. Thus, it appears that flicker-induced depth is temporally tuned and optimal at moderate temporal frequencies. This feature makes it different from depth signaled by differential velocities of moving fields related to motion parallax. Similarly, it is not tenable to account for our depth effect in terms of occlusion cues, even if the temporal change adjacent to a stationary edge is considered to be a cue indicating disappearance behind opaque regions. One would expect occlusion to work whether the temporal changes at a stationary edge were fast or slow. In fact, for occlusion to function as a reliable cue for depth segregation, it must be transparent to the rate of temporal change. If occlusion were tied to temporal tuning, only objects moving at a certain rate would be seen as moving behind other objects. This effect would defeat the whole purpose of occlusion as a cue to depth segregation.

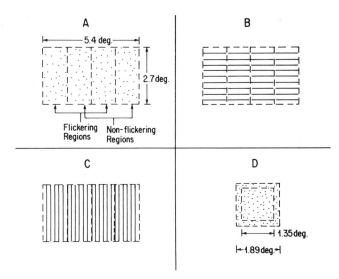

Figure 2.8   Stimulus displays used in investigating the effect of flicker in the segregation of flickering and nonflickering regions in depth.

III.B. Spatial and Temporal Tuning of Flicker-Induced Depth

Because flicker-induced depth is uniquely related to temporal frequencies, we decided to look at the aspect of temporal tuning in greater detail. First, we tested whether the effect was dependent on the pattern elements making up the visual field. In the initial investigation we used fields of random dots. Figure 2.8 shows four types of displays used in an experiment that looked at flicker-induced depth, with different display elements making up the flickering and nonflickering regions.

In panels A, B, and C (Figure 2.8), alternating regions were flickered; in panel D, either the center or the surrounding area was flickered. The average temporal luminance across all of the regions was kept equal. On–off square–wave flicker was used. The depth of the temporal modulation was always 100%. Figure 2.9 shows the results of this study. The effect of depth segregation between flickering and nonflickering areas was obtained in all the pattern fields. The temporal tuning of depth is again prominent. It peaks between 6 and 8 Hz across all of the displays. This result indicates no interaction of temporal frequency and display pattern in the inducement of depth between the flickering and nonflickering areas.

We next looked at both the spatial and temporal properties of flicker-induced depth using alternating flickering and nonflickering "bars" of

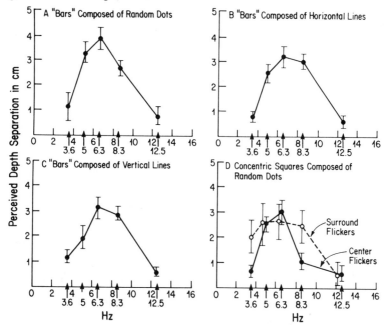

Figure 2.9   Results of experiment investigating the effect of temporal frequencies and display patterns on the separation of flickering and nonflickering regions in depth.

random dots (Wong & Weisstein, 1984a). In the experiment, temporal frequencies ranged from 1 to 12.5 Hz. The width of the bars varied from .34° to 2.7° per bar. The average temporal luminance of the flickering and nonflickering regions was kept equal, and a square–wave flicker of 100% depth modulation was used. The amount of depth perceived between the flickering and nonflickering areas was measured as a function of barwidth and temporal frequency and was plotted in two-dimensional space. Whenever depth was seen between the flickering and nonflickering areas, the flickering regions were always seen in depth behind the nonflickering regions. Figure 2.10 shows the isodepth contours contained. The contours joining the coordinate points connect spatial (barwidth) and temporal loci, giving a similar level of depth segregation perceived between flickering and nonflickering areas.

Larger barwidths and higher temporal frequencies produce the maximum segregation in depth between the flickering and nonflickering areas. At temporal frequencies of 6.3 and 7.1 Hz, and at barwidths of 1.35° and .68°, the depth effect is greatest. The upper spatial limit (in terms of barwidth) is bounded by 2.7°, while the depth effect disappears below a temporal frequency of 2 Hz. Depth is perceived up to the highest flicker

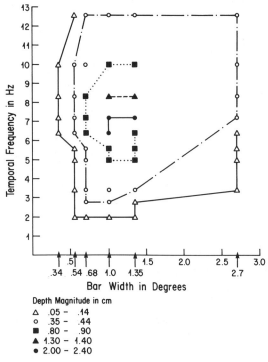

Figure 2.10   Perceived separation in depth of flickering and nonflickering bars as a function of bar width and temporal frequency.

rate used in our study (12.5 Hz), although it is substantially diminished. At the lower end of smaller barwidths, the depth segregation occurs down to .34°.

The amount of depth perceived between flickering and nonflickering areas is also affected by the amplitude of the temporal modulation. We took spatial and temporal parameters, which gave sizable amounts of depth separation between flickering and nonflickering regions, and modulated the flickering areas at amplitudes of 25%, 50%, 75%, and 100%. The amplitude of modulation is defined as $L_{max} - L_{min} / L_{max} + L_{min}$. At 100% modulation, the stimulus is identical to those studies discussed earlier. The average temporal luminance across all of the spatial regions and at all of the modulation amplitudes was kept constant. Perceived depth segregation between the flickering and nonflickering regions was maximal at 100% modulation. At 75% modulation, depth segregation diminished. At barwidths and temporal frequencies where depth was maximum at 100% modulation (1.35° and .68°; 6.3, 71, and 8.3 Hz), the amount of perceived depth is much lower compared to that at 100% modulation (Figure 2.11).

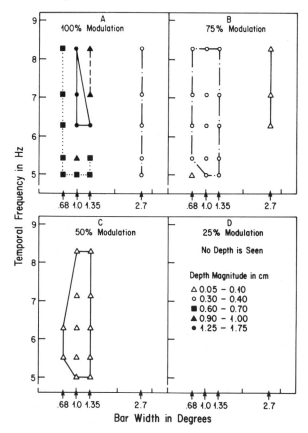

Figure 2.11   Perceived depth separation of flickering and nonflickering bars as a function of barwidth, temporal frequency, and depth of temporal modulation.

At 50% modulation, the amount of depth segregation is only marginal for barwidths and flicker rates where depth had been maximal at 100% modulation. Where depth was marginal at 75% modulation, depth segregation disappeared at 50% modulation. At 25% modulation, no depth was seen at all in the stimulus, although good segregation of regions of random dots was still seen.

Bright areas of the visual field are often perceived as being nearer than dim regions (Ittelson, 1960). Although the average temporal luminance of the flickering and nonflickering areas of our display was equal, if the nonflickering regions somehow looked brighter, this perceived difference might make the area appear to be nearer the observer.

We systematically examined the effect of luminance and brightness on the amount of depth perceived between the flickering and nonflickering regions. The luminance of the nonflickering fields was kept constant throughout the experiment, while the luminance of the flickering areas varied. Seven luminance differences between flickering and nonflickering fields (defined by the ratio of flickering to nonflickering fields) were used: .75, 1, 1.25, 1.5, 1.75, and 2. A ratio of 1 indicates that the average temporal luminance of the flickering and nonflickering areas were equal. A ratio of 1.5 indicates that the average temporal luminance of the flickering area was 1½ times that of the average temporal luminance of the nonflickering regions. Square–wave on–off flicker at 100% modulation depth was used throughout the experiment. The display was the same—alternating flickering and nonflickering random-dot bars. Only the barwidths and temporal frequencies which gave the optimal depth in the earlier experiments were used.

It is interesting that for all of the luminance differences between the flickering and nonflickering areas that we used, at no time was the flickering region seen in front of the nonflickering region. This observation held true even when the flickering area's average temporal luminance was twice that of the nonflickering area.

The effect of luminance between flickering and nonflickering regions on the amount of depth perceived is shown in Figure 2.12. When the flickering regions had an average temporal luminance .75 times that of the non-flickering regions' temporal luminance, the depth separation between the two areas was greatest (see panel A in Figure 2.12). While a substantial amount of depth was seen across all temporal frequencies and barwidths used, not much difference in perceived depth existed among luminance ratios of 1, 1.25, and 1.5. At luminance ratios of 1.25 and above, the flickering areas were invariably seen as brighter than the nonflickering areas. Although the amount of depth diminished as the average temporal luminance of the flickering areas increased, the flickering regions were never seen to appear in front of the nonflickering regions. Thus, although the brightness of an area affects the perceived relative distance of objects, flicker is a much stronger determinant of depth; as a conflicting cue to depth information, brightness can only diminish depth segregation, not reverse it.

III.C. Flickering Regions of a Reversible Picture

Figure 2.13 is a reversible faces–vase picture filled with random dots. If the flanking areas are flickered, the central region appears as a vase filled with random dots standing in front of a backdrop of flickering dots. If the dots in the central area are flickered, the flanking areas are seen as two faces standing out in front of the flickering areas. The visual impression is that of figures of faces filled with dots standing in front of a flickering

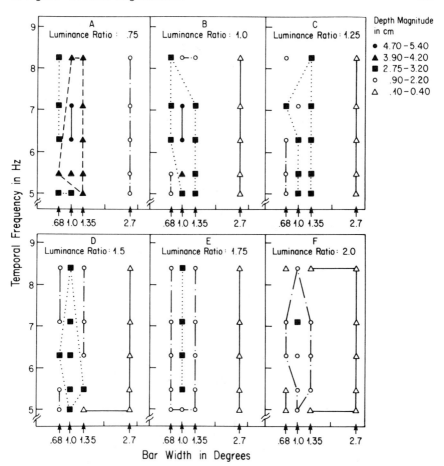

Figure 2.12   Perceived depth separation of flickering and nonflickering bars as a function of barwidth, temporal frequency, and the luminance ratios of flickering/nonflickering areas.

background. This flicker-induced "ground" effect is coupled with the perception of depth segregation of figure and ground areas (Wong & Weisstein, 1984c). In fact, whenever a region is seen as a figure, it is always perceived in front of the background. We examined the effect of flicker rates on the percentage of time that a region is seen as a figure or as ground. At the same time, we measured the amount of depth perceived between the flickering and nonflickering regions. Figure 2.14 shows results from an experiment in which the flickering and nonflickering regions were bounded by an outline defining the vase and faces. We found that the percentage of time a region is seen as background is strongly

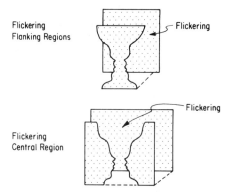

Figure 2.13   Visual impressions of figure–ground organization and perceived depth between flickering and nonflickering areas of regions of the Rubin faces–vase picture filled with random dots.

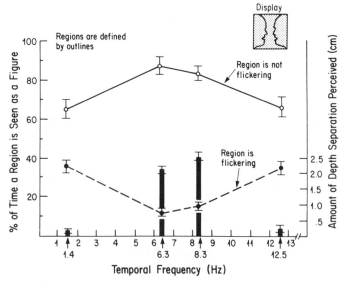

Figure 2.14   Perceived depth separation and percentage of time a region is perceived as a figure or ground as a function of the temporal frequency of flickering regions. Data are from the condition in which the regions of the Rubin picture are defined by a solid outline.

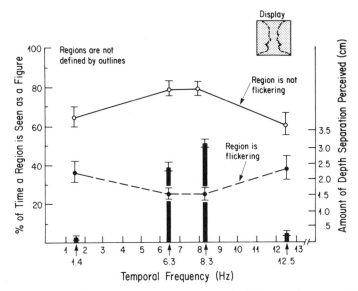

Figure 2.15   Perceived depth separation and percentage of time a region is perceived as a figure or ground as a function of the temporal frequency of the flickering regions. Data are from the condition in which the regions of the Rubin picture are not defined by a solid outline.

dependent on the flicker rate. At temporal frequencies of 6.3 and 8.3 Hz, the flickering regions were seen as ground about 80% of the time, while at 1.4 and 12.5 Hz, figure–ground fluctuated and each organization was seen about 50% of the time. In other words, at very high and very low flicker rates, no dominant organization occurred.

The same trend of results occurred when the flickering and nonflickering regions were not defined by a solid outline. In this condition, when none of the regions flickered, the visual field consisted of a field of random dots. Once a field started flickering, segregation of the field into different regions became apparent. At 6.3 and 8.3 Hz, again the percentage of time a region was seen as ground was greatest at the high and low flicker rates. No region was anchored as ground more than 50% of the time. Figure 2.15 shows the results of this test.

Besides the Rubin faces–vase reversible picture, we also used a display that exhibited reversal properties. This display is shown in Figure 2.16. When the central region flickered, the flanking regions were perceived as two triangles in front of a flickering background. When the flanking areas flickered, the central region was seen as a diagonal strip in front of a flickering backdrop.

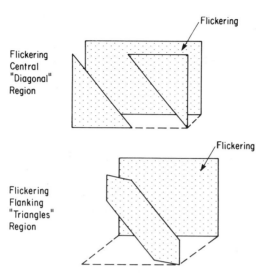

Figure 2.16   Visual impressions of a reversible picture which could be organized as a diagonal strip in front of a background or as two triangles in front of a background as a function of flicker.

Once again we looked at the effect of temporal frequency on the percentage of time a region is seen as a figure or as ground. The results we obtained were similar to those we found with the reversible faces–vase display. When an area was flickered between 6.3 and 8.3 Hz, it was seen as ground more than 80% of the time. However, at very high and very low flicker rates, the flicker was unable to effectively anchor the region as ground. Figure 2.17 shows results from a condition in which the regions were defined by a solid contour. Figure 2.18 shows results from a condition in which the regions were undefined by any solid contour.

Accompanying the "flicker-induced ground" is a perceived separation in depth between the flickering ground areas and the static figure areas. This association strongly suggests a relationship of temporal frequency, figure–ground organization, and perceived depth separation. The tuning functions of flicker-induced depth and ground resemble those of visual channels maximally sensitive to high temporal and low spatial frequencies (Breitmeyer & Ganz, 1977; Burbeck & Kelly, 1981; Legge, 1978; Robson, 1966; Tolhurst, 1975). Given this resemblance of the tuning characteristics of spatiotemporal channels and the tuned temporal effect of flicker on the perception of ground and depth, it is tempting to look at our experimental manipulation as activating figure and ground perceptual processes. Channels tuned to high temporal/low spatial frequencies responding to

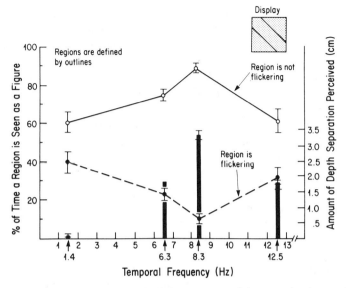

Figure 2.17   Perceived depth separation and percentage of time a region is perceived as a figure or ground as a function of the temporal frequency of the flickering regions. Data are from the condition in which the regions of the "diagonal–triangles" picture are defined by a solid outline.

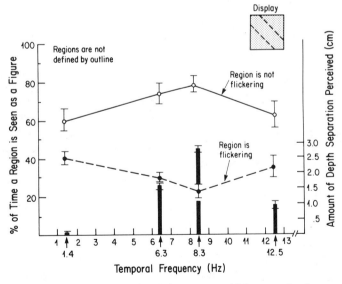

Figure 2.18   Perceived depth separation and percentage of time a region is perceived as a figure or ground as a function of the temporal frequency of the flickering regions. Data are from the condition in which the regions of the "diagonal–triangles" picture are not defined by a solid outline.

flicker would "signal" ground, and channels responding maximally to low temporal/high spatial frequencies would signal figure.

That we have established a connection of figure–ground perception and spatial frequency sensitivity (see Section II) strengthens the association of high spatial/low temporal frequencies with figure processing and of low spatial/high temporal frequencies with ground processing. The organization of figure and ground can affect how spatial frequency and orientation are processed. Conversely, the spatiotemporal responses of the visual system can also determine whether an area will be perceived as a figure or as ground.

IV. CONCLUDING REMARKS

Although figure–ground perception has been the subject of much research, there is a viewpoint which regards figure–ground segregation as a problem that can and should be avoided. Computational approaches to object and shape perception using image segmentation procedures often have difficulty determining objects, shapes, and backgrounds. Thus, figure–ground segregation has been a major obstacle in developing computational theories of form and object perception. Theorists such as Marr (1982, p. 279) have attempted to avoid these difficulties by having the system deal with the surface properties of an image rather than its segmentation into regions.

In Marr's scheme of visual processing, the representation of the visual world is built up in stages by way of sketches. Initially, intensities of the image are coded. Operations are then performed using this information to construct primary sketches of representations which make explicit information about edges, lines, blobs, boundaries, and groupings. Successive computational operations extract surface orientations and textures, depth and distances from these givens and arrive at curvature, discontinuity, and surface properties directly without having to segment the image into regions. Segregating a figure from ground does not become a problem, since surface contours (and occlusions) can be arrived at once the appropriate computational procedures are carried out on the information made explicit in the representations formed in earlier stages of processing.

Understandably, this approach (and other, related computational approaches) has a tremendous advantage over the earlier image segmentation approaches in computer vision in terms of arriving at a representation that closely matches the real world. Although computational expediency might be gained where machine vision is concerned, this approach would nevertheless have difficulty incorporating a number of the visual phenomena associated with figure–ground perception described in this chapter.

In a computational theory such as Marr's, the extraction of surface textures and contours is based on the givens of groupings made explicit in the primal sketches. The higher primitives in the primary sketch incorporate groupings of dots, and lines in which discontinuities, depth, and surface structures are inferred. If the visual information flow is such that the transition from one representation to another is constrained only by the information made explicit in the representation and by the algorithms in the intepretation of the givens, there is no problem (at least logically) in arriving at surface structure properties. However, this is not the case in human visual processing. Orientation resolution and discrimination are very different depending on whether line segments are lying in a figural or ground region. This means that the grouping of lines, at least in the orientation dimension, is different for elements in the two areas. Moreover, the detection of edge and contour continuation—in fact, even the detection of blobs—is dependent on figure and ground. This fact reintroduces the problem of figure and ground at a level of processing before surface properties are extracted.

While the difficulties of image segmentation and figure–ground segregation are avoided in the transition from primal sketch to the emergence of surface structures and depth, the problem returns in that the effects of figure–ground organization have to be contended with in an even earlier stage of processing. Therefore, Marr's (1982) computational approach does not totally avoid the problem of figure–ground organization in human vision. Indeed, any theory of human vision would have to recognize the place of figure–ground perception in constructing a view of how the world is represented and experienced.

We hope that our summary of the existing research in figure–ground perception will motivate further explorations of the processes underlying stimulus extraction and percept formation. We also hope that our initial explorations into how the visual system responds to spatial and temporal stimuli in connection with figure–ground organization will be helpful in charting the operations that mediate figure–ground perception.

REFERENCES

Allman, J., Campbell, C. B. G., & McGuinness, E. (1979). The dorsal third tier area in Galugo senegalensis. *Brain Research, 179,* 355–361.

Bahnsen, P. (1928). Eine Untersuchung über Symmetrie und Asymmetrie bei visuellen Wahrnehmugen. *Zeitschrift für Psychologie, 108,* 129–154.

Blakemore, C., & Campbell, F. W. (1969). On the existence of neurons in the human visual system selectively sensitive to the orientation and size of retinal images. *Journal of Physiology, 203,* 237–260.

Blakemore, C., & Nachmias, J. (1971). The orientation specificity of two visual after-effects. *Journal of Physiology*, **213**, 157–174.

Breitmeyer, B. G. (1975). Simple reaction time as a measure of the temporal response properties of transient and sustained channels. *Vision Research*, **15**, 1411–1412.

Breitmeyer, B. G., & Ganz, L. (1976). Implications of sustained and transient channels for theories of visual pattern masking, saccadic suppression, and information processing. *Psychological Review*, **83**, 1–36.

Breitmeyer, B. G., & Ganz, L. (1977). Temporal studies with flashed gratings: Inferences about human transient and sustained channels. *Vision Research*, **17**, 861–865.

Bridgemann, B. (1981). Cognitive factors in subjective stabilization of the visual world. *Acta Psychologica*, **48**, 111–121.

Broadbent, D. E. (1977). The hidden preattentive process. *American Psychologist*, **32**, 109–118.

Burbeck, C. A., & Kelly, D. H. (1981). Contrast gain measurements and the transient/sustained dichotomy. *Journal of the Optical Society of America*, **71**, 1335–1342.

Calis, G., & Leeuwenberg, E. (1981). Grounding the figure. *Journal of Experimental Psychology*, **7**, 1386–1397.

Campbell, F. W., & Kulikowski, J. J. (1966). Orientational selectivity of the human visual system. *Journal of Physiology*, **187**, 437–445.

Carpenter, P. A., & Ganz, L. (1972). An attentional mechanism in the analysis of spatial frequency. *Perception & Psychophysics*, **12**, 57–60.

Coren, S. (1969). Brightness contrast as a function of figure–ground relations. *Journal of Experimental Psychology*, **80**, 517–524.

Festinger, L., Coren, S., & Rivers, G. (1970). The effects of attention on brightness contrast and assimilation. *American Journal of Psychology*, **83**, 189–207.

Frank, H. (1923). Uber die Beeinflussung von Nachbildeen durch die Gestalteigenschaften der Projektionflache. *Psychologische Forschung*, **4**, 33–41.

Frost, B. J., & Nakayama, K. (1983). Single visual neurons code opposing motion independent of direction. *Science*, **220**, 744–745.

Goldhammer, H. (1934). The influence of area, position, and brightness in the visual perception of a reversible configuration. *American Journal of Psychology*, **46**, 189–206.

Graham, C. H. (1929). Area, color, and brightness difference in a reversible configuration. *Journal of General Psychology*, **2**, 470–481.

Harrower, M. R. (1936). Some factors determining figure–ground articulation. *British Journal of Psychology*, **26**, 407–424.

Henning, G. B., Hertz, B. C., & Broadbent, D. E. (1975). Some experiments bearing on the hypothesis that the visual system analyses spatial patterns in independent bands of spatial frequency. *Vision Research*, **15**, 887–898.

Hochberg, J. (1971). Perception. In L. A. Riggs & J. W. Kling (Eds.), *Woodworth and Schlossberg's Experimental Psychology* (3rd ed.), pp. 396–546. New York: Holt, Rinehart, & Winston.

Hochberg, J. (1981). Levels of perceptual organization. In M. Kubovy & J. Pomerantz (Eds.), *Perceptual organization*, pp. 255–278. Hillsdale, NJ: Erlbaum.

Hood, D. C. (1973). The effects of edge sharpness and exposure duration on detection threshold. *Vision Research*, **13**, 759–766.

Ittelson, W. H. (1960). *Visual space perception*. New York: Springer-Verlag.

Julesz, B. (1971). *The Foundations of Cyclopean perception*. Chicago: University of Chicago Press.

Julesz, B. (1978). Perceptual limits of texture discrimination and their implications to figure–

ground separation. In E. Leeuwenberg & H. Buffart (Eds.), *Formal theories of perception*, pp. 205–216. New York: Wiley.

Koffka, K. (1935). *Principles of Gestalt psychology*. New York: Harcourt Brace.

Köhler, W. (1946). *Dynamics in psychology*. New York: Liveright.

Kulikowski, J. J., Abadi, R., & King-Smith, E. (1973). Orientational selectivity of grating and line detectors in human vision. *Vision Research*, **13**, 1479–1486.

Künnapas, T. M. (1957). Experiments on figure dominance. *Journal of Experimental Psychology*, **53**, 31–39.

Legge, G. E. (1978). Sustained and transient mechanisms in human vision: Temporal and spatial properties. *Vision Research*, **18**, 69–81.

Lupp, U., Hauske, G., & Wolf, W. (1976). Perceptual latencies to sinusoidal gratings. *Vision Research*, **16**, 969–972.

Marr, D. (1982). *Vision*. San Francisco: Freeman.

Marr, D., & Poggio, T. (1979). A computational theory of human stereo vision. *Proceedings of the Royal Society*, **B204**, 301–328.

Nachmias, J. (1967). Effect of exposure duration on visual contrast sensitivity with square-wave gratings. *Journal of the Optical Society of America*, **57**, 421–427.

Oyama, T. (1960). Figure–ground dominance as a function of sector angle, brightness, hue, and orientation. *Journal of Experimental Psychology*, **60**, 299–305.

Oyama, T., & Sasamoto, S. (1957). Experimental studies of figure–ground reversal: II. The effects of brightness, brightness gradient, and area in the tachistoscopic presentation. *Japanese Journal of Psychology*, **28**, 18–27; 64–65.

Oyama, T., & Torii, S. (1955). Experimental studies of figure–ground reversal: I. The effects of area, voluntary control, and prolonged observation in the continuous presentation. *Japanese Journal of Psychology*, **26**, 178–188; 217–218.

Phillips, G. C., & Wilson, H. R. (1984). Orientation bandwidths of spatial mechanisms measured by masking. *Journal of the Optical Society of America*, **1**, 226–232.

Regan, D., & Beverely, K. I. (1984). Figure–ground segregation by motion contrast. *Journal of the Optical Society of America*, **1**, 433–442.

Robson, J. G. (1966). Spatial and temporal contrast sensitivity functions of the visual system. *Journal of the Optical Society of America*, **56**, 1141–1142.

Rubin, E. (1958). Figure and ground. In D. C. Beardslee & M. Wertheimer (Eds.), *Readings in perception*, pp. 194–203. Princeton, NJ: Van Nostrand (original work published in 1921).

Thomas, J. P., & Gille, J. (1979). Bandwidths of orientation channels in human vision. *Journal of the Optical Society of America*, **69**, 652–660.

Thomas, J. P., Gille, J., & Barker, R. A. (1982). Simultaneous visual detection and identification: Theory and data. *Journal of the Optical Society of America*, **72**, 1642–1651.

Tolhurst, D. J. (1975). Sustained and transient channels in human vision. *Vision Research*, **15**, 1151–1155.

Van Nes, F. L., Koenderink, J. J., & Bouman, M. A. (1967). Spatio-temporal modulation transfer in the human eye. *Journal of the Optical Society of America*, **57**, 1082–1087.

Vassilev, A., & Mitov, D. (1976). Perception time and spatial frequency. *Vision Research*, **16**, 89–92.

Watanabe, A., Mori, T., Nagata, S., & Hiwatashi, K. (1968). Spatial sine-wave responses of the human visual system, *Vision Research*, **8**, 1245–1263.

Watson, A. B., & Nachmias, J. (1977). Patterns of temporal interaction in the detection of gratings. *Vision Research*, **17**, 893–902.

Weaver, E. G. (1928). Attention and clearness in the perception of figure and ground. *American Journal of Psychology*, **40**, 51–74.

Weisstein, N., & Harris, C. S. (1974). Visual detection of line segments: An object superiority effect. *Science, 186,* 752–755.

Weisstein, N., Ozog, G., & Szoc, R. A. (1975). A comparison and elaboration of two models of metacontrast. *Psychological Review, 82,* 2325–343.

Weitzman, B. (1963a). A figural aftereffect produced by a phenomenal dichotomy in a uniform contour. *Journal of Experimental Psychology, 66,* 195–200.

Weitzman, B. (1963b). A threshold difference produced by a figure–ground dichotomy. *Journal of Experimental Psychology, 66,* 201–205.

Westheimer, G., & McKee, S. (1980). Stereoscopic acuity with defocused and spatially filtered retinal images. *Journal of the Optical Society of America, 70,* 772–778.

Williams, M., & Weisstein, N. (1981). Spatial frequency response and perceived depth in the time course of object superiority. *Vision Research, 21,* 631–674.

Wilson, H. R., McFarlane, D. K., & Phillips, G. C. (1983). Spatial frequency tuning of orientation selective units estimated by oblique masking. *Vision Research, 23,* 873–882.

Wong, E., & Weisstein, N. (1982). A new perceptual context-superiority effect: Line segments are more visible against a figure than against a ground. *Science, 218,* 587–589.

Wong, E., & Weisstein, N. (1983). Sharp targets are detected better against a figure and blurred targets are detected better against a background. *Journal of Experimental Psychology: Human Perception and Performance, 9,* 194–202.

Wong, E., & Weisstein, N. (1984a). Flicker induces depth: Spatial and temporal factors in the perceptual segregation of flickering and non-flickering regions in depth. *Perception & Psychophysics, 35,* 229–236.

Wong, E., & Weisstein, N. (1984b). The effects of perceived figure and ground on the orientation discrimination of sharp and blurred targets. *Perception,* in press.

Wong, E., & Weisstein, N. (1984c). *Flickering regions of a reversible figure are seen as backgrounds and non-flickering regions are seen as figures.* Paper presented at the Association for Research in Vision and Ophthalmology meeting, Sarasota, Florida, May 1984.

Wong, E., & Weisstein, N. (1986). A new visual phenomenon: Flickering fields are localized in a depth plane behind non-flickering fields. *Perception, 14,* 13–17.

CHAPTER 3

Eye Movements and Visual Pattern Perception

Bruno G. Breitmeyer

Department of Psychology, University of Houston,
Houston, Texas 77004

I. INTRODUCTION

Our commerce with the world around us relies to a major extent on our ability to actively look, visually scan, and selectively pick up information on the basis of which effective, visually guided action can be deployed. Such visual scanning and deployment of "effectivities" or goal-directed behavior in turn requires spatial as well as temporal coordination between sensory and motor processes. Spatially, what is required in sensory–motor coupling is that the outer would be projected systematically onto a motor map of the body. Much of this sensory–motor coupling is reflexive and by and large innate, although this does not rule out an appreciable degree of plasticity. A detailed discussion of these basic aspects of behavioral space are beyond the scope of this chapter; however, they have been treated at some length by Trevarthen (1974, 1978). We restrict ourselves here to that subclass of visual exploratory and orienting behavior requiring directed movements of the eyes to selectively garner specific information from the extensive fund that is potentially available to the observer. In this regard, what is required temporally is a remarkably exquisite orchestration of the visuosensory, attentional, and oculomotor processes that make up active perception.

On one hand, insofar as we have mentioned a spatial coupling between the world and the motor map of an observer, it is perhaps more appropriate to talk in terms of *perceptual systems* rather than of perception disembodied from the organism–environment matrix. On the other hand, since our particular focus is on the spatiotemporal orchestration of visuosensory attentional and oculomotor processes involved in active visual exploration, it is more appropriate to talk in terms of perceptual cycles

65

(Neisser, 1976) characterized by (1) the directing of sensory apparatus to (2) selectively pick up information which serves to (3) modify and update the schemata that in turn direct the further pick-up of information. In these terms, perception is (to use a hackneyed phrase) an active process. However, let us not lose sight of the fact that much of what supports and even necessitates active perception is rather passive mechanisms and boundary conditions, characterizing the functional architecture of the visual system. In the following we review such structural and functional aspects of the visual system, which are intimately tied to active perception.

II. STRUCTURES AND MECHANISMS: PASSIVE COMPONENTS IN ACTIVE LOOKING

Despite the phenomenal isotropy of the visual field's spatial layout, we can nonetheless, with an effort of introspection, become aware of an essential anisotropy of visual space. The area at and within the vicinity of our center of gaze appears more distinct and differentiable than areas progressively farther from our center of gaze. This anisotropy is, of course, tied to the existence of a foveal area in which spatial resolution is highest and outside of which it rapidly deteriorates at progressively greater distances. In primates, the anatomical bases of such high-resolution vision are not only the correspondingly high cone–receptor density found at the foveae but also the smaller visual receptive fields found there, as well as the cortical magnifications of the foveal projections of both monocular visual fields (Cowey & Rolls, 1974; Daniel & Whitteridge, 1961; Hubel & Wiesel, 1974; Myerson, 1977; Rolls & Cowey, 1970; Rovamo & Virsu, 1979; Talbot & Marshall, 1941). Berkley (1976) has speculated on the role of foveal vision in binocular single vision. According to his argument, the two foveae as areas of highest spatial resolution act like a pair of cross-hairs which allow the precise aligning of the two monocular fields required for stereoscopic vision. This approach seems particularly reasonable if one notes that the central area of binocular overlap corresponds to that part of behavioral space associated with consummatory responses that are critically dependent on object discrimination, identification, and manipulation, whereas the more lateral and monocular fields are associated with orienting movements toward the location of objects in the behavioral field (Trevarthen, 1978).

Despite the benefits for binocular single vision and object perception gained by the presence of the two foveae, according to Steinman (1975) and Robinson (1976) they nevertheless pose a most serious complication to the oculomotor system. In the entire visual field, problems can arise in several ways. For example, it is often the case that two or more widely separated objects or areas in the visual field require foveal attention and scrutiny. The oculomotor problems posed here are solved by conjugate, ballistic saccades which allow the eyes to move rapidly from one area of foveal gaze to another. The small size of the foveae also poses the problem of maintaining foveal regard on an object when either the object or the observer moves over an extensive distance. The former problem is solved by executing smooth ocular pursuit movements, the latter by smooth, conjugate, compensatory eye movements.

Associated with these eye movements are sensory events which at relatively early stages of visual processing facilitate the efficient pick-up of information. Discussion of these events relies on drawing distinctions and noting functional relations between two classes of neurons—sustained and transient. These two types of visual neurons have been identified throughout the visual pathways of higher mammals. In cats and monkeys they are found in the retina (De Monasterio, 1978; Enroth-Cugell & Robson, 1966; Gouras, 1968; Kaas, Huerta, Weber, & Harting, 1978), in the lateral geniculate nucleus (Dreher, Fukuda, & Rodieck, 1976; Friedlander, Lin, & Sherman, 1979; Kratz, Webb, & Sherman, 1978; Schiller & Malpeli, 1978), and in the visual cortex (Dow, 1974; Dreher, Leventhal, & Hale, 1980; Ikeda & Wright, 1974; Singer, Tretter, & Cynader, 1975). Psychophysical evidence also points to their existence in humans (Breitmeyer & Ganz, 1976, 1977; Breitmeyer, Levi, & Harwerth, 1981; Kulikowski & Tolhurst, 1973; Legge, 1978; Lennie, 1980a,b).

Several response properties allow us to functionally distinguish between these two cell types. These have been enumerated elsewhere (Breitmeyer, 1980; Breitmeyer & Ganz, 1976) and are presented in summary fashion here: (1) Sustained relative to transient channels are characterized by both a longer response latency and a longer response persistence. (2) Sustained activity is most heavily concentrated in the fovea, whereas transient activity appears to dominate extrafoveally. (3) Sustained channels are responsive to stationary stimuli and have a relatively high spatial resolution which is required for the detailed analysis of pattern information; transient channels respond to the sudden on- or off-set of a stimulus, or to its rapid motion, and are characterized by a relatively higher temporal resolution. (4) Transient and sustained channels, at least at postretinal levels (Singer & Bedworth, 1973; Singer et al., 1975; Tsumoto, 1978; Tsumoto & Suzuki, 1976), can mutually inhibit each other. These and ancillary properties have been incorporated in several neurologically based models of visual masking (Breitmeyer, 1980; Breitmeyer & Ganz, 1976; Weisstein, Ozog, & Szoc, 1975), and their relevance to our understanding of active visual exploration is outlined here.

Consider the situation of scanning across an extensive but static visual scene, such as inspecting a road map or reading a book. The pick-up of information is characterized by successive fixation intervals lasting on the order of 200 msec, separated by rapid saccades lasting about 20 msec. What are the sensory consequences of such fixation–saccade sequences? During a fixation, the eyes are stationary, and since the scene being inspected is also stationary, one would expect only the sustained channels to be responding actively to the patterns present in the scene. However, during a saccade, whose velocity can attain several hundred degrees per second, one would obtain abrupt and rapid image displacements across the retina. Here the sustained channels, due to their relatively low temporal resolution, would not be active; instead, one would obtain strong transient activity. As noted by Breitmeyer (1980), short-latency transient activity retroactively inhibits the longer-latency sustained activity generated in the latter portion of the prior fixation interval and thus prevents that activity from persisting across the saccade and integrating with the sustained activity generated during the initial portion of the succeeding fixation interval. In effect, transient-on-sustained neural inhibition, as noted by several investigators (e.g., Breitmeyer & Ganz, 1976; Matin, 1974, 1976; Singer & Bedworth, 1973), acts as a mechanism of saccadic suppression of sustained response persistence in the retino-geniculo-cortical pathway, so that the pattern information picked up by the visual system during one fixation interval is segregated from that picked up in the following interval.

Why is such a segregation desirable, or even necessary? The answer lies in the fact that the sustained pathways carrying pattern information from the retina to the striate cortex are retinotopically organized. Since with successive saccade-directed fixations we typically pick up very disparate pattern information, it would be undesirable for such spatially discordant information to reside simultaneously (i.e., to be integrated) in the same retinotopic pathways. As noted by Hochberg (1978), our successive glimpses of the world would then mask each other, at least partially, and this would certainly slow our ability to pick up information. Of course, saccadic suppression as a solution to the problem of response persistence and integration in retinotopically organized sustained pathways during saccade-directed changes of gaze in turn poses a problem. Why is perception continuous or temporally integrated rather than segregated at the later, spatiotopically organized level of visual processing, which is reflected in our phenomenal experience of a stable world despite ever-changing inputs along the earlier, retinotopically-organized pathways (Matin, 1976)? We simply do not experience the saccadic suppression in retinotopic channels as temporal gaps between fixations.

Up to now we have discussed the role of transient-on-sustained neural inhibition as a form of saccadic suppression. We now suggest a possible role of the reverse, sustained-on-transient neural inhibition in maintaining clear foveal vision during either visual pursuit of a moving pattern or fixation of a stationary pattern while the observer is moving past it. In either case, except for some retinal slip, the image of a pursued or fixated pattern remains more or less fixed on the fovea, whereas images of patterns or objects not pursued or fixated are displaced rapidly across the extrafoveal and peripheral areas of the retina. As a result, a more or less stationary image falling on the fovea would activate sustained channels which are particularly strongly represented there, whereas moving images in the immediately surrounding extrafoveal and more remote peripheral areas of the retina would activate transient channels. As argued elsewhere (Breitmeyer, 1980; Breitmeyer & Valberg, 1979), this nearby and remote transient activity is capable of inhibiting sustained activity at the fovea. If such inhibition were to go unchecked, foveal pattern vision and acuity would deteriorate severely during visual pursuit or compensatory movements. However, the sustained channels strongly activated at the fovea during pursuit or compensatory eye movements (but not during saccades) are in turn capable of reciprocally inhibiting or checking this effect of the extrafoveal transient activity. Consequently, the role of sustained-on-transient neural inhibition, particularly at the fovea, can be viewed as a mechanism that facilitates a clear, sharp foveal pattern percept during active visual pursuit and compensation.

We have discussed some structural aspects of the visual system which necessitate active visual exploration as it is effected by a variety of eye movements. We have also pointed out some of the sensory consequences of such active looking which follow rather passively from the functional architecture of the peripheral afferent visual pathway, particularly that characterizing the retinotopically organized sustained and transient pathways projecting from the retina to the striate cortex. In the following section we focus on some possible central processes, corollary to the execution of eye movements executed during visual exploratory behavior, which actively modulate the signals arriving at the central, cortical levels via the afferent sensory pathways.

III. CENTRAL PROCESSES IMPLICATED IN THE CONTROL OF VISUAL GAZE AND SELECTIVE ATTENTION

To set the stage for the following discussion, we briefly sketch several situations in which the control of visual gaze and focal attention aids in our selective pick-up of information. We have already mentioned ocular pursuit and compensatory movements, which allow continued foveal scrutiny of an object when either it or the observer is in motion. We have also noted that saccades mediate the abrupt, rapid change of gaze when we are inspecting or reading a static display such as a road map, a text, or a painting at a gallery. Here the sequential search or inspection is guided by cognitive as well as extrafoveal, sensory information (Hochberg, 1978; Malt & Seaman, 1978; McConkie & Rayner, 1975; Neisser, 1976; Rayner, Inhoff, Morrison, Slowiaczek, & Bertera, 1981; Rayner, Well, Pollatsek, & Bertera, 1982). Henceforth, we designate such saccades and associated shifts of attention and gaze as *information-guided.* However, saccade-directed changes of gaze and the accompanying change of attention can also occur when, for instance, a new object is suddenly introduced into the periphery of the visual field, or when a previously stationary object located in the extrafoveal regions suddenly moves. In both situations, execution of a saccade is required to effect a rapid shift of foveation to the peripheral event. Henceforth, we refer to such saccades and associated shifts of attention as *event-triggered.*

In each of these three basic settings, some visual processing must occur prior to the shift of attention and gaze to, or their maintenance on, a given object. As pointed out by Robinson and Goldberg (1978b) such processing relies on analysis of the visual object in terms of the following set of questions: Where is it, what is it, and is it behaviorally relevant? In what follows, we concentrate on the visually responsive areas of the brain: the superior colliculus, the visual cortex, the posterior parietal cortex, and the frontal eye fields. Additionally, the brain stem reticular areas will be discussed vis-à-vis their role in the control and direction of eye movements and visual attention.

III.A. Superior Colliculus and Visual Cortex

Collicular and cortical influences on eye movement control and directed attention have been investigated extensively. Robinson and Goldberg (1978b) differentiate between the general functions of the superior colliculus and visual cortex as follows. The superior colliculus seems to be involved in rather coarsely localizing and detecting the presence of a visual stimulus which may be potentially informative and behaviorally significant. However, it does not appear to be involved in the detailed qualitative analysis or identification of the stimulus. By contrast, the visual cortex seems to be involved primarily in the fine localization of a stimulus (e.g., vernier acuity tasks) and in analyzing its qualitative and figural aspects. Unlike the superior colliculus, the visual cortex, except for area 19 (Fischer & Boch, 1981a–d; Fischer, Boch, & Bach, 1981), does not respond selectively to behaviorally relevant (as compared to irrelevant) stimuli. These differential functional assignments to the superior colliculus and visual cortex concur in part with the differential roles ascribed to these structures by Trevarthen (1968, 1978), Schneider (1969), and Humphrey (1974). These investigators have demonstrated, on the basis of selective lesions, that focal and ambient vision—that is, the ability to discriminate, recognize, and identify stimuli and to locate and orient toward stimuli—are predominantly under the control of cortical and midbrain/collicular structures, respectively. As we shall see, other visual structures also differentially support focal and ambient vision. However, we now take a closer look at the superior colliculus.

Located in the midbrain, it comprises three general subdivisions: the superficial, the intermediate, and the deep layers. Cells in the superficial layer of the super colliculus are particularly responsive to visual stimuli, and their receptive fields are relatively large. Perhaps of greatest behavioral significance, their response is selectively enhanced from approximately 200 msec prior to and up to the onset of a goal-directed saccade. The latter must be made to a behaviorally relevant stimulus falling in their receptive fields but not elsewhere (Goldberg & Wurtz, 1972b; Robinson & Goldberg, 1977; Schiller & Koerner, 1971; Wurtz, 1976; Wurtz & Mohler, 1974, 1976). As noted by Goldberg and Wurtz (1972b), such selective response enhancement may be a neurophysiological event corresponding to the psychological phenomenon evidenced by shifts of visual attention or target selection from an area being currently fixated to a behaviorally relevant stimulus introduced into or already located in some portion of the peripheral visual field. Based on several human psychophysical studies (see Posner, 1980; Posner, Snyder, & Davidson, 1980; Remington, 1980), when shifts of visual attention are associated with eye movements such as saccades, the attentional shift appears to be obligatory. Moreover, like the selective response enhancement of superficial collicular cells, the shift occurs prior to the onset of saccadic eye movements.

The superior colliculus projects to the pulvinar nuclei (Benevento & Fallon, 1975; Benevento & Rezak, 1976; Lin & Kaas, 1979, 1980), which in turn project to the primary visual cortex (area 17) (Benevento & Rezak, 1976; Cooper, Kennedy, Magnin, & Vital-Durand, 1979) as well as the adjacent visual association (circumstriate and inferotemporal) areas (Diamond & Hall, 1969; Jones, 1974). Thus an enhanced collicular response to a stimulus at a given extrafoveal location of the visual field could render that location more salient to the pulvinar (Keys & Robinson, 1979; Perryman, Lindsley & Lindsley, 1980) and thus to its cortical recipient areas

(Chalupa, Anchel, & Lindsley, 1973; Chalupa, Coyle, & Lindsley, 1976; Goldberg & Robinson, 1978; Gross, Bender, & Roch-Miranda, 1974; Rezak & Benevento, 1979).

The superficial layers of the superior colliculus are known to be innervated by fast-conducting transient fibers arriving either cortifugally from the visual cortex or directly from the retina. In both pathways, visual receptive fields are topographically organized, thus providing a sensory map of the retinal surface (Cynader & Berman, 1972; Goldberg & Wurtz, 1972a; McIlwain, 1973a, 1973b, 1975; McIlwain & Lufkin, 1976; Schiller & Koerner, 1971). These collicular transient neurons can be regarded as event detectors (Schiller & Koerner, 1971) which, due to their short-latency activation, constitute an "early warning system" that alerts the visual system to the presence and location of novel objects suddenly introduced or set into motion in the visual field. It is plausible that the activity of these event detectors is thus involved in generating and directing event-triggered saccades and associated shifts of attention to the location of the novel object(s).

What evidence exists to support this alerting and early warning function of transient cells in the superficial layers of the superior colliculus? Goldberg and Wurtz (1972b) and Oyster and Takahashi (1975) have reported that the responses of cells in the superficial layers of the colliculus habituate to repetitive stimuli applied to their receptive fields. Similarly, Robinson, Baizer, and Dow (1980) have found such habituation in prestriate neurons of the rhesus monkey. (Recall that the superior colliculus projects, via the pulvinar, to the prestriate areas of the visual cortex.) In effect, an initially novel stimulus is "recognized" as a non-novel one after several repetitive presentations. In related psychophysical studies, Singer, Zihl, and Pöppel (1977) and Frome, McLeod, Buck, and Williams (1981) have shown that with steady fixation, the detection threshold in humans for stimuli repeatedly flashed in the same location of the peripheral visual field increases over that of their initial presentation. This loss of sensitivity is not due simply to a local adaptation effect occurring at, say, the receptor or postreceptor levels activated by the repetitive stimulus, since, as reported by Singer et al. (1977), such a loss could be prevented if subjects were allowed to switch attention and make saccades to the location of a peripheral stimulus each time it was presented.

Cells in the deep layers of the superior colliculus may also contribute to these alerting and selective enhancing functions. These cells were long believed to be visually unresponsive; however, Berson and McIlwain (1982) have demonstrated that direct and indirect input from retinal transient cells can exert an influence on the output of the deep layer cells of the cat's superior colliculus. These cells respond prior to saccades. Via ascending fibers, they may provide the previously mentioned response enhancement found prior to saccades in the superficial layer cells (Goldberg & Robinson, 1978; Mohler & Wurtz, 1976; Wurtz & Mohler, 1976). In fact, on physiological and cytological grounds, Edwards, Ginsburgh, Henkel, and Stein (1979) argue that the deeper cells ought to be classified as reticular rather than collicular. As we show here, reticular activity, particularly when associated with saccades, generally facilitates activity in the geniculo-striate pathway during the postsaccade fixation interval.

What are the consequences of such alerting and enhancement effects for perceptual performance? Based on several psychophysical studies (e.g., Bashinski & Bacharach, 1980; Crovitz & Davis, 1962), we can infer that shifts of attention to a given spatial location do enhance perceptual sensitivity there. In a particularly apropos series of studies, Posner et al. (1980) arrived at the following relevant conclusions: (1) The detection of visual signals is facilitated by selectivity attending to their location; and (2) subjects cannot split their attention so that it is allocated to two separate locations in space.

This latter finding is further corroborated by psychophysical results reported by Wilson and Singer (1981). These investigators found that the ability to discriminate a single from a double flash of a target light at a given location in the visual field could be suppressed by another such flash occurring within about 100 msec, and up to distances as large as 20° from the first flash. Interesting parallels exist between these psychophysical results and neurophysiological findings showing that the responses of transient neurons which constitute the set of collicular event detectors associated with event-triggered saccades and shifts of attention can be suppressed by remote stimulation falling outside their conventionally spot-mapped receptive fields (Rizzolatti, Camarda, Grupp, & Pisa, 1973, 1974; Wurtz, Richmond, & Judge, 1980). Moreover, the timing of the remote flash relative to the target flash falling on the transient cell's receptive field center is such that suppressive effects can be obtained at flash asynchronies ranging from 0 to about 100 msec, a range approximating that obtained in Wilson and Singer's (1981) study. From this information one may infer that roughly 100 msec are required to allow the switching of attention from one location in space to another, a value that closely approximates other psychophysical estimates of attention-switching time (LaBerge, 1973; Posner, 1980; Posner & Cohen, 1980).

In view of this assumption, it is perhaps not coincidental that the response latency of pattern-analyzing sustained neurons at the cortical level is also approximately 100 msec longer than that of the faster-responding transient neurons (Dow, 1974). Hence, an event-triggered shift of the functional locus of attention to a novel stimulus in an extrafoveal location is completed at about the time that the visual cortex begins to process in preliminary, coarse fashion the pattern information carried in the extrafoveal, sustained channels. This process is followed by a saccade which brings the foveal sustained channels to bear on the more fine-grained analysis of the figural aspects of the novel stimulus.

Until now we have focused on the visual exploration triggered by stimuli suddenly introduced or moved in extrafoveal areas of the visual field. However, the superior colliculus and visual cortex are also involved in what we have termed "information-guided" changes of attention and visual gaze. Recall that the information-guided control of vision arises in situations in which one serially scans or reads a stationary display. Such exploration depends not only on determining where a stimulus is located but also what it is. Hence, the involvement of visual cortical activity may be more evident here than in event-triggered exploration. Due to the generally smaller receptive field of its neurons and a more precise topographic map of the retina, the visual cortex is very likely involved in the more finely tuned localization of visual stimuli (Mohler & Wurtz, 1977). As noted previously, in conjunction with cortical visual association areas, it is also involved in the qualitative and figural analysis of visual stimuli required to guide attention and saccades on the basis of extrafoveal pattern information.

Despite the crucial role of cortical visual areas, the superior colliculus appears to play an important role in information-guided exploration. The transient event detectors found in the superior colliculus would be of little use here, since the visual display is assumed to be static. Collicular neurons are additionally required which can signal, tonically rather than transiently, the location of stationary stimuli. Such tonically responding cells have been identified by Peck, Schlag-Rey, and Schlag (1980) and by Mays and Sparks (1980a, 1981). Moreover, these collicular cells signal the location of a stimulus in terms of spatial or environmental coordinates rather than retinal ones. That is, the cells are capable of holding or storing information about both retinal error (i.e., the retinal location of the stimulus relative to the fovea) and the orbital position of the eyes (i.e., the direction in which the eyes are gazing). Peck et al. (1980) note that the existence of such tonically activated collicular cells may be related to the execution of spatially (rather than retinally) coded, goal-directed saccades which have been shown to exist in monkeys (Mays & Sparks, 1980b). This is an important aspect of visual exploration, for it indicates that our attention and gaze are guided by objects located in the environment rather than by optical images falling on the retina. Thus, the selective attentional system in active visual exploration seems to work on spatiotopically rather than retinotopically coded representations of the visual field.

III.B. Posterior Parietal Cortex and Frontal Eye Fields

The posterior parietal cortex also appears to be involved in the control of eye movements and visual orientation. Mountcastle and his associates (Lynch, 1980; Lynch, Mountcastle, Talbot, & Yin, 1977; Mountcastle, 1976; Mountcastle, Lynch, Georgopoulos, Sakata, & Acuna, 1975; Mountcastle, Motter, & Anderson, 1980; Yin & Mountcastle, 1977) have found neurons in the parietal lobe of alert, behaving monkeys which may be involved in directing eye movements and visual attention in several ways. One class of cells, called *"visual tracking neurons,"* responds during ocular pursuit of moving stimuli but not during fixation on stationary stimuli. The responses of these cells are suppressed before and during saccades superimposed on the smooth pursuit movements. Furthermore, their response to moving stimuli is directionally selective (Goldberg & Robinson, 1977; Robinson & Goldberg, 1978b; Robinson, Goldberg, & Stanton, 1978). Such neurons seem to be involved in maintaining a central gaze on a moving visual object.

A second neuron type, called *"saccade neurons,"* discharges phasically prior to visually guided saccades. They fail to respond before saccadic eye movements made in the absence of a behaviorally significant stimulus. Like the cells of the superficial layers of the superior colliculus, the response of saccade neurons to the onset of an extrafoveal stimulus is enhanced only if that stimulus is the target of a saccade (Goldberg & Robinson, 1977; Robinson & Goldberg, 1978b; Robinson et al., 1978). In addition, their activity is suppressed postsaccadically during the new fixation interval. Of particular importance is the finding reported by Robinson and his co-workers (Bushnell, Goldberg, & Robinson, 1978, 1981; Goldberg & Robinson, 1980; Robinson, Bushnell, & Goldberg, 1980; Robinson et al., 1978) that the selective enhancement effects found in parietal saccade neurons can be dissociated from saccadic eye movements. This neural facilitatory effect may have its perceptual correlate when an extrafoveal stimulus is attended to but is not the target of a saccade (Klein, 1979; Posner, 1980; Posner et al., 1980; Remington, 1980; Shulman, Remington, & McLean, 1979). In fact, Posner (1980) reports that while a saccade is overtly executed toward one location in the visual field, attention can nevertheless covertly shift to another location.

These psychophysical phenomena are interesting because they demonstrate that a change of visual attention, or what can be termed the *"functional fovea,"* is not necessarily effected by a corresponding change of central gaze (i.e., of the anatomical fovea; Posner, 1980; Zinchenko & Vergiles, 1972). Rather, what happens under normal viewing conditions is that the change of attention precedes and is subsequently accompanied by (but not tied to) a change of fixation. A third variety of parietal neurons, called *"visual fixation neurons,"* discharges tonically while a stationary stimulus is being fixated. Like visual tracking neurons, their responses are suppressed during a saccade and, as might be expected, their receptive fields always contain the fovea. These neurons would be involved in maintaining one's gaze on an object during the fixation intervals when one is, for instance, reading or actively exploring a static visual scene.

The frontal eye fields are also involved in the control of eye movements and the orientation of attention (Crowne, Yeo, & Russell, 1981; Guitton, 1981; Latto, 1978; Robinson & Fuchs, 1969; Schiller, True, & Conway, 1979). The responses of many visual neurons in the frontal eye fields, like the collicular neurons discussed earlier, are selectively enhanced prior to and only when a goal-directed saccade is made to the saccade-eliciting stimuli flashed on their receptive fields, but not elsewhere (Goldberg & Bushnell, 1981a,b; Wurtz, 1976). Hence, they may also be neural correlates of the covert shift of attention that precedes a saccadic eye movement.

At the same time, other investigators (e.g., Bizzi, 1968; Bizzi & Schiller, 1970; Mohler, Goldberg, & Wurtz, 1973) have found a different class of frontal eye field neurons whose response facilitation occurs after any (rather than a specifically goal-directed) saccade is executed. Although the connection has not been firmly established, such postsaccadic enhancement may be related to the possibility suggested by Tsumoto and Suzuki's (1976) findings that frontal eye field stimulation facilitates transmission through lateral geniculate sustained neurons immediately after a saccade is completed and a new fixation interval begins. We elaborate on this possibility after we review similar findings reported when investigating subcortical reticular areas.

III.C. Midbrain Reticular Formation

Electrical stimulation of the midbrain reticular formation is known to produce saccade eye movements (Büttner, Büttner-Ennever, & Henn, 1977; Singer & Bedworth, 1974). It is also known that reticular activity corollary to saccades modulates the excitability of cortical and lateral geniculate neurons (Cohen, Feldman, and Diamond, 1969; McIlwain, 1972; Ogawa, 1963; Pecci-Saacedra, Wilson, & Doty, 1966; Singer, 1973a,b, 1977; Singer & Bedworth, 1974; Singer, Tretter, & Cynader, 1976; Tatton & Crapper, 1972). According to Singer and his co-workers (Singer, 1977; Singer & Bedworth, 1974; Singer et al., 1976), this modulation of activity generally takes the form of response enhancements. The latency of this facilitation effect after activation of the reticular areas is approximately 60–100 msec. This value also represents the latency of enhancement effects found in sustained neurons of the lateral geniculate nucleus after activation of frontal eye fields (Tsumoto & Suzuki, 1976). Thus, when saccadic eye movements occur, both the frontal eye field and reticular corollary facilitatory effects would, due to latency, be maximal at and after the termination of a saccade. As Singer and his co-workers (Singer, 1977; Singer & Bedworth, 1974; Singer et al., 1976) and Tsumoto and Suzuki (1976) suggest, this effect would thus reset the excitability of sustained neurons in the geniculate–cortical pathway. This reset would occur at the beginning of each new fixation interval by counteracting any persisting effects of saccadic suppression exerted on the response of these sustained neurons as a result of the activation of transient channels during the saccade.

IV. OVERVIEW AND EXTENSIONS

At this point, it may be worthwhile to recapitulate the main themes raised in Sections II and III. As one vehicle to illustrate how these themes relate to each other, we again consider scanning a static visual scene as, for instance, when reading. Since this task is accomplished by an extended fixation–saccade sequence, we noted in Section II that interactions between two afferent visual pathways—the sustained pathways activated during fixations and the transient pathways activated by and during saccades—contribute to the efficient pick-up of pattern information. The role of the sustained pathways is to process the pattern information contained in the visual field during a given fixation. The role of the transient pathways activated by saccades is to inhibit the sustained pathways' activity, generated during the latter portion of a prior fixation interval, from persisting and thus carrying over into the following fixation interval. In this way the retinotopically organized afferent pathways do not simultaneously carry discordant pattern information from two separate fixations. On the contrary, the pattern information picked up during the fixation interval is temporally segregated in the retinotopically organized pathways.

Superimposed on these early, afferent visual processes are central ones concerned with the control of eye movements and the orienting of attention. We noted in Section III that these central processes can produce two general kinds of enhancements of the activity of the afferent pattern-processing channels. One process, presumably tied to activity generated in the superior colliculus, parietal cortex, and frontal eye fields, produces a presaccadic facilitation of activity only at the extrafoveal location of the visual field to which attention is oriented and to which the gaze is subse-

quently directed by the saccade. We noted how this process in turn facilitates the sequential pick-up of information during fixation–saccade sequences. In addition to this presaccadic facilitation (which corresponds to
the reorientation of attention preceding a saccade), we also noted a general (i.e., nonselective), postsaccadic faciliation in afferent, geniculocorti-
cal sustained pathways tied to activity presumably generated in the brain
stem and midbrain reticular areas and in the frontal eye fields. As noted,
this postsaccadic facilitation is necessary to prevent the saccadic suppression of the retinotopically organized sustained pathways produced by
transient channels activated by and during a saccade from extending into
the following fixation interval. In other words, at the end of each saccade,
a resetting of sensitivity in the suppressed sustained pathways occurs so
that they can expeditiously respond to the newly gained pattern information contained in the present fixation interval. This sequence of events
illustrates the close temporal orchestration of activity in the afferent visual pathways, on one hand, and, on the other hand, in central areas
concerned with the orientation of attention and gaze, which facilitates the
efficient pick-up of information during active looking, reading, and so on.

Finally, I would like to address briefly an issue of broader theoretical
concern—namely, that regarding the approach to perception which can
be classified as "ecological." There are several identifiable versions of
this approach, although the ecological optics advocated by Gibson (1966,
1979) and eloquently promoted by others, such as Turvey (1977), Michaels and Carello (1981), and Shaw and Bransford (1977), has captured
much enthusiasm. This latter version rests on an assumption of direct
realism that is consequential for considering how we ought to focus on the
study of visual perception. The emphasis of ecological optics seems to be
on the *what* of perception; that is, on an optics concerned with the description of information picked up by the visually perceiving organism.
Such a description does not rely on the traditional categories of light rays,
pointillist sense data, and so on, but rather on descriptors, whatever they
may be, more attuned to an account of the affordances offered or the
effectivities directed by visual information.

Such efforts ought to be lauded; however, not to the exclusion of the
study of *how* visual information is processed in the service of an organism's commerce in its world of objects and events. The position implicit
throughout this chapter is similar to that taken by Neisser (1976, 1977). It
fully recognizes the validity of the ecological approach and emphases
advocated by Gibsonians but without deemphasizing a process-oriented
study of visual perception concerned with how perceptions occur and
function—but, more inclusively still, with *why* such perception functions
as it does (Breitmeyer, 1980). I hope the current chapter illustrates that an

effort directed at studying visual perception in the context of at least the three queries of *what, how* and *why* can be a fruitful, ecologically valid approach (Neisser, 1976) to the study of visual perception.

REFERENCES

Bashinski, H. S., & Bacharach, V. R. (1980). Enhancement of perceptual sensitivity as the result of selectively attending to spatial locations. *Perception & Psychophysics*, **28**, 241–248.

Benevento, L. A., & Fallon, J. H. (1975). The ascending projections of the superior colliculus in the rhesus monkey (Macaca mullatta). *Journal of Comparative Neurology*, **160**, 339–362.

Benevento, L. A., & Rezak, M. (1976). The cortical projections of the inferior pulvinar and adjacent lateral pulvinar in the rhesus monkey (*Macaca mulatta*): An autoradiographic study. *Brain Research*, **108**, 1–24.

Berkley, M. A. (1976). Visual acuity. In R. M. Masterton, M. E. Bitterman, C. B. G. Campbell, & N. Hotton (Eds.), *Evolution of brain and behavior in vertebrates*, pp. 73–88. Hillsdale, NJ: Erlbaum.

Berson, D. M., & McIlwain, J. T. (1982). Retinal Y-cell activation of deep-layer cells in superior colliculus of the cat. *Journal of Neurophysiology*, **47**, 700–714.

Bizzi, E. (1968). Discharge of frontal eye field neurons during saccadic and following eye movements in unanesthetized monkeys. *Experimental Brain Research*, **6**, 69–80.

Bizzi, E., & Schiller, P. H. (1970). Single unit activity in the frontal eye fields of unanesthetized monkeys during eye and head movement. *Experimental Brain Research*, **10**, 151–158.

Breitmeyer, B. G. (1980). Unmasking visual masking: A look at the "why" behind the veil of the "how." *Psychological Review*, **87**, 52–69.

Breitmeyer, B. G., & Ganz, L. (1976). Implications of sustained and transient channels for theories of visual pattern masking, saccadic suppression, and information processing. *Psychological Review*, **83**, 1–36.

Breitmeyer, B. G., & Ganz, L. (1977). Temporal studies with flashed gratings: Inferences about human transient and sustained channels. *Vision Research*, **17**, 861–865.

Breitmeyer, B. G., Levi, D. M., & Harwerth, R. S. (1981). Flicker-masking in spatial vision. *Vision Research*, **21**, 1377–1385.

Breitmeyer, B. G., & Valberg, A. (1979). Local foveal, inhibitory effects of global, peripheral excitation. *Science*, **203**, 463–465.

Bushnell, M. C., Goldberg, M. E., & Robinson, D. L. (1978). Dissociation of movement and attention: Neuronal correlates in posterior parietal cortex. *Neuroscience Abstracts*, **4**, 621.

Bushnell, M. C., Goldberg, M. E., & Robinson, D. L. (1981). Behavioral enhancement of visual response in monkey cerebral cortex. I. Modulation in posterior parietal cortex related to selective attention. *Journal of Neurophysiology*, **46**, 755–772.

Büttner, U., Büttner-Ennever, J. A., & Henn, V. (1977). Vertical eye movement related unit activity in the rostral mesencephalic reticular formation of the alert monkey. *Brain Research*, **130**, 239–252.

Chalupa, L. M., Anchel, H., & Lindsley, D. B. (1973). Effects of cryogenic blocking of pulvinar upon visually evoked responses in the cortex of cat. *Experimental Neurology* **39**, 112–122.

Chalupa, L. M., Coyle, R. A., & Lindsley, D. B. (1976). Effect of pulvinar lesion on visual pattern discrimination in monkeys. *Journal of Neurophysiology, 39,* 354–369.

Cohen, B., Feldman, H., & Diamond, S. P. (1969). Effects of eye movement, brain-stem stimulation, and alertness on transmission through lateral geniculate body of monkey. *Journal of Neurophysiology, 32,* 583–594.

Cooper, H. M., Kennedy, H., Magnin, M., & Vital-Durand, F. (1979). Thalamic projections to area 17 in a prosimian primate, *Microcebus murinus. Journal of Comparative Neurology, 187,* 145–168.

Cowey, A., & Rolls, F. T. (1974). Human cortical magnification factor and its relation to visual acuity. *Experimental Brain Research, 21,* 447–454.

Crovitz, H. F., & Davis, W. (1962). Tendencies to eye movements and perceptual accuracy. *Journal of Experimental Psychology, 63,* 495–498.

Crowne, D. P., Yeo, C. H., & Russell, I. S. (1981). The effects of unilateral frontal eye field lesions in the monkey: Visual–motor guidance and avoidance behavior. *Behavioral Brain Research, 2,* 165–167.

Cynader, M., & Berman, N. (1972). Receptive-field organization of monkey superior colliculus. *Journal of Neurophysiology, 35,* 187–201.

Daniel, P. M., & Whitteridge, D. (1961). The representation of the visual field on the cerebral cortex in monkeys. *Journal of Physiology (London) 159,* 203–221.

De Monasterio, F. M. (1978). Properties of concentrically organized X and Y ganglion cells of macaque retina. *Journal of Neurophysiology, 41,* 1139–1417.

Diamond, I. T., & Hall, W. C. (1969). Evolution of neocortex. *Science, 164,* 251–262.

Dow, B. M. (1974). Functional classes of cells and their laminar distribution in monkey visual cortex. *Journal of Neurophysiology, 37,* 927–946.

Dreher, B., Fukuda, Y., & Rodieck, R. W. (1976). Identification, classification and anatomical segregation of cells with X-like and Y-like properties in the lateral geniculate nucleus of old-world primates. *Journal of Physiology (London), 258,* 433–452.

Dreher, B., Leventhal, A. G., & Hale, P. T. (1980). Geniculate input to cat visual cortex: A comparison of area 19 with areas 17 and 18. Journal of *Neurophysiology, 44,* 804–826.

Edwards, S. B., Ginsburgh, C. L., Henkel, C. K., & Stein, B. E. (1979). Sources of subcortical projections to the superior colliculus in the cat. *Journal of Comparative Neurology, 184,* 309–330.

Enroth-Cugell, C., & Robson, J. G. (1966). The contrast sensitivity of retinal ganglion cells of the cat. *Journal of Physiology (London), 187,* 517–552.

Fischer, B., & Boch, R. (1981a). Activity of neurons in area 19 preceding visually guided eye movements of trained rhesus macaques. In A. F. Fuchs & W. Becker (Eds.), *Progress in oculomotor research,* pp. 211–214. Amsterdam: Elsevier/North-Holland.

Fischer, B., & Boch, R. (1981b). Enhanced activation of neurons in prelunate cortex before visually guided saccades of trained rhesus monkey. *Experimental Brain Research, 44,* 129–137.

Fischer, B., & Boch, R. (1981c). Selection of visual targets activates prelunate cortical cells in trained rhesus monkey. *Experimental Brain Research, 41,* 431–433.

Fischer, B., & Boch, R. (1981d). Stimulus vs. eye movements: Comparison of neural activity in the striate and prelunate cortex (A17 and A19) of trained rhesus monkey. *Experimental Brain Research, 43,* 69–77.

Fischer, B., Boch, R., & Bach, M. (1981). Stimulus vs. eye movements: Comparison of neural activity in the striate and prelunate visual cortex (A17 and A19) of trained rhesus monkey. *Experimental Brain Research, 43,* 69–77.

Friedlander, M. J., Lin, C. S., & Sherman, S. M. (1979). Structure of physiologically identified X and Y cells in the cat's lateral geniculate nucleus. *Science, 204,* 1114–1117.

Frome, E. S., McLeod, D.I.A., Buck, S. L., & Williams, D. R. (1981). Large loss of visual sensitivity to flashed peripheral targets. *Vision Research, 21,* 1323-1328.

Gibson, J. J. (1966). *The Senses considered as perceptual systems.* Boston: Houghton, Mifflin.

Gibson, J. J. (1979). *The ecological approach to visual perception.* Boston: Houghton, Mifflin.

Goldberg, M. E., & Bushnell, M. C. (1981a). Behavioral enhancement of visual responses in monkey cerebral cortex. II. Modulation in frontal eye fields specifically related to saccades. *Journal of Neurophysiology, 46,* 773-787.

Goldberg, M. E., & Bushnell, M. C. (1981b). Role of frontal eye fields in visually guided saccades. In A. F. Fuchs & W. Becker (Eds.), *Progress in oculomotor research,* pp. 185-192. Amsterdam: Elsevier/North-Holland.

Goldberg, M. E., & Robinson, D. L. (1977). Visual mechanisms underlying gaze: Function of the cerebral cortex. In R. A. Baker & A. Berthoz (Eds.), *Developments in neuroscience* (Vol. 1), pp. 445-451. Amsterdam: Elsevier/North-Holland Biomedical Press.

Goldberg, M. E., & Robinson, D. L. (1978). Visual system: Superior colliculus. In R. B. Masterton (Ed.), *Handbook of behavioral neurobiology,* pp. 119-164. New York: Plenum.

Goldberg, M. E., & Robinson, D. L. (1980). The significance of enhanced visual responses in posterior parietal cortex. *Behavioral and Brain Sciences, 3,* 503-505.

Goldberg, M. E., & Wurtz, R. H. (1972a). Activity of superior colliculus cells in monkey. I. Visual receptive fields of single neurons. *Journal of Neurophysiology, 35,* 542-559.

Goldberg, M. E., & Wurtz, R. H. (1972b). Activity of superior colliculus in behaving monkey. II. Effect of attention on neuronal responses. *Journal of Physiology (London),* **199,** 533-547.

Gouras, P. (1968). Identification of cone mechanisms in monkey ganglion cells. *Journal of Physiology (London),* **199,** 533-547.

Gross, C. G., Bender, D. B., & Roch-Miranda, C. E. (1974). Inferotemporal cortex: A single unit analysis. In (F. O. Schmitt & F. G. Worden (Eds.), *The neurosciences third study program,* pp. 229-238. Cambridge, MA: MIT Press.

Guitton, D. (1981). On the participation of the feline ''frontal eye field'' in the control of eye and head movements. In A. F. Fuchs & W. Becker (Eds.), *Progress in oculomotor research,* pp. 193-201. Amsterdam: Elsevier/North-Holland.

Hochberg, J. (1978). *Perception.* Englewood Cliffs, NJ: Prentice-Hall.

Hubel, D. H., & Wiesel, T. N. (1974). Uniformity of monkey striate cortex: A parallel relationship between field size, scatter, and magnification factor. *Journal of Comparative Neurology, 158,* 295-306.

Humphrey, N. K. (1974). Vision in a monkey without striate cortex: A case study. *Perception, 3,* 241-255.

Ikeda, H., & Wright, M. J. (1974). Evidence for ''sustained'' and ''transient'' neurons in the cat's visual cortex. *Visual Research, 14,* 133-136.

Jones, E. G. (1974). The anatomy of extrageniculate visual mechanisms. In F. O. Schmitt & F. G. Worden (Eds.), *The neurosciences third study program,* pp. 215-227. Cambridge, MA: MIT Press.

Kaas, J. H., Huerta, M. F., Weber, J. T., & Harting, J. K. (1978). Patterns of retinal terminations and laminar organization of the lateral geniculate nucleus of primates. *Journal of Comparative Neurology, 182,* 517-554.

Keys, W., & Robinson, D. L. (1979). Eye movement-dependent enhancement of visual responses in the pulvinar nucleus of the monkey. *Society of Neuroscience Abstracts,* **5,** 791.

Klein, R. (1979). Does oculomotor readiness mediate cognitive control of visual attention? In (R. S. Nickerson (Ed.), *Attention and performance VIII*, pp. 259–276. Hillsdale, NJ: Erlbaum.

Kratz, K. E., Webb, S. V., & Sherman, S. M. (1978). Electrophysiological classification of X- and Y-cells in the cat's lateral geniculate nucleus. *Vision Research*, **18**, 489–492.

Kulikowski, J. J., & Tolhurst, D. J. (1973). Psychophysical evidence for sustained and transient detectors in human vision. *Journal of Physiology (London)*, **232**, 149–162.

LaBerge, D. (1973). Identification of the time to switch attention: A test of a serial and parallel model of attention. In S. Kornblum (Ed.), *Attention and performance* (Vol. 4), pp. 71–85. New York: Academic Press.

Latto, R. (1978). The effects of bilateral frontal eye-field lesions on the learning of visual search tasks by rhesus monkey. *Brain Research*, **147**, 370–376.

Legge, G. E. (1978). Sustained and transient mechanisms in human vision: Temporal and spatial properties. *Vision Research*, **18**, 69–81.

Lennie, P. (1980a). Parallel visual pathways: A review. *Vision Research*, **20**, 561–594.

Lennie, P. (1980b). Perceptual signs of parallel pathways. *Philosophical Transactions of the Royal Society (London)*, **290B**, 23–37.

Lin, C. S., & Kaas, J. H. (1979). The inferior pulvinar complex in owl monkey: Architectonic subdivisions and patterns of input from the superior colliculus and subdivisions of the visual cortex. *Journal of Comparative Neurology*, **187**, 655–678.

Lin, C. S., & Kaas, J. H. (1980). Projections from the medial nucleus of the inferior pulvinar complex to the middle temporal area of the visual cortex. *Neuroscience*, **5**, 2219–2228.

Lynch, J. C. (1980). The functional organization of posterior parietal association cortex. *Behavioral and Brain Sciences*, **2**, 485–499.

Lynch, J. C., Mountcastle, V. B., Talbot, W. H., & Yin, T. C. T. (1977). Parietal lobe mechanisms for directed visual attention. *Journal of Neurophysiology* **40**, 362–389.

Malt, B. C., & Seaman, J. G. (1978). Peripheral and cognitive components of eye guidance in filled-space reading. *Perception & Psychophysics*, **23**, 399–402.

Matin, E. (1974). Saccadic suppression: A review and analysis. *Psychological Bulletin*, **81**, 899–917.

Matin, E. (1976). Saccadic suppression and the stable world. In R. A. Monty & J. W. Senders (Eds.), *Eye movements and psychological processes*, pp. 113–119. Hillsdale, NJ: Erlbaum.

Mays, L. E., & Sparks, D. L. (1980a). Dissociation of visual and saccade-related responses in superior colliculus neurons. *Journal of Neurophysiology*, **43**, 207–232.

Mays, L. E., & Sparks, D. L. (1980b). Saccades are spatially, not retinotopically, coded. *Science*, **208**, 1163–1165.

Mays, L. E., & Sparks, D. L. (1981). The localization of saccade targets using a combination of retinal and eye position information. In A. F. Fuchs & W. Becker (Eds.), *Progress in oculomotor research*, pp. 39–47. Amsterdam: Elsevier/North-Holland.

McConkie, G. W., & Rayner, K. (1975). The span of the effective stimulus during a fixation in reading. *Perception & Psychophysics*, **17**, 578–586.

McIlwain, J. T. (1972). Nonretinal influences on the lateral geniculate nucleus. *Investigative Ophthalmology and Visual Science*, **5**, 311–322.

McIlwain, J. T. (1973a). Retinotopic fidelity of striate cortex-superior colliculus interactions in the cat. *Journal of Neurophysiology*, **36**, 702–710.

McIlwain, J. T. (1973b). Topographic relationships in projection from striate cortex to superior colliculus of the cat. *Journal of Neurophysiology*, **36**, 690–701.

McIlwain, J. T. & Lufkin, R. B. (1976). Distribution of direct Y-cell inputs to the cat's superior colliculus: Are there spatial gradients? *Brain Research*, **103**, 133–138.

Michaels, C. F., & Carello, C. (1981). *Direct perception.* Englewood Cliffs, NJ: Prentice-Hall.

Mohler, C. W., Goldberg, M. E., & Wurtz, R. H. (1973). Visual receptive fields of frontal eye field neurons. *Brain Research,* **16,** 385–409.

Mohler, C. W., & Wurtz, R. H. (1976). Organization of monkey superior colliculus: Intermediate layer cells discharging before eye movements in monkeys. *Journal of Neurophysiology,* **39,** 722–744.

Mohler, C. W., & Wurtz, R. H. (1977). Role of striate cortex and superior colliculus in visual guidance of saccadic eye movements in monkeys. *Journal of Neurophysiology,* **40,** 74–94.

Mountcastle, V. B. (1976). The world around us: Neural command functions for selective attention. *Neuroscience Program Research Bulletin,* **14,** Suppl., 1–47.

Mountcastle, V. B., Lynch, J. C., Georgopoulos, A., & Sakata, H., & Acuna, C. (1975). Posterior parietal association cortex of the monkey: Command functions for operations within extrapersonal space. *Journal of Neurophysiology,* **38,** 871–908.

Mountcastle, V. B., Motter, B. C., & Anderson, R. A. (1980). Some further observations of the functional properties of neurons in the parietal lobe of the waking monkey. *Behavioral and Brain Sciences,* **3,** 520–523.

Myerson, J. (1977). Magnification in striate cortex and retinal ganglion cell layer of owl monkey: A quantitative comparison. *Science,* **198,** 855–857.

Neisser, U. (1976). *Cognition and reality.* San Francisco: Freeman.

Neisser, U. (1977). Gibson's ecological optics: Consequences of a different stimulus description. *Journal of the Theory of Social Behavior,* **7,** 17–28.

Ogawa, T. (1963). Midbrain reticular influences upon single neurons in lateral geniculate nucleus. *Science,* **139,** 343–344.

Oyster, C. W., & Takahashi, E. S. (1975). Responses of rabbit superior colliculus neurons to repeated visual stimuli.*Journal of Neurophysiology,* **38,** 301–312.

Pecci-Saacreda, J., Wilson, P. D., & Doty, R. W. (1966). Presynaptic inhibition in primate lateral geniculate nucleus. *Nature (London),* **210,** 740–742.

Peck, C. K., Schlag-Rey, M., & Schlag, J. (1980). Visuo-oculomotor properties of cells in the superior colliculus of the alert cat. *Journal of Comparative Neurology,* **194,** 97–116.

Perryman, K. M., Lindsley, D. F., & Lindsley, D. B. (1980). Pulvinar neuron responses to spontaneous and trained eye movements and to light flashes in squirrel monkeys. *Electroencephalography & Clinical Neurophysiology,* **49,** 152–161.

Posner, M. I. (1980). Orienting of attention. *Quarterly Journal of Experimental Psychology,* **32,** 3–25.

Posner, M. I., & Cohen, Y. (1980). Attention and the control of movements. In G. E. Stelmach & J. Requin (Eds.), *Tutorials in motor behavior,* pp. 243–258. Amsterdam: Elsevier/North-Holland.

Posner, M. I., Snyder, C.R.R., & Davidson, B. J. (1980). Attention and the detection of signals. *Journal of Experimental Psychology: General,* **109,** 160–174.

Rayner, K., Inhoff, A. W., Morrison, R. E., Slowiaczek, M. L., & Bertera, J. H. (1981). Masking of foveal and parafoveal vision during eye fixations in reading. *Journal of Experimental Psychology: Human Perception and Performance,* **7,** 167–179.

Rayner, K., Well, A. D., Pollatsek, A., & Bertera, J. H. (1982). The availability of useful information to the right of fixation in reading. *Perception & Psychophysics,* **31,** 537–550.

Remington, R. W. (1980). Attention and saccadic eye movements. *Journal of Experimental Psychology: Human Perception and Performance,* **6,** 726–744.

Rezak, M., & Benevento, L. A. (1979). A comparison of the organization of the projections

of the dorsal lateral geniculate nucleus, the inferior pulvinar and adjacent lateral
pulvinar to primary visual cortex (area 17) in the macaque monkey. *Brain Research,*
167, 19–40.

Rizzolatti, G., Camarda, R., Grupp, L. A., & Pisa, M. (1973). Inhibition of visual responses
of single units in the cat superior colliculus by the introduction of a second visual
stimulus. *Brain Research,* **61,** 390–394.

Rizzolatti, G., Camarda, R., Grupp, L. A., & Pisa, M. (1974). Inhibitory effect of remote
visual stimuli on visual responses of cat superior colliculus: Spatial and temporal factors. *Journal of Neurophysiology,* **37,** 1262–1274.

Robinson, D. A. (1976). The physiology of pursuit eye movements. In A. Monty & J. W.
Senders (Eds.), *Eye movements and psychological processes,* pp. 19–31. Hillsdale, NJ:
Erlbaum.

Robinson, D. L., Baizer, J. S., & Dow, B. M. (1980). Behavioral enhancement of visual
responses of prestriate neurons of the rhesus monkey. *Investigative Ophthalmology
and Visual Science,* **19,** 1120–1123.

Robinson, D. L., Bushnell, M. C., & Goldberg, M. E. (1980). Role of posterior parietal
cortex in selective visual attention. In A. F. Fuchs & W. Becker (Eds.), *Progress in
oculomotor research,* pp. 203–210.

Robinson, D. A., & Fuchs, A. (1969). Eye movements evoked by stimulation of frontal eye
fields. *Journal of Neurophysiology,* **32,** 637–648.

Robinson, D. L., & Goldberg, M. E. (1977). Visual mechanisms underlying gaze: Function
of the superior colliculus. In R. Baker & A. Berthoz (Eds.), *Control of gaze by brain
stem neurons* (Vol. 1), pp. 445–451. Amsterdam: Elsevier/North-Holland.

Robinson, D. L., & Goldberg, M. E. (1978a). Sensory and behavioral properties of neurons
in posterior parietal cortex of the awake, trained monkey. *Proceedings of the Federa-
tion of the American Society of Experimental Biology,* **37,** 2258–2261.

Robinson, D. L., & Goldberg, M. E. (1978b). The visual substrate of eye movements. In J.
W. Senders, D. F. Fisher, & R. D. Monty, (Eds.), *Eye movements and the higher
psychological functions,* pp. 3–14. Hillsdale, NJ: Erlbaum.

Robinson, D. L., Goldberg, M. E., & Stanton, G. B. (1978). Parietal association cortex in
the primate: Sensory mechanisms and behavioral modulations. *Journal of Neurophysiology,* **41,** 910–932.

Rolls, E. T., & Cowey, A. (1970). Topography of the retina and striate cortex and its
relationship to visual acuity in rhesus monkeys and squirrel monkeys. *Experimental
Brain Research,* **10,** 298–310.

Rovamo, J., & Virsu, V. (1979). An estimation of the human cortical magnification factor.
Experimental Brain Research, **37,** 495–510.

Schiller, P. H., & Koerner, F. (1971). Discharge characteristics of single units in superior
colliculus of alert rhesus monkey. *Journal of Neurophysiology,* **35,** 920–936.

Schiller, P. H., & Malpeli, J. G. (1978). Functional specificity of lateral geniculate nucleus
laminae of the rhesus monkey. *Journal of Neurophysiology,* **41,** 788–797.

Schiller, P. H., True, S. D., & Conway, J. L. (1979). Effects of frontal eye field and superior
colliculus ablations on eye movements. *Science,* **206,** 590–592.

Schneider, G. E. (1969). Two visual systems. *Science,* **163,** 895–902.

Shaw, R., & Bransford, J. (1977). *Perceiving, acting, and knowing.* Hillsdale, NJ: Erlbaum.

Shulman, G. L., Remington, R. W., & McLean, J. P. (1979). Moving attention through
visual space. *Journal of Experimental Psychology: Human Perception and Performance,* **5,** 522–526.

Singer, W. (1973a). Brain stem stimulation and the hypothesis of presynaptic inhibition in
cat lateral geniculate neurons. *Brain Research,* **61,** 55–68.

Singer, W. (1973b). The effect of mesencephalic reticular stimulation on intracellular potentials of cat lateral geniculate neurons. *Brain Research,* **61,** 35–54.

Singer, W. (1977). Control of thalamic transmission by corticofugal and ascending reticular pathways in the visual system. *Physiological Review,* **57,** 386–420.

Singer, W., & Bedworth, N. (1973). Inhibitory interaction between X and Y units in cat lateral geniculate nucleus. *Brain Research,* **49,** 491–307.

Singer, W., & Bedworth, N. (1974). Correlation between the effects of brain stem stimulation and saccadic eye movements on transmission in the cat lateral geniculate nucleus. *Brain Research,* **72,** 185–202.

Singer, W., Tretter, F., & Cynader, M. (1975). Organization of cat striate cortex: A correlation of receptive-field properties with afferent and efferent connections. *Journal of Neurophysiology,* **38,** 1080–1998.

Singer, W., Tretter, F., & Cynader, M. (1976). The effect of reticular stimulation on spontaneous and evoked activity in the cat visual cortex. *Brain Research,* **102,** 71–90.

Singer, W., Zihl, J., & Pöppel, E. (1977). Subcortical control of visual thresholds in humans: Evidence for modality specific and retinoptically organized mechanisms of selective attention. *Experimental Brain Research,* **29,** 173–190.

Steinman, R. M. (1975). Oculomotor effects in vision. In G. Lennerstrand & P. Bach-Y-Rita (Eds.), *Basic mechanisms of ocular motility and their clinical implications,* pp. 395–415. Oxford: Pergamon Press.

Talbot, S. A., & Marshall, W. H. (1941). Physiological studies on neural mechanisms of visual localization and discrimination. *American Journal of Ophthalmology,* **24,** 1244–1263.

Tatton, W. G., & Crapper, D. R. (1972). Central tegmental alteration of cat lateral geniculate activity. *Brain Research,* **47,** 371.

Trevarthen, C. B. (1968). Two mechanisms of vision in primates. *Psychologische Forschung,* **31,** 299–337.

Trevarthen, C. B. (1974). Cerebral embryology and the split brain. In M. Kinsbourne (Ed.), *Hemispheric disconnection and cerebral function,* pp. 208–235. Springfield, IL: Charles C. Thomas.

Trevarthen, C. B. (1978). Manipulative strategies of baboons and origins of cerebral asymmetry. In M. Kinsbourne (Ed.), *Asymmetrical function of the brain,* pp. 329–391. Cambridge: Cambridge University Press.

Tsumoto, T. (1978). Inhibitory and excitatory binocular convergence to visual cortical neurons of the cat. *Brain Research,* **159,** 85–97.

Tsumoto, T., & Suzuki, D. A. (1976). Effects of frontal eye field stimulation upon activities of the lateral geniculate body of the cat. *Experimental Brain Research,* **25,** 291–306.

Turvey, M. T. (1977). Contrasting orientations to the theory of visual information processing. *Psychological Review,* **84,** 67–88.

Weisstein, N., Ozog, G., & Szoc, R. (1975). A comparison and elaboration of two models of metacontrast. *Psychological Review,* **82,** 325–343.

Wilson, J. T. L., & Singer, W. (1981). Simultaneous visual events show a long-range spatial interaction. *Perception & Psychophysics,* **30,** 107–113.

Wurtz, R. H. (1976). Extraretinal influences on the primate visual system. In R. A. Monty & J. W. Senders (Eds.), *Eye movements and psychological processes,* pp. 231–244. Hillsdale, NJ: Erlbaum.

Wurtz, R. H., & Mohler, C. W. (1974). Selection of visual targets for the initiation of saccadic eye movements. *Brain Research,* **71,** 209–214.

Wurtz, R. H., & Mohler, C. W. (1976). Organization of monkey superior colliculus: Enhanced visual response of superficial layer cells. *Journal of Neurophysiology,* **39,** 745–765.

Wurtz, R. H., Richmond, B. J., & Judge, S. J. (1980). Vision during saccadic eye movements. III. Visual interactions in monkey superior colliculus. *Journal of Neurophysiology,* **43,** 1168–1181.

Yin, T. C. T., & Mountcastle, V. B. (1977). Visual input to the visuo-motor mechanisms of the monkey's parietal lobe. *Science,* **197,** 1381–1383.

Zinchenko, V. P., & Vergiles, N. Y. (1972). *Formation of visual images.* New York: Consultants Bureau.

CHAPTER 4

A Computer Vision Model
Based on Psychophysical Experiments*

Deborah K. W. Walters

*Department of Computer Science, State University of
New York at Buffalo, Buffalo, New York 14260*

"A picture is worth a thousand words." Or more accurately, a simple image can contain more than 25 million bits of information.[1] This is too much information for the human visual system to process in detail, yet we have the impression that we "see" all of the information in an image. Indeed, visual perception even feels to us like a trivial task. There is a high level of redundancy in visual information, so perhaps the visual system does not process all of the available information in detail; rather, it may be selective and concentrate on those aspects of the image which are most likely to contain useful information. But which image features provide information? This is a hard question to answer, but one indirect way of approaching it is to use psychophysical experiments to determine which features appear to be selectively processed by the human visual system. For example, in line drawings, segments joined at their ends appear to have higher contrast than unconnected segments (Walters & Weisstein, 1982a,b). Such a difference in contrast probably indicates selective processing of end-connected lines (see Section V).

---

* Some of the psychophysical experiments described in this chapter were performed in the Psychology Department, State University of New York at Buffalo. They were funded by Grants 5RO1EY0343203 and 5RO1EY0304703 from the National Eye Institute, awarded to Naomi Weisstein. The computational model research was supported in part by a Research Development Fund Award from the State University of New York Research Foundation and by Grant IST-8409827 from the National Science Foundation, both awarded to the author.

[1] This figure is true for a standard image with a resolution of 1024 by 1024 pixels and eight bits of intensity in each of three colors. Higher-resolution images, such as those used in computer-generated animation, would result in substantially more bits of information.

PATTERN RECOGNITION BY HUMANS
AND MACHINES: Visual Perception
Volume 2

Psychophysical results can demonstrate which image features are selectively processed, but it is not always clear why certain features are important. To continue the example just introduced, above, it is not immediately obvious why end-connected lines should contain more relevant information than unconnected lines, or, indeed, how such information can be utilized in visual perception. One way of answering these questions is to develop models of specific visual tasks using techniques developed in the field of computer vision. To understand these techniques, it is first necessary to understand the motivations of computer vision research.

I. WHAT IS COMPUTER VISION?

Computer vision is the construction of explicit, meaningful descriptions of physical objects from images by computers (Ballard & Brown, 1982). That is, it is the attempt to have computers perform the tasks of visual perception. The visual tasks that computer scientists want to implement are the same tasks that psychologists study. The manner in which the two fields profit from each other can be understood by looking at two approaches to computer vision research: machine vision, with its roots in robotics, and computational vision, which is a later development.

I.A. Machine Vision

Early computer vision research consisted of attempts to make machines "see." The idea was to build a complete vision system which would receive visual input from some type of video camera and provide a useful description of the scene. That goal proved to be very difficult (Brady, 1981). Only relatively simple and very restricted tasks have been performed successfully. For example, there are systems that can read and interpret engineering drawings. The strict rules followed by such drawings, and their standard interpretations, make this task simple enough to be performed by an artificial vision system. Another task that has had success is the inspection of parts on an assembly line (Bolles & Cain, 1983). In this task domain, there are several parameters which can be controlled to help simplify the task. For example, the distance between the viewing system and the objects can be held constant, as can the orientation in which the objects are presented. The lighting can also be controlled. The main drawback with the machine vision approach has been the lack of extensibility of the techniques used. Algorithms that work fine in a simple domain often fail when the domain is extended.

I.B. Computational Vision

The difficulty of creating a total vision system led to a change in emphasis in computer vision research. There is now more concentration on developing general theories of vision (Brady, 1982; Marr, 1982). This is the computational vision approach, which attempts to understand the basic nature of vision. One way to do this is to study vision abstractly, independent of any particular "hardware" system (man or machine) that implements vision. The work of Barrow and Tenenbaum (1981) is an example of this approach. They have investigated how the visual process can be broken down into a number of separate modules, as well as studied the processes that must be involved in each module.

Another approach relies on the fact that the human visual system rapidly and effortlessly accomplishes those visual tasks which we would like a computer to be able to do. Thus, by studying human vision, we may be able to develop a computational theory of vision that we can then implement by machine. This means that we want to study *what* the human visual system does rather than *how* a particular algorithm it might use is implemented in terms of neurons. This approach has been productive in several areas (Marr, 1982; Ullman, 1979; Winston, 1975). Again, most research has concentrated on understanding specific visual modules such as stereopsis, or the determination of surface orientation from texture (Brady, 1981).

II. WHAT CAN COMPUTATIONAL VISION OFFER PSYCHOLOGY?

Computational vision attacks the nature of the problem of vision rather than considering any particular implementation. It provides psychologists with a means of expressing their perceptual theories in a way that makes it possible to test them rigorously—namely they can be expressed as algorithms. There are two reasons for the use of algorithms. First, translating a theory into an algorithm requires a full and complete expression of the theory. The translation stage often leads to the discovery of holes in the theory, and the filling in of the holes enriches the theory. However, the second, more important reason is that algorithms can be implemented and thus used to test the theory. Once the theory is expressed in algorithmic form, it can be programmed on a computer, and the performance of the program on real or simulated data can be observed.

Expressing visual theories as algorithms leads to the development of computational models of vision. In creating computational models, several important issues must be addressed. The next section discusses the more general of these issues.

III. ISSUES INVOLVED IN COMPUTATIONAL MODELS

The first issue concerns the importance of distinguishing between the processing that occurs at the earliest stages—low-level processing—and that occurring later—high-level processing. The second issue concerns the type of processing that occurs at the different levels—is it serial or parallel processing? The third issue is the extent to which information is automatically processed (i.e., all information is processed) or selectively processed (i.e., only certain selected aspects are processed). The fourth issue involves whether information is expressed as visual signals or as cognitive symbols. The fifth issue concerns which features should be processed, and the last issue concerns the extent to which visual information is processed globally or locally.

III.A. Low-Level versus High-Level Visual Processing

Visual processing is a complex process that involves not only the analysis of visual stimuli from the outside world but also an interaction between these stimuli and the viewer's knowledge about the world. A useful conceptual simplification is to divide the process into two levels: low-level visual processing and high-level visual processing.

Low-level processing deals directly with the incoming visual stimuli. The intrinsic characteristics of the image are extracted, such as color, lightness, or range information (Barrow & Tenenbaum, 1981; Horn, 1977; Marr, 1976). Simple features may be extracted and simple patterns recognized. Object perception may also occur at this low level of processing.

The high level of visual processing is concerned with cognitive processing and makes use of knowledge about the world when processing visual information. Hence, it deals with geometric models, and with goals and plans. High-level processing accomplishes such tasks as object classification and scene interpretation.

Traditionally, these two levels of visual processing have been studied separately. They are often represented by different types of models: high-level processing deals with propositional models, relational structures, and knowledge-based systems, while low-level processing is more directly tied to the physical characteristics of an image. The question naturally arises as to how these two levels interface with each other. The traditional artificial intelligence approach assumes that certain information has already been extracted from the visual image and is available in symbolic form. This approach makes assumptions about what is output by the early stages of visual processing, but the assumed symbols might not be readily computable by the lower level of processing.

Which visual cues are chosen to be processed by the lowest levels is obviously an important consideration, as all further processing depends in some sense on how well this initial stage is carried out. The computational model developed in this chapter deals with low-level processing, with the aim of extracting image information directly useful for higher stages. The work presented in this chapter is one example in which the right type of initial processing of the image generates information that makes some aspects of object representation (which were previously thought to require high-level processing) "fall out." Thus, it can be useful to consider how low- and high-level processing interface, even when expressly studying one or the other.

III.B. Serial versus Parallel Processing

There is a distinction between parallel and serial processing, but it is not always straightforward. That is, a system may be described as serial at the top level of description and as parallel at the most detailed level (Anderson & Hinton, 1981). For example, many motor neurons operate together in the contraction of a single muscle. Thus, at the motor neuron level of description, this is a parallel process. At the muscle level, however, movements occur serially, one at a time. Visual tasks may also be viewed as serial at the top level of description but are probably performed in parallel at the most detailed level of description.

In spite of these caveats, it is useful to distinguish between the type of processing used by high- and low-level visual processes in terms of serial versus parallel processing. This framework assumes that the low level of visual processing is primarily performed in parallel. Humans can recognize objects in a visual image in a few milliseconds. Taking into account the speed of neural elements, this means that there is only time to perform a few steps of the computation. Thus, the computations must be performed in parallel. Further evidence for this assumption comes from four different areas. The neurophysiology of the visual system shows us that there are vast arrays of neurons which operate in parallel on the retinal image. In fact, the nature of the visual signal itself is parallel—light wavelength and intensity information for thousands of points in two-dimensional space. There is also psychophysical evidence that humans perform the early stages of visual processing in parallel (Julesz & Schumer, 1981; Treisman & Gelade, 1980). Also, the machine vision evidence supports an initial stage of parallel processing (Rosenfeld & Kak, 1982). Finally, several computational theories of vision provide motivation for assuming that most low-level processing is performed in parallel (Feldman, 1981; Marr, 1982; Ullman, 1986).

Serial processing is more likely to occur at the high levels of visual processing. This is especially true when considering cognitive processes that do not allow for divided attention. For example, objects located at separate points in an image may need to be sequentially processed. Treisman and Gelade (1980) have demonstrated the difference between visual tasks that are apparently performed in parallel and those that appear to be more serial. One of their tasks was to search for a particular visual attribute in the presence of distracters (e.g., the presence of a red T in a field of green T's). Some attributes appear to be processed in parallel, as detection is independent of the number of distracters. Other attributes appear to require serial search, as the reaction times are linear functions of the number of distracters. Treisman and Gelade argue that the parallel processing of an attribute suggests processing at an early, low level of vision.

The computational model developed in this chapter deals with low-level visual processing. Thus, it is developed as a parallel model, being composed of many identical units which simultaneously process information present at each location of the visual image.

III.C. Automatic versus Selective Processing

As just argued, low-level visual processing involves parallel computations performed simultaneously at many locations on the image. Much of this processing would be best performed automatically, without intervention from higher levels. In fact, it would be advantageous if certain parallel computations could be "hardwired" into the system so that basic types of processing could always be performed.

As mentioned earlier, high-level processing is more likely to be serial and to require flexible control of the operations to be performed. It also must allow for the selective inclusion of operations, depending on the available computational resources.

Another way to discuss the automatic versus selective issue is in terms of bottom-up versus top-down processing. Automatic processing can be performed bottom-up without using information from higher levels. On the other hand, selective processing might require top-down processing where there is feedback between the different stages of processing.

In the model developed in this chapter, the processing is performed automatically at each point on the visual image. It is assumed that the type of processing performed is so basic that it should be done for all image locations. The model shows how simple hardware could easily be designed to perform these computational operations.

At the low level, processing can be done in parallel, automatically, without flexible control; it can also be done more efficiently. Thus, it would be advantageous to have as much as possible of the visual processing performed at the low level. The research presented in this chapter gives an example in which processing that had previously been thought possible only if top-down processing were used is performed instead by parallel, bottom-up processing, thus simplifying the visual task.

III.D. Signals versus Symbols

Low-level processing is closely tied to the image, or the visual signal. By contrast, high-level processing deals with cognitive symbols rather than visual signals.

The main task of the early stages of visual processing is to extract the meaningful information from the total visual information and to pass it on to the higher levels of processing. The problem is in deciding how the information should be represented. Either the useful visual features could be labeled and that information transmitted symbolically, or else a scheme not requiring the explicit labeling of features could be employed.

III.D.1. Labeled Features

The simplest case of labeled features would involve labeling particular features which are present in the image, such as oriented line segments or angles. An example of this type of theory is Barlow's (1972) neuron doctrine, stating that each particular neuron is activated by a particular stimulus and that such activation indicates the presence of a stimulus. If this theory were used, then visual features would be labeled early in the process; thus, symbols would be used in low-level processing.

A more complex example of labeling features does not use the delimited representation of the previous theory; instead, it uses a distributed representation, of which there are many possible types. One frequently used in theories of visual perception is the Fourier representation, in which spatial position information is transformed into apatial frequency information (Campbell & Robson, 1968; see also the review by Graham, 1980). The attractiveness of the Fourier transform is due to its mapping information from a delimited domain into a distributed domain. It is not the representation of the image as a series of sinusoidal functions that is important, since many other orthogonal functions could be used equally well to yield a distributed representation.

An example of a simple distributed representation will show how it differs from Barlow's symbolic labeling. Imagine that a and b are particular visual features or cues. In Barlow's scheme, neuron 1 would respond if and only if a were present, and neuron 2 would fire if and only is b were present. In a distributed representation, neuron 1 would fire when either a or b was present but would fire twice as much to a, while neuron 2 would fire equally for a and b but twice as much when both were present. Using either representation, it is possible from the output of both neurons to tell whether a, b, or both a and b were present. Notice that in the distributed representation, the information about the presence of a and b is there, but it is not labeled in a simple way. If we do not need the information in an explicit form, but only need to use it in some intermediary stage of processing, then the distributed representation may be preferable, since reducing the amount of explicit labeling can reduce the complexity of a computational task.

III.D.2. Unlabeled Features

Many cognitive scientists assume that humans, like serial, digital computers, are simply symbol processors (e.g., Pylyshyn, 1980). However, as Hinton (1983) points out, there are alternative theories. For example, distributed patterns of activity could provide a more accurate representation. Such schemes could also avoid labeling visual features. For example, a local computational network might "decide" whether a particular feature is present, but instead of sending that information (expressed symbolically) to a higher stage, it might use the information locally to modify the response to the visual stimulus of some part of the network.

The main reason that the distinction between signals versus symbols is important is that they lead to two different types of representations, and thus to different types of computations. Unlabeled features have been used less frequently, and thus that type of computation is less well understood. Yet there appear to be many similarities between the later style of computation and the computations that might be performed by neurons in the low levels of the visual system.

It is advantageous to restrict the use of symbolic labeling to the highest possible levels. The more symbols that are involved in the computations, the more complex they become. Hence, restricting the use of explicit labeling should reduce the complexity. Minsky's (1980) K-line model is an example of this type of representation. It comprises a network of parallel computational units which represent information in the excitation and inhibition passed between units, rather than using symbolic expressions. The model developed in this chapter also uses this type of unlabeled representation.

III.E. Which Features Should Be Processed?

There is an immense amount of information present in a visual image. The role of early visual processing is to extract the meaningful information—that is the useful cues—from the image. This first step is important because all further processing depends on how well this initial step is carried out.

As mentioned earlier in reference to distributed representations, there are several ways to capture all of the information in an image. For example, the intensity at each spatial location is one representation, while the amplitude and phase of the separate spatial frequency components is another. Both representations contain the same information, yet spatial edges might offer a more useful visual clue than spatial frequency peaks. This would depend on what the higher stages were interested in computing.

In early computer vision research, the decision of which image information was important was ad hoc. There have since been attempts to base the decision on geometric considerations of the physical world (Kanade, 1981). This approach has made many contributions, but these considerations do not fully constrain the decision. One problem is that an image is a two-dimensional projection of a three-dimensional world. If we are given a three-dimensional object, the distance of that object from the projection plane, and the angle of the object in relation to the plane, we can determine what the two-dimensional projection of the object will be. But from the two-dimensional projection we cannot completely determine the three-dimensional object. Generally, there is an infinity of three-dimensional objects that can produce a given two-dimensional projection.

Another approach is to look to the human visual system for inspiration. We know the human system works, so we can hope that its solutions will generalize to other vision systems. Many of the insights in computer vision have actually come through introspection about how humans see. However, there is a problem in relying on introspection. In humans, the earliest stages of visual processing are not available for conscious introspection. This is where psychophysical techniques come in handy. They give us ways of "looking into" early visual processing. Thus, it is clear that computer vision has a lot to offer psychologists, and also that visual psychophysics has a lot to offer computer vision.

III.F. Global versus Local Analysis

An active issue in visual psychophysics is the extent to which global features are extracted from an image prior to the extraction of local features (McArthur, 1982; Navon, 1977; Pomerantz, 1981). The related issue in computational vision is whether low-level visual processing requires global information or can be performed using only local information. For example, in line drawing interpretation systems, the computation to determine if a line segment is present at a given location in an image can be a time-consuming procedure. Shirai (1975) has developed a system that greatly speeds line drawing analysis by using knowledge about where lines are likely to occur and then searching for lines only in those locations. This type of use of top-down processing is common in artificial intelligence. However, Marr (1976) has pointed out that we need not therefore assume that humans require top-down processing to perform such tasks. Marr argues that the edge-finding computation of humans is superior to that used by Shirai and does not need to resort to knowledge-based processing to do the task. This is a common theme in computer vision work: Use one initial transform or set of features, and top-down processing and knowledge about global variables becomes necessary. Use another transform or set of visual cues, and the same task can be performed with local, botom-up processing.

IV. ANALYSIS OF LINE DRAWINGS

One area of visual perception that has been repeatedly studied through computer vision models is the interpretation of line drawings. It is a portion of the problem that will be dealt with by the computational model developed in this chapter. The interpretation of line drawings may seem like a simple task to study, yet its solution continues to elude both psychologists and computer scientists.

IV.A. Why Study Line Drawing Interpretation?

One reason to study line drawings is that lines contain a lot of information. Lines are used to represent edges (abrupt changes in image intensity) and the boundaries of objects (which do not always correlate with the edges in an image). Another reason is that there is neurophysiological evidence that edges are important stimuli in the mammalian visual system (Hubel & Weisel, 1968). The importance of edges as basic visual features for humans has been shown in psychophysical experiments (Barrow & Tenenbaum, 1981; Gregory, 1970). In addition, humans can provide rich interpretations of sparse line drawings, suggesting that this type of representation captures a lot of the essence of an object, or that it is actually very close to an internal representation.

There is growing evidence that images are represented as edges in at least one stage of analysis—for example, Marr's (1982) zero-crossings. Even if this is not the case, however, line drawings are still useful, as we can readily compare the performance of humans and machines. Even if humans do not represent all visual images as edges, when given a line drawing, an image will always be represented as edges in a trivial sense.

IV.B. Review of Computer Vision Research Using Line Drawings

McArthur (1982) provides a review of computer vision models, including many of the early models dealing with line drawings. Later work is well represented in Brady (1981). A brief review of various models will illustrate the three approaches to answering the question of which visual cues should be used in scene interpretation. Roberts (1965) produced one of the first line drawing interpretation models. It takes a digitized image of a scene of polyhedra and produces a line drawing from any specified viewpoint. Both the Roberts program and a later program by Guzman (1969) can interpret line drawings of polyhedral scenes, but they can interpret scenes only containing a few specified polyhedra. These programs have to be given models of the specific objects to be recognized; thus, they are not general-purpose line drawing interpreters. In both programs, the decisions concerning which image features to use for recognition were ad hoc. Roberts used certain topological features (configurations of faces, lines, and vertices), while Guzman labeled different lines at vertices as links between two regions.

The step from ad hoc decisions about image features to the use of geometric constraints was made by both Clowes (1971) and Huffman (1971). They developed polyhedral vertex labeling schemes by considering all possible vertex types and then showing that only a few are physically possible. Waltz (1975) continued this classification by including edges formed by shadows. These edges had previously been ignored as providing only noise. Waltz was able to show that the inclusion of shadow edges added even more constraints: On average, only 0.03% of all possible labels could physically occur. Waltz was also one of the first to use constraint propagation, a kind of parallel computation model that allows only local interactions between computational units and requires many iterations to reach a final, stable solution. These three models could still deal only with trihedral vertices and could not handle the accidental alignment of line segments forming accidental junctions.

Mackworth's (1973) model extended the use of geometrical constraints by representing objects in gradient space. This model was able to deal with both nontrihedral vertices and accidental alignment. However, Draper (1981) has since demonstrated that it is not the gradient space representation itself that is responsible for the improved performance. Draper points out that representation as plane equations is adequate but not very intuitive. He considers which side of a plane a point lies on and develops a recognition scheme based on such "sidedness."

The last model to be mentioned that relies solely on geometrical considerations to determine which visual features to use as cues is that of Kanade (1981). His is a line-labeling scheme that can even deal with nonsolid objects made up of planar surfaces—an origami world. This algorithm does not rely on having models of the objects given to it. Also it does not produce just a single interpretation of a scene; rather, it gives all geometrically possible interpretations. Thus, it is not an attempt to model human performance, where generally just one "best" interpretation is desired.

Other models have been introduced which use our knowledge about human vision to decide which visual features to use in interpreting line drawings. One example is that of Binford (1981), which uses evidence about how humans segment curves to interpret scenes. Binford stresses that the main limitation in computational vision is the problem of determining how to transform the visual signal into symbolic form. Barrow and Tenenbaum (1981) also rely on the results of psychological experiments to aid in the decision of which visual features to use. They compute intrinsic images and assume that global information is necessary for this process. Local information alone is not adequate for their algorithm, which also uses constraint propagation.

A model that again takes seriously the human vision system is the connectionist model of Feldman (1981). His system requires that an object model be present, but it is present in the connections between elements in the model rather than in symbolic form.

These computer vision models represent three approaches to answering the question of which visual cues are important and should be analyzed at the lowest levels of visual processing: ad hoc choices, considerations of geometrical constraints, and the use of psychological knowledge about human vision. The model developed in this chapter uses the last approach. Note that looking to visual psychology for clues does not preclude the consideration of geometrical constraints. Indeed, it is to be

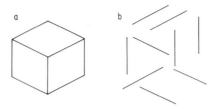

Figure 4.1   Line drawing patterns used in psychophysical experiments. (a) Three-dimensional, connected drawing; (b) flat, unconnected drawing.

assumed that the solutions developed by the human visual system are consistent with such constraints.

V. PSYCHOPHYSICAL EXPERIMENTS

This section presents the results of the psychophysical experiments used to suggest visual cues to be incorporated in the computational model.

V.A. Perceived Brightness and Object Superiority

In terms of global properties, the two patterns in Figure 4.1 differ in several ways: The pattern in 4.1a is connected and appears three-dimensional, while the pattern in 4.1b is unconnected and appears flat. Weisstein and Harris (1974) have demonstrated the object-superiority effect found with such patterns. Basically, this effect shows that it is easier to detect a line segment when it forms part of a line drawing, such as that in Figure 4.1a, than when the same line segment is part of a pattern, such as that in Figure 4.1b, even though both patterns are formed from identical line segments. The same figures also demonstrate a new phenomenon: The line segments in 4.1a appear brigher than the line segments in 4.1b (Walters & Weisstein, 1982a).

Why is there a difference in the perceived brightness? The object superiority theory states that line segments in the pattern of Figure 4.1a are easier to see because of the global, wholistic properties of this pattern— its three-dimensionality, its objectness, and so forth. A natural assumption might then be that the line segments in this pattern appear brighter because the two patterns differ in terms of these and other global properties such as connectedness, closure, and area. This hypothesis was tested by comparing the perceived brightness of many pairs of patterns designed to differ in terms of their global properties. The results indicated that

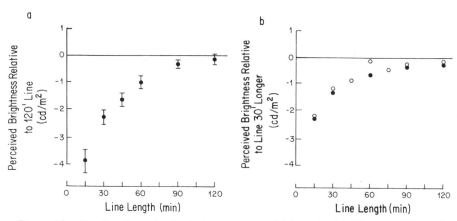

Figure 4.2   Results of psychophysical experiments. (a) Perceived brightness of lines of various lengths, judged relative to a single line that subtended 120′ of visual arc; (b) open circles denote perceived brightness of line segments of various lengths, judged relative to a line 30′ longer. Closed circles denote data from (a) replotted relative to line 30′ longer.

perceived brightness did not systematically vary with any of these global properties (Walters & Weisstein, 1982a). However, two local stimulus properties did correlate highly with perceived brightness—the length of the line segments and the way in which the line segments were connected (Walters & Weisstein, 1982b).

V.B. Local Properties That Enhance Perceived Brightness

V.B.1. Line Length

The importance of line length is demonstrated in Figure 4.2. Figure 4.2a shows the perceived brightness relative to a control line for a series of line segments of increasing lengths. The control line subtended 120′ of visual arc on the retina. The 0 point on the vertical axis represents no difference in perceived brightness between the test and control lines. The negative numbers on that axis indicate the amount by which the control line appeared brighter than the test line.

Note that as the length of the test line increases, the difference in the perceived brightness decreases. This effect could be interpreted as an increase in perceived brightness corresponding to increases in line length for lengths up to 60′. However, there is an alternative interpretation: For differences in line length greater than 60′, there may be a decrease in perceived brightness. To rule out this interpretation, another experiment was performed. In it, subjects compared the perceived brightness of two

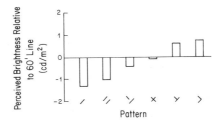

Figure 4.3   Perceived brightness of various simple patterns measured relative to a single line that subtended 60′ of visual arc. The line segments in the patterns each subtended 30′ of arc.

line segments that always differed in length by 30′. The filled circles in Figure 4.2b represent the data from the previous experiment replotted, while the open circles symbolize the data from the new experiment. Since both experiments give the same pattern of results, it is possible to deduce that perceived brightness increases with length for lengths up to 60′.

V.B.2. Local Connectedness

The other local property that determined perceived brightness was the way in which line ends were connected. Experiments showed that there is actually a hierarchy of types of end connections: Figure 4.3 shows the results of one such experiment. Here the perceived brightness of various patterns was measured relative to a line twice as long as the individual line segments making up the patterns. From these measurements we can see that lines joined at their ends appear brighter than lines of which one end abuts the middle of the other. These abutting lines appear brighter than lines that intersect, while intersecting lines appear brighter than unconnected lines. Note that although the intersecting lines could be interpreted as four end-to-end connected lines, they are not, as collinear lines joined at their ends are considered to be a single line.

We now know that long lines appear brighter than short lines, and that lines joined at their ends are brighter than lines that are not connected. The question naturally arises: Are the end-connected lines brighter simply because of the increase in total connected line length? Note that the two 30′ segments connected end to end (right angle pattern) form a total connected length of 60′, yet they actually appear brighter than the single 60′ control line. Thus, the increase in brightness observed with end-connected lines cannot be explained solely in terms of the increase in total connected line length.

V.B.3. Summary

In short, the psychophysical results are that long lines are brighter than short lines. End–end connected lines are brighter than end–middle connected lines, which in turn are brighter than middle–middle connected lines, which are brighter than unconnected lines. This enhancement of perceived brightness indicates that the early visual processing system treats stimuli with these local properties differently from stimuli without them. This does not necessarily mean that brightness enhancement per se is significant, but it does suggest that the local properties are in some sense important, as they are differentially processed. We may be able to use this difference in perceived brightness as a hint concerning which visual features are important in an image.

VI. CREATION OF A COMPUTATIONAL MODEL

VI.A. Rationale

A computational model based on the psychophysical findings was developed for two reasons. First, such a module can throw light on why both the type of end connections between line segments and the length of line segments are important visual cues. Thus, it may become clear why the human visual system should be interested in such local properties. Second, a computational model can demonstrate whether or not it is possible to compute perceived brightness using parallel processing that does not involve the explicit labeling of local cues in the image.

The computational model should take as its input a line drawing and give as its output the perceived brightness of the line segments. The module results should agree with the results of the psychophysical experiments described earlier.

VI.B. Tessellation

The first step is to digitize the image. That is, the line drawing's brightness is sampled at many points. These samples can be thought of as finite-sized cells which cover the surface of the image. These cells are called pixels, short for picture elements. The digitized line drawing is an array of pixels, with the value of each pixel representing the physical brightness of the image at that point. The pattern with which the pixels cover the line drawing is its tessellation. The most often used tessellation in computer vision is a rectangular tessellation (see Figure 4.4). In this tessellation, the image is sampled at points that correspond to a rectangular array. Be-

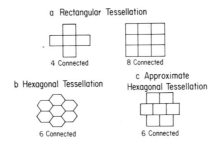

Figure 4.4   (a) Rectangular tessellation. The center pixel is connected to its four horizontal and vertical neighbors in the four-connected definition and to all eight neighbors in the eight-connected definition. (b) Hexagonal tessellation with the six-connected definition. (c) Approximation to the hexagonal tessellation with a six-connected definition.

cause one of the local image properties which appear to be important to perceived brightness is the connection between line segments, a tessellation is needed that makes this property easy to compute.

Connectedness is defined for a particular tessellation by defining which pixels will be considered to be neighbors. The problem with the rectangular tessellation is that there are two definitions of connectedness—four-connectedness, in which each pixel is considered to be connected to the four neighbors shown in Figure 4.4a, and eight-connectedness, with each pixel connected to all eight neighbors (Figure 4.4a). The problem is that an arbitrary figure can be connected by the eight-connected definition and unconnected by the four-connected definition. This paradox poses complications for geometric algorithms in general and for the calculation of line end connections in particular, so the rectangular tessellation was rejected.

Recall that the human visual system can provide inspiration for computational vision. The human visual system also samples an image. What kind of tessellation does it use? The answer has been elegantly demonstrated by Wassle (1982). The output of the retinal ganglion cells corresponds to the sample of the visual image. But how are the ganglion units distributed? Previous attempts at uncovering this distribution were unsuccessful because they looked at the distribution of all of the ganglion cells and found no regular pattern. Wassle found the pattern by looking separately at the four basic types of ganglion cells. This structure was a hexagonal packing of circles with some overlap. Interestingly, Wassle found that the amount of overlap was that which gave a complete covering with minimal overlap.

The visual system uses a hexagonal tessellation. This tessellation was used in the model for that reason and because the hexagonal tessellation has only one definition of connectedness: It uses six-connectedness (Figure 4.4b). Actually, due to hardware limitations, an approximation to the hexagonal tessellation was used (see Figure 4.4c).

VI.C. Domain Limitations

The input to the model consists of line drawings. This domain was further limited to line drawings composed of line segments with just three possible orientations. Although this condition simplifies the implementation of the model, the results of the simplified model will generalize to an unlimited domain.

Line drawings were generated using a computer graphics system. These were input to the model as raster images (a two-dimensional array of pixels).

VI.D. Local Productions

The psychophysical results can be expressed as a set of rules which can form the basis of a set of productions to be used in the model. The rules are: (1) If a local region of a line segment is longer than length x, enhance each element of the segment in the region in accordance with some rule L. (2) If and only if two line segments meet at their ends, enhance each element in each segment by amount A. (3) If the ends of three noncollinear line segments meet, enhance each element in each segment by amount B. (4) If the end of a line abuts another line segment, enhance each element of the first segment by amount C. (5) Amount A is greater than amount B, which is greater than amount C.

Only the third production needs further explanation. The meeting of three noncollinear lines can be viewed as a special case of abutment or as a special case of two lines forming an end–end connection. Thus, the amount of enhancement lies between that for the second and fourth productions.

VI.E. Local Calculators

As the enhancement depends only on local features of the image, it is possible to do the computation in parallel—that is, to have many identical "calculators" act on some small, local region of the image. Figure 4.5a shows a representation of the small region used. It consists of only 13 pixels, which can be thought of as being arranged into six arms, with three pixels per arm. There is an arm for each possible orientation of a line

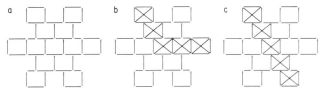

Figure 4.5 (a) Local region, used by each individual calculator, consisting of 13 pixels arranged into six arms. (b) Local region showing two noncollinear arms. (c) Local region showing two collinear arms.

segment, and the length of the arms is determined by the line length x of the first production.

Imagine a digitized image with a little calculator at each pixel in the image. Each of these calculators acts on its pixel and its 12 neighboring pixels as defined by this local region. The little calculators will implement all local productions. As a first step, they must determine whether there are any long line segments or end-connected lines in the local region. One way of doing this would be to use a series of templates, or masks, which cover all the possible combinations of such features. This is an unreasonable approach, as it would require 53 templates for just this small region. Another method has been developed based on the possible arrangement of occupied arms in the region. Occupied arms are those in which the value of each of the three pixels indicates the presence of a portion of a line segment at that pixel. These arms can either be noncollinear, as in Figure 4.5b, or collinear, as in Figure 4.5c. All collinear arms should be enhanced, as they represent line segments of at least length 5.

Figure 4.6 shows the six possible arrangements of noncollinear arms in one orientation. From this figure we can see that each arrangement has a distinct combination of the number of collinear and noncollinear arms. Thus, if we count the number of collinear and noncollinear arms, we can determine which type of arms pattern is present and thus know which type of enhancement to apply. The letters in Figure 4.6 refer to the type of enhancement mentioned in the set of productions. This table and the set of productions form the heart of the model.

VI.F. Connectionist Implementation

The model rules can easily be implemented as a computer program, but it is conceptually more interesting to implement them using parallel processing that does not involve the use of labels or symbols in the way that a computer program does. The formalism of connectionist models (Feldman & Ballard, 1982) can be used to satisfy these criteria. Connectionist

Deborah K. W. Walters

Enhancement Matrix

Number of Colinear Arms

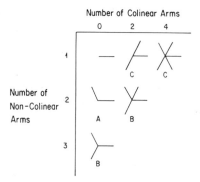

Figure 4.6 Matrix used to determine the type of enhancement to apply to line segments based on the connections between the ends of the line segments. The letters below the six possible configurations indicate the appropriate enhancement type.

models are highly parallel, highly connected networks built from individual computational units which resemble neurons.

An example of one type of connectionist unit, here called a U unit, is shown in Figure 4.7. This unit has multiple numerical inputs and a single output which can signal only a limited range of numerical values. The output of the unit is a function of its input and is determined by the equation

$$U \text{ output} = \text{Min}\left(\left(I + \sum_{k=1}^{13}\sum_{j=1}^{6} I_{2,j,k} + \sum_{k=1}^{13}\sum_{j=1}^{6} I_{3,j,k}\right), \text{BMAX}\right).$$

The U unit sums the model input, the length enhancement input, and the end enhancement input. It has the added property that if the total sum

The U Unit

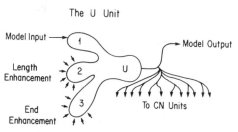

Figure 4.7 The U unit—the basic input/output unit used in the connectionist model. The numbers refer to the separate input sites. Input site 1 has a single input; input sites 2 and 3 have 78 inputs each. The output goes to 78 different CN units and to 78 different A units.

exceeds the maximum value that the unit can signal (i.e., BMAX), the output of the unit is BMAX. This type of unit is similar to Minsky and Papert's (1969) perceptrons, but there are differences. This type of connectionist unit can have a kind of local memory, although that property is not used here. Also, these units can have disjunctive firing conditions and conjunctive connections. For example, its output could be the maximum of the total input at each of the three disjunctive input sites.

The second type of connectionist unit basically includes classical finite automata. Examples of these are described later.

VI.F.1. Connectionist Units as Little Calculators

The model uses connectionist units to build local calculators. One of the U units is associated with each pixel in an image. It receives the input to the model, the numerical value representing the brightness of the associated pixel. As the input image is simply a line drawing, the original image needs to have only two brightness levels—0, representing no line segment at a given pixel, and x, representing a line segment of brightness x. The U unit provides the output of the model as well—an integer representing the enhanced brightness of the associated pixel. This same unit also adds enhancement due to both length and end connections to the input to get the output.

The U units are connected with other types of units to form local calculators. The local calculator is best described by breaking it down into its two functional parts—the length enhancement network, which will increase the brightness of long lines, and the end connection enhancement network, which will increase the brightness of end-connected lines.

The complexity of the model is linear, as local calculators are only locally interconnected. Thus, as we increase the size of the model in terms of the number of pixels modeled, we also increase the number of units required by a constant times the number of increased pixels. This effect means that the model is easily expandable, with no difference in connectivity or performance.

VI.F.2. Length Enhancement Network

The length enhancement network comprises six identical subnetworks, each associated with two collinear arms of the local region. Figure 4.8 shows one such subnetwork. It is composed of the five U units associated with the five pixels in the collinear arms. The output of the U units goes to the CN unit. It "decides" whether there is a single, short, noncollinear line segment, two collinear line segments, or no line segment present in the five-pixel region of the image. The CN unit has two disjunctive input

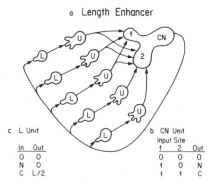

Figure 4.8   The subnetwork that computes the enhancement contributed by the length of the line segments. The numbers refer to distinct input sites. The arrows indicate the direction of information flow (see text for detailed description). (b) State table for the CN unit in the subnetwork. The 0's represent inactive sites, while the 1's represent active sites. (c) State table for the L units in the subnetwork.

sites. Each site "fires" if and only if all the inputs to that site are nonzero (i.e., if they represent the presence of a line segment). Thus, site 1 fires if the top three U units indicate the presence of a line segment, while site 2 fires if all five pixels are parts of line segments.

The output of the CN unit has three possible states, and its behavior is characterized by the table in Figure 4.8b. If neither input site is active, it signals 0, indicating that no line segments are present. If just site 1 is active, it signals N, indicating that one noncollinear segment is present. If both sites are active, the CN unit signals C, indicating that two collinear segments are present.

The output of the CN unit goes to the L units. They fire in accordance with the table in Figure 4.8c. Their output is 0 unless their input is the collinear signal, C. The L output is the amount of brightness enhancement based on the length of the line segment. All line segments of length equal to or greater than five pixels are enhanced. Recall that there are six of the length enhancement subnetworks making up the length-enhancing network for each local region. Each pair of collinear arms in the region has two subnetworks acting on them. If all five pixels in the collinear arms signal the presence of line segments, then both of the associated subnetworks will enhance the brightness of all five pixels. Thus, each contributes just half of the total enhancement.

VI.F.3.   End Connection Enhancement Network

The second enhancement network enhances end-connected lines. Again, it has six identical subnetworks, one of which is illustrated in

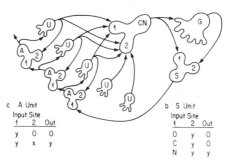

Figure 4.9 (a) The subnetwork that computes the enhancement which is attributable to the presence of end-connected lines. The numbers refer to distinct input sites. The arrows indicate the direction of flow of information. (b) State table for the S unit in the subnetwork. The y's are variables, indicating the presence of any one of a number of possible signals. When the input at site 1 is N, the output of the S unit is equal to the input present at site 2. (c) State table for the A units of the subnetwork. Again, the y's are variables. The x represents any nonzero value.

Figure 4.9. It shares the CN and the U units with the length-enhancing network, but here the output of the CN unit goes to the G unit. There is just one G unit for each local calculator. It receives input from the six CN units that are associated with the six pairs of collinear arms in the local region. The G unit does the hard work of the network—it "decides" which type of end connection, if any, is present in the local region and determines the appropriate type of enhancement. The state table for the G unit is the end enhancement matrix of Figure 4.6. It has four possible types of enhancement—0 for no enhancement, A for end–end enhancement, B for multiple end–end enhancement, and C for end–middle enhancement.

The output of the G unit goes to the S unit, which also receives input from the CN unit. The S unit acts as a gate and lets the end enhancement through only if the CN unit signals that a noncollinear segment is present. Thus, collinear line segments do not receive end-related enhancement. The S unit output is just the input at site 2, if and only if the input at site 1 indicates the presence of a noncollinear segment. The S unit output travels to the A unit, which functions as another gate; its output is gated by its input from the U unit. Thus, it passes the end enhancement along to the U unit, if and only if the U unit is signaling the presence of a line segment. The A unit also sends its output to the next A unit in its arm. Thus, the end-related enhancement can travel along the entire length of a line segment, stopping only when it reaches an endpoint.

VI.G. Possible Neural Implementation

The connectionist implementation of the model consists of a local calculator associated with each pixel of the image. These calculators are composed of simple units having only a limited number of states. It is conceivable that a single neuron could perform the function of any of these units. The units have only local connections, although they are highly connected (each U unit receives input from 157 units and sends output to 157 units). This structure resembles that of a neuronal nucleus in that it has simple inputs which are highly connected to each other and to interneurons within the nucleus and yet have simple output.

In the model structure, the units are laid out so that they maintain the spatial relations between the pixels they represent. This is also true of the primate visual system at the retinal, ganglion, and even cortical levels. The information from the retina is distributed to the visual cortex in an orderly fashion, with spatial relations kept intact. This process is called retinotopic mapping (Tootell, Silverman, Switkes, De Valois, 1982).

The model has no timing considerations that could not be met by neurons. It can even be implemented as a continuous time system. The only assumption is that the input is continuously present, which is the case in the primate visual system.

VI.H. Computer Implementation

The formal connectionist model was implemented on a serial computer, with the computation at each pixel computed serially. This arrangement is possible because the procedure is totally local and uses additive enhancement. In the computer implementation, the same local region was used, as were the same enhancement rules. Furthermore, the program modules corresponded to the separate networks, and the computational steps within the modules were identifiable with the separate units in the networks.

VII. RESULTS OF THE EDGE-ENHANCEMENT MODEL

The model was implemented using a Grinnell image processing system. The input line drawing was displayed on the screen. The model program was run, and the enhanced line drawing was presented on the screen. However, it was not really adequate to view the results from the screen. We immediately realized that we had to use our visual system to view the screen, and since we know that our visual system alters the perceived brightness, another way of presenting the results was necessary.

Brightness Levels

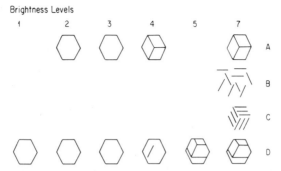

Figure 4.10   Threshold representation of the results computed by the connectionist model for four patterns used in the psychophysical experiments. Brightness level 1 contains only the brightest lines in the pattern. The brightness threshold decreases for the subsequent levels, with level 7 containing all the lines of the pattern.

Instead of drawing different lines at different luminances, all lines can be drawn as shown in Figure 4.10. The patterns on the right were drawn with the lowest threshold—all lines in the patterns are visible. The threshold is increasingly higher for each column of patterns across to the left pattern, which has the highest threshold—only the very brightest lines in the patterns being displayed.

VII.A. Psychophysical Patterns

The four patterns in Figure 4.10 are examples of those used in the psychophysical experiments, and the model results do simulate the psychophysical results for these patterns. The two patterns which appeared similar in perceived brightness in the experiments (A and D) also have similar brightnesses here, while the two patterns perceived to be less bright (B and C) are obviously less bright in the model. The same agreement between experiments and model was seen for all of the psychophysical patterns.

Nevertheless, the computer model is not meant to be just a simulator; rather, it is meant to be used as a means of going beyond the psychophysical results. One limitation with the psychophysical results is that subjects were able to make only global judgments of brightness. They could say that pattern A was overall brighter than pattern B, but they could not say whether a particular line segment in pattern A was brighter than the others. Yet the model gives such results, which can show us why such a brightness enhancement system is useful.

VII.B. What Brightness Enhancement Buys You

Some of the reasons for the system's value are apparent from the simple stimuli of Figure 4.10. Lines that are part of object contours (A) and enhanced relative to lines that form textures (C). Also, lines that form part of object contours (A) are enhanced relative to lines that are perceived as "sticks" (B). Finally, the model shows that the outer contours of objects are enhanced relative to the inner lines (see A).

VII.B.1. Automatic Filtering

Why would these enhancements be useful for a visual system? As previously mentioned, a major problem for a visual system is that there is too much information in a visual image to process all of it in detail. One solution is to have some automatic system to determine which lines or areas contain the most important information, and then to process those areas in detail while ignoring other, possibly less fruitful areas. This algorithm automatically enhances those line segments which have a high probability of being part of object contours, rather than just part of texture or noise. If the next stage of processing has to be selective, it can "attend" only to the enhanced lines and thus will not waste resources processing spurious edges.

VII.B.2. Image Segmentation

Edge enhancement can also aid higher processing stages by indicating regions of an image likely to contain a single object, as the outer object contours are enhanced relative to the inner contours. A higher stage of processing could label these regions as containing a single object, thus aiding in image segmentation. Looking at another example shows how the algorithm goes one step further.

VII.B.3. Partially Occluded Objects

Figure 4.11 shows two distinct objects, one partially occluded by the other. At the highest threshold, the line segments making up the two objects are separated from each other. Thus, the algorithm helps to segment the lines into two sets which correspond to the two objects. Also, the object in the foreground is enhanced relative to the object in the background. Again, the outer contours are enhanced more than the inner contours.

A more complex case of occlusion is seen in the model output shown in Figure 4.12. Here there are three objects, all of which are again separated at the highest threshold. Note also that the texture, the fine detail of the

Brightness Levels

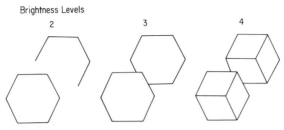

Figure 4.11   Model results for pattern demonstrating partial occlusion by three-dimensional objects.

parallelogram, is not enhanced. This again fits with our perception as humans. We could perceive the parallelogram as 16 separate parallelograms whose edges are touching, in which case all of the edges should be enhanced. Instead, we perceive it as one object that is textured or patterned.

VII.B.4. Accidental Alignment

Figure 4.13 gives an example of accidental alignment. The algorithm results at the highest threshold indicate that all of the line segments are likely to be part of the same object. It is not obvious until the lowest threshold that there might be two distinct objects. Again, this agrees with human perception: If we were to catch only a brief glimpse of this pattern, we would think we had seen a single object.

Another example of accidental alignment is shown in Figure 4.14. Note that the two patterns differ only by a single short line segment, yet the algorithm separates them into two objects at the highest threshold. Again, as humans we perceive these patterns as being very different.

VII.B.5. Impossible Objects

Figure 4.15 shows the results of the algorithm for an impossible object and a possible object. The algorithm results at an early level (second

Brightness Levels

Figure 4.12   Model results for two-dimensional pattern illustrating partial occlusion and texture effects.

Brightness Levels

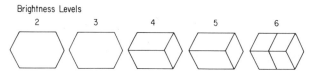

Figure 4.13   Model results for pattern demonstrating accidental alignment.

highest threshold) already show the main properties of the object pattern—a blob with a hole in it. That is, the algorithm is giving the topological structure of the object at a very early level. But what happens with the
impossible object? At the second highest threshold, the algorithm again
agrees with our perception that this is a connected blob, but this time it is
not represented as having a hole in it. Instead, by having two sets of
unconnected interior lines, it is indicating the possible presence of two
objects or object components. This effect relates well to our perception of
one object if we concentrate on the lower right corner, and of another
object if we concentrate on the upper left corner. Neither we nor the
algorithm can get our perceptions to merge.

VII.C. Summary of Model Performance

1. Contour lines are enhanced relative to texture lines or lines seen as
   "sticks."
2. Outer object contours are enhanced relative to inner contours.
3. Foreground objects are enhanced relative to occluded objects.
4. Regions containing distinct objects are segmented.
5. For accidentally aligned and impossible objects, the algorithm
   results agree with human perception.

The algorithm demonstrates an edge-enhancing process that is strictly

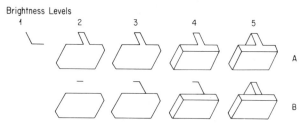

Figure 4.14   Model results for two patterns, A and B. Pattern A illustrates concave effects,
while pattern B shows a case of accidental alignment.

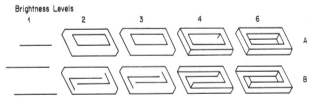

Figure 4.15   Model results for a possible figure (pattern A) and an impossible figure (pattern B).

local, although the results correlate well with the global, topological properties of an image.

VIII. RELATION TO OTHER WORK

VIII.A. Perception of Outer Contours of Objects

The results of this end-enhancement model show that the outer contours of objects are enhanced relative to the inner contours. From this outcome it is possible to predict that humans should process outer contours preferentially over inner contours. Experiments by Rock, Halper, and Clayton (1972) have shown that this is the case.

Ullman (1986) also discusses how the outer contours of objects can receive preferential processing. In his scheme, visual images are first processed in a local, parallel stage to form the base representation. Certain regions of the image are then processed by higher-level, more serial, iterative, and universal routines. Ullman concludes that it would not be possible to selectively represent an object's outer contour in the local, parallel representation. However, this end-enhancement model shows a way of doing just that.

Why can the end-enhancement model make selective representations while the base representation cannot? Both schemes suggest that perceptual single units are not feature detectors. Rather, they participate in local computations and network operations. Both schemes also let attention be grabbed by the image region with the highest signal strength. They also assume a local, parallel stage followed by a more serial higher level—the only difference being in how much processing is done by each stage. The end-enhancement model differs in assuming that much more can be computed by the lowest stages. This is shown to be the case when visual features are chosen that yield the greatest amount of information.

VIII.B. Relation to Edge-Finding Algorithms

The edge-enhancement model relates to several levels of computer vision work. It enhances lines or edges, and so is relevant to low-level edge-finding algorithms, but its enhancement correlates with the global properties of objects, making it relevant to higher-level scene interpretation modules as well.

There are a host of edge-finding algorithms in existence. One of the simplest is Roberts' (1965) edge-finder. It detects all of the edges in an image and thus generates a large number of edges. The simplest way to select which edges should be further analyzed is to consider only those edges with intensity slopes greater than a particular threshold value. The problem with this method is that not all of the edges that humans perceive as important are further analyzed. However, if the edge-enhancing model were applied to the output of such a simple edge-finder before the thresholding stage, some of the perceptually important edges would be enhanced enough to guarantee further analysis.

Other edge-enhancement techniques are based on iterative (relaxation) techniques such as those devised by Schachter, Lev, Zucker, & Rosenfeld (1977) and by Prager (1980). The disadvantage of such systems is that the elements must first be labeled with a probability of inclusion in a line segment, after which several iterations must be performed to adjust that probability. The edge-enhancement model requires no labeling and can be performed in one step, without iterations.

VIII.C. Relation to Line Drawing Interpretation Systems

The edge-enhancement model appears to be related to the line drawing interpretation systems that relie on categorizing vertices formed by line segments, such as those mentioned in Section IV,B. However, the edge-enhancement model does something very different. In the previous schemes, vertex labeling of complex scenes leads to a combinatorial explosion of the number of labels needed, while the edge-enhancement model uses just three types of end connections. More important, this model does not interpret scenes; rather, it generates a filtered version of a scene that gives an interpretation system a head start. Thus, the edge-enhancer operates at an early, preattentive level (corresponding to the first few milliseconds of processing in humans), while interpretation modules operate at a directed attention level.

IX. THEORETICAL POINTS RAISED BY THE EDGE-ENHANCEMENT MODEL

IX.A. Basic Perceptual Features

One of the remaining questions in both human and computer vision is whether it is helpful to break an image down into basic elements such as individual line segments. The problem with trying to answer the question is that if you use the wrong candidate for the basic elements, the answer appears to be "no." Unfortunately, the right candidates may not be intuitively obvious. The edge-enhancement model is one instance in which looking for certain counterintuitive basic features (line segments and the relation between their ends) did prove useful. Thus, it appears that visual psychophysics can make a significant contribution to computer vision by suggesting that such counterintuitive transforms be used in the early stages of visual processing. Similarly, computer vision can contribute to visual perception and cognition by expressing theories in a rigorously testable form.

IX.B. Local–Global Analysis

Another theoretical point made by this research concerns the global–local question, showing that it is possible to use simple local computations to extract quantities that correlate well with the global properties of an image. Why might we want to do this? Minsky and Papert (1969) have shown that local units such as perceptions could not compute certain global properties such as connectedness. However, the model used here shows that local connectedness can be computed with local units. Moreover, this local connectivity is highly correlated with global connectivity (Walters & Weisstein, 1982a). Again, we might be asking the wrong questions when we reject local units on the basis of their failure to compute some abstract quality. Perhaps we would be as happy, or happier, with a correlate of that quality which could be locally computed.

IX.C. Initial Transformations

This point is related to another: When the right initial image transformations are used, and the right global correlates are computed, then some stages of visual processing can be accomplished with bottom-up control—you don't have to resort to a knowledge-based system that uses top-down processing. However, just how many stages of visual processing can rely on this purely data-dependent, bottom-up processing remains an interesting question.

IX.D. Brightness Pyramids

The display of the results of the model in terms of different brightness levels (as in Figure 4.10) illustrates how the results might be used by a higher stage of processing. If the higher stage were interested in segmenting the image, it might look at only the brightest levels, where even an occluded object is separated from the object occluding it. Also, the brightness levels will contain the lines most likely to be part of an object's outer contours, so a higher stage interested in object contours could obtain more useful information from the brighter levels than from the dimmer levels. This organization of the information into a kind of pyramidal structure, with each layer of the pyramid representing one brightness level, would enable later stages requiring selective processing to determine easily which line segments are likely to yield the most information and thus should be processed first, fastest, or best.

X. PSYCHOPHYSICAL RESEARCH AND COMPUTATIONAL VISION

The results of the computational model suggest ways in which the presence of certain local cues could be used to perform further useful visual processing, such as image segmentation. It remains to be seen if the human visual system actually does use local cues for these purposes. Yet we can see the contribution that computational models make: They enable us to rigorously test hypotheses generated from psychophysical results, and they can suggest new hypotheses to be tested by further psychophysical experiments.

The benefits of collaborative research between psychologists and computer scientists are not one-sided: Psychophysical research contributes to computer vision. The research presented here is one example of this process. The psychophysical results suggest which visual features are likely to convey the most useful information and should therefore be processed selectively in a computational model.

REFERENCES

Anderson, J. A., & Hinton, G. E. (1981). Models of information processing in the brain. In G. E. Hinton, & J. A. Anderson (Eds.), *Parallel models of associative memory*, pp. 9–48. Hillsdale, NJ: Erlbaum.

Ballard, D. H., & Brown, C. P. (1982). *Computer vision.* Englewood Cliffs, NJ: Prentice-Hall.

Barlow, H. B. (1972). Single units and sensation: A neuron doctrine for perceptual psychology? *Perception,* **1,** 371–394.

Barrow, H. G., & Tenenbaum, J. M. (1981). Interpreting line drawings as three-dimensional surfaces. *Artificial Intelligence,* **17,** 75–116.

Binford, T. O. (1981). Inferring surfaces from images. *Artificial Intelligence,* **17,** 205–244.

Boles, R. C., & Cain, R. A. (1983). Recognizing and locating partially visable objects: The local-feature-focus method. In A. Pugh (Ed.), *Robot vision,* pp. 43–82. London: IFS.

Brady, M. (1981). Preface—The changing shape of computer vision. *Artificial Intelligence,* **17,** 1–15.

Brady, M. (1982). Computational approaches to image understanding. *Computing Surveys,* **14,** 3–71.

Campbell, F. W., & Robson, J. G. (1968). Application of fourier analysis to the visability of gratings. *Journal of Physiology,* **197,** 551–556.

Clowes, M. B. (1971). On seeing things. *Artificial Intelligence,* **2,** 79–116.

Draper, S. W. (1981). The use of gradient and dual space in line drawing interpretation. *Artificial Intelligence,* **17,** 461–508.

Feldman, J. A. (1981). A connectionist model of visual memory. In G. E. Hinton & J. A. Anderson (Eds.), *Parallel models of associative memory,* pp. 49–82. Hillsdale, NJ: Erlbaum.

Feldman, J. A., & Ballard, D. H. (1982). Connectionist models and their properties. *Cognitive Science,* **6,** 205–254.

Graham, N. (1980). Spatial-frequency channels in human vision: Detecting edges without edge detectors. In C. Harris (Ed.), *Visual coding and adaptability,* pp. 215–262. Hillsdale, NJ: Erlbaum.

Gregory, R. L. (1970). *The intelligent eye.* New York: McGraw-Hill.

Guzman, A. (1968). *Computer recognition of three-dimensional objects in a scene.* Cambridge, MA: MIT Report MAC-TR-59.

Hinton, G. E. (1983). *The computational metaphor.* Panel discussion at the Fifth Annual Conference of the Cognitive Science Society, Rochester, NY, May 1983.

Horn, B. K. P. (1977). Understanding image intensity. *Artificial Intelligence,* **8,** 201–231.

Hubel, D. H., & Weisel, T. N. (1968). Receptive fields and functional architecture of monkey striate cortex. *Journal of Physiology,* **195,** 215–243.

Huffman, D. A. (1971). Impossible objects as nonsense sentences. In B. Meltzer & D. Mitchie (Eds.), *Machine intelligence* (Vol. 6), pp. 295–323. Edinburgh: Edinburgh University Press.

Julesz, B., & Schumer, R. A. (1981). Early visual perception. *Annual Review of Psychology,* **32,** 575–627.

Kanade, T. (1981). Recovery of the three-dimensional shape of an object from a single view. *Artificial Intelligence,* **17,** 409–460.

Mackworth, A. K. (1973). Interpreting pictures of polyhedral scenes. *Artificial Intelligence,* **4,** 121–137.

Marr, D. (1976). Early processing of visual information. *Philosophical Transactions of the Royal Society, Series B,* **275,** 483–524.

Marr, D. (1982). *Vision.* San Francisco: Freeman.

McArthur, D. J. (1982). Computer vision and perceptual psychology. *Psychological Bulletin,* **92,** 283–309.

Minsky, M. (1980). K-lines: A theory of memory. *Cognitive Science,* **4,** 117–133.

Minsky, M., & Papert, S. (1969). *Perceptrons.* Cambridge, MA: MIT Press.

Navon, D. (1977). Forest before trees: The precedence of global features in visual perception. *Cognitive Psychology*, **9**, 353–383.

Pomerantz, J. R. (1981). Perceptual organization in information processing. In M. Kubovy & J. Pomerantz (Eds.), *Perceptual organization*, pp. 141–180. Hillsdale, NJ: Erlbaum.

Prager, J. M. (1980). Extracting and labeling boundary segments in natural scenes. *IEEE Transactions on Pattern Analysis and Machine Intelligence*, **PAMI-2**, 16–27.

Pylyshyn, Z. (1980). Computation and cognition: Issues in the foundations of cognitive science. *The Behavioral and Brain Sciences*, **3**, 111–169.

Roberts, L. G. (1965). Machine perception of three-dimensional objects. In J. P. Tippett (Ed.) *Optical and electro-optical information processing*, pp. 159–197. Cambridge, MA: MIT Press.

Rock, I., Halper, F., & Clayton, T. (1972). The perception and recognition of complex figures. *Cognitive Psychology*, **3**, 655–673.

Rosenfeld, A., & Kak, A. C. (1982). *Digital picture processing*. New York: Academic Press.

Schachter, B. J., Lev, A., Zucker, S. W., & Rosenfeld, A. (1977). An application of relaxation methods to edge reinforcement. *IEEE Transactions on Systems, Man and Cybernetics*, **7**, 813–816.

Shirai, Y. (1975). Analyzing intensity arrays using knowledge about scenes. In P. H. Winston (Ed.), *The psychology of computer vision*, pp. 93–114. New York: McGraw-Hill.

Tootell, R. B. H. Silverman, M. S., Switkes, E., & De Valois, R. L. (1982). Deoxyglucose analysis of retinotopic organization in primate striate cortex. *Science*, **218**, 902–904.

Treisman, A. M., & Gelade, G. (1980). A feature integration theory of attention. *Cognitive Psychology*, **12**, 97–136.

Ullman, S. (1979). *The interpretation of visual motion*. Cambridge, MA: MIT Press.

Ullman, S. (1986). Visual routines: Where bottom-up and top-down processing meet. *Syntax and Semantics*. this volume, pp. 000–000.

Walters, D. K. W., & Weisstein, N. (1982a). Perceived brightness is a function of line length and perceived connectivity. *Bulletin of the Psychonomic Society*, **Sept.,** 130.

Walters, D. K. W., & Weisstein, N. (1982b). Perceived brightness is influenced by global structure of line drawings? *Investigative Ophthalmology and Visual Science*, **22**, 124.

Waltz, D. I. (1975). Understanding line drawings of scenes with shadows. In P. H. Winston (Ed.), *The psychology of computer vision*, pp. 19–92. New York: McGraw-Hill.

Wassle, H. (1982). *The structural basis of the ganglion cell receptive field center*. Paper presented at the 13th Symposium of the Center for Visual Science, Rochester, NY., June 1982.

Weisstein, N., & Harris, C. S. (1974). Visual detection of line segments: An object superiority effect. *Science*, **186**, 752–755.

Winston, P. H. (Ed.), (1975). *The psychology of computer vision*. New York: McGraw-Hill.

CHAPTER 5

Schemas and Perception: Perspectives from Brain Theory and Artificial Intelligence*

Michael A. Arbib

Computer and Information Sciences, University of Massachusetts, Amherst, Massachusetts 01002

I. INTRODUCTION

This chapter attempts to provide a perspective on theories of perception by combining artificial intelligence, the art of programming computers to exhibit seemingly intelligent behavior, with brain theory, the study of the brain's function via mathematical modeling and computer simulation. The aim of the chapter is to provide a conceptual framework for the single-topic chapters that follow. It is not intended to provide a detailed, up-to-date survey of the literature.

Much of brain theory to date has tended to be *bottom-up*, either working from models of membranes up to neuronal function or analyzing the behavior of small or regular neural networks. By contrast, artificial intelligence has worked *top down* to provide decompositions of overall processes such as solving problems, planning, perceiving a visual scene, or understanding natural language. While many workers in the field of artificial intelligence believe that introspection on the way they solve problems can help them program computers to solve those problems, a majority of such workers feel that the detailed analysis of biological prototypes is

---

* Portions of this chapter were adapted from Arbib (1975a, 1978, 1981b). These articles are used here with the kind permission of the publishers: Academic Press, Inc., the Mathematical Association of America, and Lawrence Erlbaum Associates, respectively. Preparation of this chapter was supported in part by National Institutes of Health Grant NS14971-04. Apart from minor editing, this chapter was written in 1981, prior to the publication of the important books on vision by Ballard and Brown (1982) and Marr (1982). For a current perspective on the themes of this chapter, see Arbib and Hanson (1986).

PATTERN RECOGNITION BY HUMANS
AND MACHINES: Visual Perception
Volume 2

irrelevant to the construction of robots or other machines. However, we develop herein a common perspective from which to view both the artificial intelligence and brain theory approaches to perception.

The need for top-down brain theory can be seen as follows: Near the periphery of the nervous system—a neuron or two in from the sensory receptors or the muscle fibers themselves—single-cell neurophysiology allows us to make moderately useful statements about the functions of neural networks. In these peripheral regions, the task of the neural modeler is fairly well-defined: to refine the description of the individual neurons and to suggest missing details about their interconnections which will allow the overall network to exhibit the posited behavior.

As we move away from the periphery, the situation becomes less clear. A given region of the brain interacts with many other regions, and it becomes increasingly hard to state unequivocally what role it plays in subserving some overall behavior of the organism. Again, the remoteness of the region from the periphery and the multiplicity of its connections make it increasingly hard to determine by the methods of single-cell neurophysiology what the "natural" patterns of afferent stimulation to that region may be. Thus, not only are we at a loss to tell what the region does on the basis of experimentation alone, but our theoretical study of the modes of response of abstract networks becomes less compelling when we must expect the input to the region to be of a highly specialized kind which is unknown to us. Finally, we may expect that central regions will often be involved in "computational bookkeeping," so that their activity will correlate poorly with stimuli or behavior. In fact, their activity will be all but incomprehensible without an appropriate theory of computation.

Half of this chapter will be devoted to successful brain models, while the other half will be more programmatic, for I believe that attempts to truly understand the brain's higher cognitive functions will have little success without the sort of vocabulary that workers in artificial intelligence are trying to develop. At the same time, it must be stressed that workers in artificial intelligence have long paid too little attention to parallelism. In fact, one of the most striking aspects of the brain is the topographical organization of its computational subsystems, and one of the major thrusts of this chapter will be to call for new concepts in a theory of *cooperative computation* which is adequate to handle this type of computational geography.

II. SCHEMAS AND ACTION-ORIENTED PERCEPTION

In this section, we start with a top-down analysis of various components required in a perceptual system. We then turn to bottom-up analyses of relevant mechanisms, from both brain theory and artificial intelligence perspectives.

II. A. The Slide-Box Metaphor

The Oxford English Dictionary defines *perceive* as "to apprehend with the mind; to become aware or conscious of; to observe, understand." Leaving aside the problems of consciousness or awareness, we can say that an important element of perception is that aspects of the external world are sampled through the senses and incorporated in the construction of an internal representation. The latter must, however indirectly, be related to action if it is in some sense to contribute to the understanding of the world being perceived. It seems plausible to suggest, then, that the act of perception must include a representation of the world in terms of "objects," these being defined as "domains of interaction." Depending on the circumstances in which the organism finds itself, an object may range anywhere from a marking on a stone, to a tree, to a whole row of trees whose detailed interrelationships are not important to the organism's current behavior.

If we think of the world as an array of domains of interaction, it then becomes appropriate to think of the internal representation of the world as an array of representations of objects. In trying to make this idea more vivid, I have introduced the "slide-box metaphor" (Arbib, 1970, 1972). In the making of moving-picture cartoons, it is far too much work to draw every frame anew; rather, the background remains unchanged through many frames and can be drawn once. The middle ground may not change anything, save its position relative to the background, and so can be drawn on a transparency and simply repositioned in front of the background from one frame to the next. Even in the foreground, only some details need to be redrawn to express current activity. In the slide-box metaphor, we think of a slide as an internal representation of an object, so that the current scene is represented by an assemblage of slides. What is important is that this assemblage is dynamic and requires relatively little updating over time as the stimuli to the organism change.

In response to internal goals and needs, as well as sensory stimulation, slides can be tuned, relocated, and replaced. In this metaphorical sense, the utility of a slide lies in the fact that it is not simply a piece of celluloid of the technology that gave rise to the metaphor but rather a structure giving access to programs appropriate for interaction with the object that the slide represents. In Section II,B, we move from this highly metaphorical presentation to a revised model of internal representation in terms of schemas. We see in Section IV,B, that this model involves heterarchical cooperative computation by autonomously active schemas.

Studies of internal representations have a long history. From psychology, we have Bartlett's (1932) notion of schema and Piaget's more elaborate theory of sensorimotor schemas (see Furth, 1969, for an exposition), in which sensory information is used to cue appropriate motor activity. Another psychological approach, based explicitly on the early artificial intelligence work of Newell, Shaw, and Simon (1960; for an overview, see Newell & Simon, 1972), is Miller, Galanter, and Pribram's (1960) theory of "plans." These authors talk of using information to get access to appropriate programs or plans that can then be followed to completion.

A number of workers in artificial intelligence have also developed ideas of internal representation whose ancestry is much the same as that of the ideas of Miller, Galanter, and Pribram. With the increasing interest in getting computers to understand natural language, workers in artificial intelligence have not only explored the representation of such linguistic knowledge as syntax and semantics but have also concerned themselves with the representation of certain social interactions required if a computer is to understand a story. Here is an example cited by Minsky (1975):

> Jane was invited to Jack's birthday party.
> She wondered if he would like a kite.
> She went to her room and shook her piggy bank.
> It made no sound.

Minsky observes that no sense can be made of this simple story unless one has available a representation (he calls it a "frame") of knowledge about birthday parties. One has to know that birthday parties require presents, that presents require money, that children get money from a piggy bank, that one can test whether there is money in a piggy bank by shaking it, and that if there is no sound, there is no money. Similar work has been done by Schank and Abelson (1975) in their study of plans and scripts, and by Schmidt (1975) in his work on belief systems, which can be seen in some ways as a successor to Searle's (1959) study of speech acts.

In this context of the representation of social knowledge, it is intriguing to consider a book entitled *Frame Analysis: An Essay on the Organization of Experience*. It is not an account of Minsky's work, but rather the attempt of a social psychologist, Goffman (1974), to represent the different types of context that determine how people behave. For example, when you walk into the doctor's office and the doctor asks, "How are you?" you probably reply, "Fine, thanks," and yet, when you are both seated and he asks you again, "How are you?" you reply with a detailed list of troublesome symptoms. Goffman suggests that all that has changed is that you have moved from the "greeting" frame to the "doctor–patient" frame.

II.B. Interacting Schemas for Perception and Motor Control

We now reserve the term *schema* for the building block of a perceptual representation or motor plan and view the current representation of the environment as being a *schema assemblage*. We explore some aspects of the schema assemblage in Figure 5.1 (Arbib, 1979). Let us hypothesize that whenever we see a duck, there is some characteristic pattern of neural activity in the brain which we shall refer to as "activation of the duck schema." Suppose also that we may speak of a "rabbit schema" as well. When we are confronted with the duck–rabbit of Figure 5.1a, we may see it either as a duck with its bill pointing to the right or as a rabbit with its ears pointing to the right, but we cannot see it as both simultaneously.

This situation might suggest that the schemas for duck and rabbit are neural assemblies with mutually inhibitory interconnections, as indicated in Figure 5.1b. However, we are quite capable of perceiving a duck and a rabbit side by side within the scene; hence, it seems more appropriate to suggest, as in Figure 5.1c, that the inhibition between the duck and rabbit schema that would seem to underlie our perception of the duck–rabbit is not so much wired in as it is based on the restriction that low-level features may activate only one of several schemas. In other words, we postulate that to the extent that a higher-level schema is activated, the features that contributed to the activation are made unavailable.

We thus have an efferent pathway within the visual system, and this finding may well tie in with the observation that the number of fibers running from the visual cortex to the lateral geniculate in mammals exceeds the number of fibers running in the "normal" direction (Singer, 1977). Finally, it must be noted that we can see a scene with, say, several ducks in it. Thus, we can no longer think of a single localized schema for each familiar object in our environment. Instead, we must imagine that the appropriate pattern of activity can be reproduced to an extent compatible with the number of occurrences of a given object within the current visual scene, as in Figure 5.1d. We must further imagine that each of these instantiations of the schema, one for each occurrence of the object that the schema represents, is tuned with appropriate parameters to represent the particularities of the occurrence so represented.

In arguing for a theory of schemas within an overall perspective of "action-oriented perception," I have viewed a schema as a system with three components (Arbib, 1975b):

Michael A. Arbib

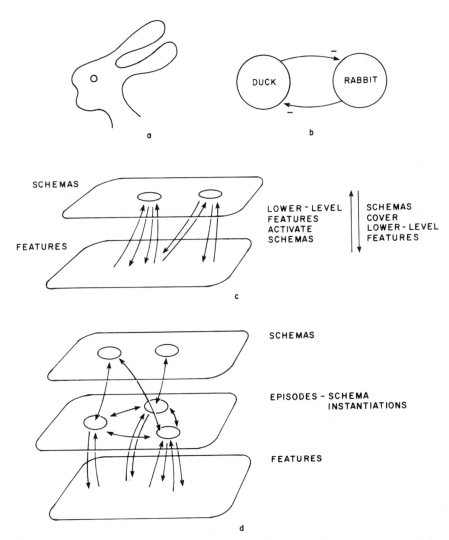

Figure 5.1   From schemas to schema assemblages. The duck–rabbit (a) suggests that the
interactions between the schemas (internal representations) of duck and rabbit are mutually
inhibitory (b). However, the fact that we can see a scene containing both a duck and a rabbit
suggests that this inhibition is not "wired in" but rather mediated by the competition for
low-level features (c). Finally, our ability to see a scene with, say, several ducks, argues that
perception does not so much activate a set of particular schemas as it does a schema
assemblage consisting of instantiations of schemas (d).

1. *Input-matching routines.* A schema corresponds to an object (though this may be at a very abstract level, such as "winter" or "a differential equation") and so requires routines whose job it is to search sensory stimuli, as well as messages from other schemas, for cues as to the correctness of the hypothesis that the object the schema represents is indeed present in the system's (conceptual) environment. These input-matching routines cooperate with segmentation routines (Section III) that are continually trying to segment the world into analyzable regions. It must be stressed that the input being matched may be multimodal: One may perceive a cat as much from its meow or the feel of its fur as from seeing it. Again, the level of detail at which the input is matched may vary greatly with the goal structure of the animal. If one is looking for a suitable stick, the detailed branching structure of a tree must be perceived, whereas if one is simply taking a walk, it may be enough simply to perceive a row of trees and thus to avoid bumping into them. Finally, in their fullest generality the input-matching routines will not simply match static aspects of the environment, but rather will match dynamic aspects. For example, when crossing the road, one is more interested in perceiving those dynamic aspects of a car required to avoid being hit than in noting the make of the car.

2. *Action routines.* From an action-oriented viewpoint, a schema must include action routines appropriate for guiding the activity of the organism in interacting with the object that the schema represents. As input-matching routines adjust the parameters of the representation, the action routines should also be adjusted so that the action they release becomes more and more appropriate for the current environment and goal structures.

3. *Competition and cooperation routines.* As pointed out in our discussion of Figure 5.1 (see also Section IV,B), some schemas will compete to "cover" objects in a given part of an animal's world, while other schemas will cooperate to provide a coherent representation of a number of regions in that world. One problem remains, however, even when, through this process of competition and cooperation, a collage of active schemas has provided an acceptable representation of the environment—namely, the animal cannot at any one time carry out more than a small fraction of the possible patterns of interaction consistent with the action routines of the activated schemas. We may say that the active schemas present, to use McCulloch's (1965, p. 397) phrase, a "redundancy of potential command": Each could, in principle, command the activity of the organism, but there are too many of them to command simultaneously. Thus, further competition and cooperation routines are required to turn the range of possibilities into a coherent plan of action for the organism.

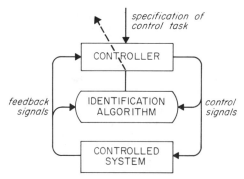

Figure 5.2   An identification algorithm provides a continually updated parametric description of the controlled system to the controller. The resultant combination of controller and identification algorithm thus yields a control system that is adaptive to changes in its environment.

However, in developing schema theory (Arbib, 1981a), I have come to the conclusion that it is not always appropriate to imagine input-matching routines and action routines as contained within the same schema. For example, many different objects may require a "grasping schema" for their manipulation (see the discussion of Figure 5.3 to follow). I thus find it convenient to now distinguish between *perceptual schemas* and *motor schemas*. Through our continuing interaction with the world, we build up an assemblage of perceptual schemas to represent our current knowledge about the environment. On the basis of our current goals, we also build up a "coordinated control program," consisting of interwoven motor schemas, which then guides our actions. Of course, as we begin to act, we are able to update the perceptual schema assemblage and thus update our plans. Our behavior is best described by an *action–perception cycle*—we act to perceive, and we perceive to act.

To analyze briefly the notion of a motor schema, we need an important concept from modern control theory—that of the identification algorithm, as shown in Figure 5.2. In the familiar realm of feedback control theory, a controller compares feedback signals from the controlled system with a statement of the system's desired performance in order to determine the control signals that will move the system into ever-greater conformity with the given plan. Of course, the appropriate choice of control signal depends on having a reasonably accurate model of the controlled system. For example, the appropriate thrust to apply depends on an estimate of the mass of the object to be moved. However, there are many cases in which the controlled system will change over time in such a way that no reliable, a priori estimate of the system's parameters can be made. It is therefore a useful practice to interpose an identification algorithm which can update a parametric description of the controlled system in such a way that the observed response of the system to its control signals comes into greater and greater conformity with that projected on the basis of the parametric description. We see that when (1) a controller is equipped with an identification algorithm, (2) the controlled system is of the class whose parameters the algorithm is designed to identify, and (3) the changes in the parameters of the controlled system are not too rapid, the combination of controller and identification algorithm then provides an adaptive control system that is able to function effectively despite continual changes in the environment.

The problem of motor control is one of sequencing and coordinating such motor schemas rather than directly controlling the vast number of degrees of freedom offered by the independent activity of all the motor units. To use the words of Greene (1964), we have to get the system "into the right ballpark" and then tune the activity within that ballpark. Thus, we are faced with the dual problems of activation and tuning.

Figure 5.3 provides one example of what I believe to be the style of a coordinated control program at a level of analysis somewhere between pure artificial intelligence and an attempt at setting forth "the style of the brain" but far from the analysis of detailed neural circuitry. Clinical studies based on lesions in human subjects should help us refine hypotheses such as that shown in Figure 5.3 so that the various "boxes" come to correspond more and more closely to the function of circumscribed layers, modules, or regions of the human brain. When the input-state-output specification of such a module becomes reasonably well established, we are then in an excellent position to pursue detailed neural modeling, with the help of animal experiments. The program shown in Figure 5.3 is designed for the task of reaching toward a visual target (some interesting data on this behavior are described by Jeannerod & Biguer, 1982). For the present purpose, it suffices simply to note that as the hand starts to reach toward a target, it is already being rotated and the separation of the fingers adjusted in anticipation of the orientation and size of the target.

The notion of a *coordinated control program* is meant to combine features of the flow diagram of the computer scientist with the block diagram of the control theorist. In the flow diagram of a conventional serial computer program, each box corresponds to a single activation of a subsystem. Only one system is activated at any time, and the lines joining the various boxes correspond to transfers of activation (in Figure 5.3, the dashed lines correspond to such activation transfers). In the block diagram of the control theorist, each box represents a physically distinct system. Each such system is imagined to be active at the same time, and

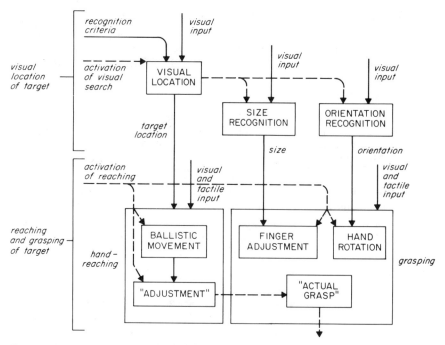

Figure 5.3 A hypothetical coordinated control program inspired by Jeannerod and Biguer's (1982) study of reaching toward a seen object.

the lines joining the different boxes correspond to the transfer of actual
data, as in the pathways conveying the control signals and feedback signals in a conventional feedback system (such data transfers are indicated
by the solid lines in Figure 5.3). In our figure, then, each box corresponds
to the activation of some subsystem. Several subsystems may be active at
the same time, but we do not imply that all systems are concurrently
active. Thus, in addition to its own internal changes, the activity of a
particular subsystem may serve both to pass messages to other activated
subsystems, as indicated by the solid lines, and to change the activation
level of other systems, as indicated by the dashed lines. In the particular
diagram shown here, we have indicated only system activation, but we
can easily picture deactivation.

Having understood the instructions, subjects first locate a target visually. This process is indicated in the upper half of Figure 5.3 by the three
boxes representing perceptual schemas for visual location, size recognition, and orientation recognition. In the lower half of the diagram, we see
that there are two motor schemas that are activated concurrently once

reaching and grasping have been initiated. Upon activation, the hand reaching schema releases a ballistic movement to the target which, in the intact subject, can be modulated at the end by visual feedback until actual contact with the target is made. The grasping schema is activated simultaneously with the reaching schema and itself involves the simultaneous activation of both finger adjustment and hand rotation.

What is particularly interesting about the hypothetical scheme shown here is that the activation of the "actual grasp" subschema of the motor schema for grasping is not internally activated by the completion of finger adjustment or hand rotation. Rather, it is separately activated when adjustment of the reaching schema yields the appropriate tactile stimulation to the palm of the hand. While this figure is certainly hypothetical, it begins to give us a language in which we can talk about the coordination and control of multiple activations of different motor schemas and thus analyze complex feats of motor coordination in terms of units (schemas) whose implementation we can explore in terms of neural circuitry.

III. SEGMENTATION OF VISUAL SCENES

It has become a commonplace in that branch of artificial intelligence called "computer vision" (Ballard & Brown, 1982; Hanson & Riseman, 1978; Marr, 1982; Nevatia, 1982) to discriminate between low-level and high-level systems. Low-level systems may carry out preprocessing to extract various features, perform motion and depth processing, extract boundaries within an image, segment the image into regions that may well correspond to the surfaces of objects represented within the image, or even come up with subtle information about the shape of the surfaces that have been sensed. While these processes may make considerable use of the physics of the world—the fact that the world tends to be made up of surfaces rather than an aggregate array of moving points, the properties of how shadows are generated, or how light is reflected from variously shaped surfaces—these low-level systems do not make any use of an organism's knowledge of what particular objects may be in the environment. Rather, it is the job of the high-level systems to build on the representations initially determined at the low level and to utilize perceptual schemas to recognize objects within the environment.

J. J. Gibson (1955, 1966, 1977) was one of the people who most forcefully made clear to psychologists that there was a great deal of information that could be picked up by low-level systems and that this information could be of great use to animals even without invoking high-level processes of object recognition. For example, if, as we walk forward, we recognize that a tree appears to be getting bigger, we can infer that the tree is in fact getting closer. What Gibson emphasized, and others (e.g., Lee, 1974; Lee & Lishman, 1977) have since developed, is the notion that we do not need object recognition to make such inferences. In particular, the "optic flow"—the vector field representing the velocity on the retina of stimuli corresponding to particular points in the environment—is rich enough to support the inference of where collisions may occur within the environment and, moreover, the time until contact.

In Section III,B, we consider a problem often glossed over in Gibson's writings—namely, that of the actual computation of the optic flow from changing retinal input. the model given there is "in the style of the brain," but it has not been related to actual neural circuitry. Rather than asking how neurons might pick up the optic flow on the basis of continuously changing retinal input, we simply offer an algorithm played out over a number of interacting layers, each of which involves the parallel interaction of local processes, in which the retinal input is in the form of two successive "snapshots." The problem is to match up corresponding features in these two frames.

Mathematically, the problem of optic flow is the same as that of stereopsis, in which two images taken from different places are to be matched so that depth can then be inferred in terms of the interocular distance. In the optic flow problem, however, the two images are separated in time, and so depth is expressed as time until contact, or adjacency. Although there are only two eyes, there may be many successive moments in time, and in Section III,B we see that the initial algorithm for matching a successive pair of frames can be improved when the cumulative effect of a whole sequence can be exploited. In Section III,A we consider the stereopsis problem itself, with a brief look at a neurallike model. In Section III,C we present a third model of segmentation that evolved from work on robot vision and uses segmentation on color and texture. In Section IV,B we study a model that uses high-level semantic information to aggregate regions into collections that constitute different portions of a single object.

I want to emphasize that these models are no longer "state of the art" but are intended rather to give the conceptual overview appropriate for an introductory chapter of this nature. We can place the three models in a methodological context as follows: The first is an example of neural modeling, the second is in a form that suggests possible neural implementation, while the third is far from a neural network implementation and suggests instead the types of data structures that must be implemented in any complex perceptual system.

III.A. Stereopsis

While each retina provides only a two-dimensional map of the visual world, between them the two retinae provide information from which the three-dimensional location of all unoccluded points in visual space can be reconstructed. We indicate this fact in the upper half of Figure 5.4, in which the right retina cannot distinguish A, B, or C ($A_R = B_R = C_R$). While the left retina can distinguish them, it cannot determine where they lie along their ray. However, the two retinae working together can locate all three points: (A_L, A_R) fixes A, (B_L, B_R) fixes B, and (C_L, C_R) fixes C. Nevertheless, two problems remain.

The first is that our observation that the two retinae contain enough information to determine the three-dimensional location of a point in no way implies that a neural mechanism exists to use that information. However, Barlow, Blakemore, and Pettigrew (1967), Pettigrew, Nikara, and Bishop (1968), and others have found cells in the visual cortex that not only respond best to a given orientation of a line stimulus but do so with a response that is sharply tuned to the disparity of the effect of the stimulus on the two retinae.

The second problem is that information is given about the three-dimensional location of points only when the corresponding points of activity on the retinae have been correctly paired. If the only stimuli activated in Figure 5.4 were at the focal point and at A, then A could only be accurately located if A_L were paired with A_R. Were A_L to be paired with F_R, the system would "perceive" an imaginary stimulus at W.

The main thrust of the model presented here will be to suggest how disparity-detecting neurons might be connected to restrict ambiguities resulting from false correlations between pairs of retinal stimulation. Before giving the details, however, let us examine some psychological data that define the overall function of the model.

Normal stereograms are made by photographing a scene with two cameras whose relative position is roughly that of a human's two eyes. When a human views the resultant stereogram (with each eye viewing only the photograph made by the corresponding camera), he or she can usually fuse the two images to see the scene in depth. Julesz (1971) has invented the ingenious technique of random-dot stereograms to show, inter alia, that this depth perception can arise even in the absence of the cues provided by monocular perception of familiar objects. The slide for the left eye is prepared by simply filling in, completely at random, 50% of the squares of an array. The slide for the right eye is prepared by transforming the first slide by shifting sections of the original pattern some small distance (without changing the pattern within the section) and otherwise

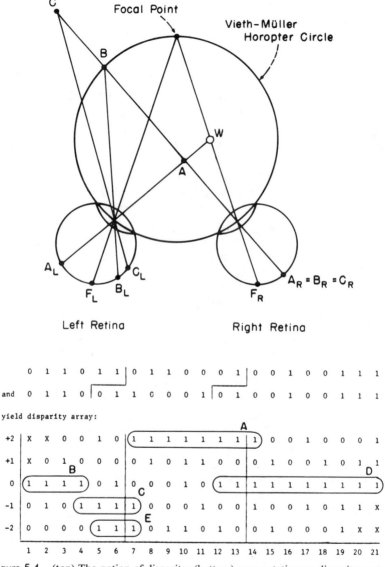

```
    0  1  1  0  1  1 | 0  1  1  0  0  0  1 | 0  0  1  0  0  1  1  1
and 0  1  1  0 | 0  1  1  0  0  0  1 | 0  1  0  0  1  0  0  1  1  1
```

yield disparity array:

	1	2	3	4	5	6	7	8	9	10	11	12	13	14	15	16	17	18	19	20	21
+2	X	X	0	0	1	0	1	1	1	1	1	1	1	1	0	0	1	0	0	0	1
+1	X	0	1	0	0	0	0	1	0	1	1	0	0	0	1	0	0	1	0	1	1
0	1	1	1	1	0	1	0	0	0	1	0	1	1	1	1	1	1	1	1	1	1
-1	0	1	0	1	1	1	1	0	0	0	1	0	0	1	0	0	1	0	1	1	X
-2	0	0	0	0	1	1	1	0	1	1	0	1	0	0	1	0	0	0	1	X	X

Figure 5.4   (top) The notion of disparity; (bottom) segmentation on disparity cues.

leaving the overall pattern unchanged, save to fill in at random the squares thus left blank. Viewing Julesz's arrays, with one slide presented to each eye, subjects start by perceiving visual "noise" but eventually come to perceive the noise as played out on surfaces at differing distances in space corresponding to the differing disparities of the noise patterns which constitute them.

Note that both stimuli of the stereogram pair are random patterns. Interesting information is contained only in the correlations between the two—that is, the fact that substantial regions of one slide are identical, save for their location, with regions of the other slide. Thus, the visual system is able to detect these correlations. If the correlations involve many regions of differing disparities, the subject may take seconds to perceive so complex a stereogram, during which time the subjective reports will be of periods in which no change is perceived, followed by the sudden emergence of yet another surface from the undifferentiated noise.

To clarify the ambiguity of disparity in Julesz's stereograms, let us caricature the rectangular arrays by the linear arrays of the lower half of Figure 5.4. The top line shows the 21 randomly generated 0's and 1's which constitute the left eye input, while the second line shows the right eye input obtained by displacing bits 7 through 13 two places to the left (so that the bit at position i goes to position $i-2$ for i between 7 and 13). The bits at positions 12 and 13 thus left vacant are filled in at random (in this case, the new bits equal the old bits—an event with a probability of 1 in 4), with all other bits left unchanged. In the remaining five lines of the figure we show a disparity array, with the ith bit of the disparity of line d being a 1 if and only if the ith bit of the right eye input equals the $(i + d)$th bit of the left eye input.

The disparity array suggests the stripped-down caricature of the visual cortex that we shall use for our model. Rather than mimic a columnar organization, we segregate our mock cortex into layers, with the initial activity of a cell in position i of layer d corresponding to the presence or absence of a match between the activity of cell i of the right retina and cell $i + d$ of the left retina. (This positioning of the elements aids our conceptualization. It is not the positioning of neurons that should be subject to experimental test, but rather the relationships that we posit between them.) As we see in the figure, the initial activity in these layers signals the "true" correlations (A signals the central surface, while B and D signal the background). However, we also see "spurious signals" (the clumps of activity of C and E, in addition to the scattered 1's, resulting from the 50% probability that a random pair of bits will agree) which obscure the true correlations.

We now turn to the stereopsis model of Dev (1975) and Amari and Arbib (1977). (Among the many other models of stereopsis, we refer the reader to those of Sperling, 1970, Nelson, 1975, and Marr & Poggio, 1977b, 1979). This model is based on the idea that the world is made up of surfaces, so that it is likely that features nearby in spatial direction will

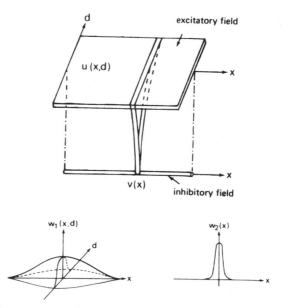

Figure 5.5   (top) the Amari–Arbib adaptation of Dev's model for stimulus-matching in stereopsis; (bottom) weighting functions of connections in the model.

also be nearby in depth (disparity). The model of Figure 5.5 has an excitatory field, divided into layers, with coordinate x for spatial direction and one layer for each discrete disparity d. There is also a single inhibitory field with coordinate x. The net effect of the interaction between the two fields is that there is moderate local cross-excitation within a layer, as well as inhibition between layers that increases as the difference in features increases.

This scheme allows a clump of actives cells in one layer to "gang up" on cells with scattered activity in the same direction but in other layers, while at the same time recruiting moderately active cells that are nearby in their own layer. The system then tends to a condition in which activity is clearly separated into regions, with each having its own unique disparity (layer of activity). In other words, such a scheme resolves ambiguity through the suppression of scattered activity, thus permitting only activity related to one disparity in any one locale. Moreover, returning to the stereopsis example, the dynamics of the model represent the Julesz phenomenon of a noise stereogram taking some time to be perceived rather immediately. This effect is simulated in the model by the fact that once a sufficient number of clumps achieve high activity, the recruitment fills in

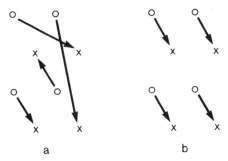

a   b

Figure 5.6   In a world made up of surfaces, nearby features are likely to have similar optic flow. Thus the flow of b is more likely to be correct than that of a.

the gaps between the clumps to form a good approximation of its final extent.

III.B. Computing the Optic Flow

The problem of computing optic flow is posed in Figure 5.6, in which we see four features extracted from frame 1, shown as circles, and four features from frame 2, represented as crosses. The *stimulus-matching problem* is to try to match up each pair of features in the two frames that correspond to a single feature in the external world. Figure 5.6a shows an assignment that seems far less likely to be correct than that shown in Figure 5.6b. Lacking other information, the reason we would prefer the latter stimulus-matching is that the world tends to be made up of surfaces, with nearby points on the same surface being displaced by similar amounts. (This use of the plausible hypothesis, that our visual world is made up of relatively few connected regions to drive a stimulus-matching process, was enunciated earlier for stereopsis.) Our algorithm, then, makes use of two consistency conditions.

1. *Feature Matching.* Where possible, the optic flow vector attached to a feature in frame 1 will come close to bringing it in correspondence with a similar feature in frame 2.
2. *Local Smoothness.* Since nearby features tend to be projections of points on the same surface, their optic flow vectors should be similar.

In developing our algorithm (Prager, 1979; Prager & Arbib, 1983) "in the style of the brain," we posit a retinotopic array of local processors which can make initial estimates of the local optic flow but will then pass messages back and forth to their neighbors in an iterative process to

Figure 5.7 Frame 1 comprises the dots indicated by circles; Frame 2 is obtained by rotating the array about the pivot at A to place the dots in the positions indicated by crosses. The dashed circle at lower right is the receptive field of a local processor. The solid arrows indicate the best local estimate of the optic flow, while the dashed arrows show the actual pairing of features under rotation about A.

converge eventually upon a global estimate of the flow. The need for interactions if a correct global estimate is to be obtained is shown in Figure 5.7, in which we see a local receptive field for which the most plausible estimate of the optic flow is greatly at variance with the correct global pattern. Our algorithm is then as shown in Figure 5.8. We fix two frames and seek to solve the matching problem for them.

An initial assignment of optic flow vectors might be made simply on the basis of the nearest match. The algorithm then proceeds through successive iterations, with the local estimate for the optic flow vector assigned to each feature of frame 1 being updated at each iteration. Consider, for example, Frame 1 feature A of Figure 5.8 and position B, which indicate the current hypothesis as to the location of the matching stimulus in frame 2. We see that if feature matching were to be the sole criterion, the new optic flow would be given by the wavy arrow that matches A to the feature in frame 2 closest to the prior estimate. On the other hand, if only local smoothness were taken into account, the new optic flow vector assigned to A would be the average of the optic flow vectors of features within a certain neighborhood. Our algorithm updates the estimate at each

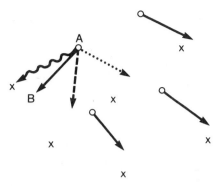

Figure 5.8   The circles indicate features in Frame 1, the crosses features in Frame 2, and the solid arrows the current estimate of the optic flow. The head of the arrow shows the posited position in Frame 2 of the feature corresponding to the Frame 1 feature at the tail of the arrow. Feature matching alone would adjust A's optic flow to the wavy arrow pointing to the Frame 2 feature nearest to B (the current estimate of A's Frame 2 position); local smoothness would yield the dotted arrow, the average of the optic flow of the neighbors, while our relaxation algorithm yields the dashed arrow as a weighted combination of these two estimates.

iteration by making the new estimate a linear combination of both the feature-matching and local smoothness updates, as indicated by the dashed arrow emanating from A in Figure 5.8. The algorithm gives a reliable estimate of optic flow within 20 iterations.

Given a sequence of frames, rather than just two, we can obtain an increasingly accurate estimate of the optic flow and yet use fewer iterations to handle each new frame as it is introduced. For example, if, having matched frame n to frame $n + 1$, we try to match frame $n + 1$ to $n + 2$, it is reasonable to assume that (to a first approximation) the optic flow advances a feature by roughly the same amount in the two frames. If we then use the repetition of the previous displacement, rather than a nearest-neighbor match, to initialize the optic flow computation of the two new frames, we find from simulations that only four or five iterations, rather than the original 20, are required and that the quality of the match on real images is definitely improved.

The algorithm just described is based on two consistency conditions—feature matching and local smoothness. It is instructive to note where these constraints break down. If one object is moving in front of another, points on the rear surface will either be occluded or disoccluded during this movement, depending on whether the front object is moving to cover or uncover the object behind it. If we look at the current estimate of the optic flow and find places where the flow vector does not terminate near a

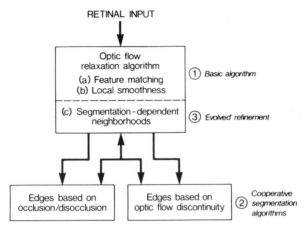

Figure 5.9 Our basic optic flow relaxation algorithm uses the consistency conditions of feature matching and local smoothness. (2) The resultant optic flow estimate permits the hypothesization of edges on cues based on both occlusion/disocclusion and optic flow discontinuity. (3) The resultant edge hypothese can be used to refine the computation of optic flow by dynamically adjusting the neighborhoods used in employing the consistency conditions.

feature similar to that from which it starts, we thus have a good indication of an occluding edge. On the other hand, the local smoothness will also break down at an edge, for the two objects on either side of the edge will in general be moving differentially with respect to the organism. Thus, we can design edge-finding algorithms which exploit the breakdown of consistency conditions to find edges in two different ways: on the basis of occlusion/disocclusion, and on the basis of optic flow discontinuity. To the extent that the estimate of edges by these two processes is consistent, we have a cooperative determination of the edges of surfaces within the image.

Note that as good edge estimates become available, the original basic algorithm can be refined, as shown in Figure 5.9 (although this refinement is yet to be implemented). Instead of having "bleeding" across edges, we can dynamically change the neighborhood of a point so that the matching of features or the conformity with neighboring flow can be based primarily on features on the same side of the currently hypothesized boundary (but not entirely, for at any time the edges will themselves be confirmed with limited confidence and so may be subject to later change).

We thus see in Figure 5.9 an *evolutionary design process*. The basic algorithm (1) provides new information which can then be exploited in the design of the cooperative segmentation algorithms (2). Once the segmentation information is available, however, the original algorithm can be refined by the introduction of segmentation-dependent neighborhoods (3). I suggest that this is not simply an interesting engineering observation but gives us some very real insight into brain evolution. Basic systems provide the substrate upon which higher-level systems may evolve, but these higher-level systems then enrich the environment of the lower systems, and the lower-level systems may then evolve to exploit the new sources of information. While it is still useful (to a first approximation) to talk of low-level and high-level systems, we see that there is no longer any univocal flow of information. Thus, we are very close to Jackson's (1898) notion of levels.

III.C. Segmentation on Ad Hoc Features

While anyone who has used the focus control of a camera will find it plausible that a small number of different disparities can yield a set of depth cues to aid other mechanisms for locating objects in the world, credulity would be strained by the suggestion that we have a prewired set of features for every color or texture that may prove to be of value in setting off one region of the visual world from another. In this section, then, we outline a scheme that creates ad hoc features for segmenting visual input (Hanson, Riseman, & Nagin, 1975). The scheme is part of a preprocessor for a visual system which is to analyze outdoor scenes. In what follows, I describe a scheme of segmentation based on their model rather than detailing their computer implementation. Few of the computations in the scheme have clear neural implementations. Nonetheless, they give us valuable insight into the top-down analysis of the computational needs of low-level vision.

The system input encodes a color photograph of an outdoor scene as three spatially coded intensity arrays, one each for the red, green, and blue components of the visual input. The first task of the system is to extract *microtextures*—features such as hue which describe small "windows" in the scene. Even in the foliage of a single tree, or in a patch of clear blue sky, the hue will change from window to window, and the system must be able to recognize the commonality among the variations. However, in segmenting a natural scene, macrotexture will be more important than microtexture. *Macrotexture* is a pattern of repetition of (one or more) microtextures across many local windows, and its recognition requires the analysis of structural relationships between types of microtexture. For example, the branching of a tree would have the microtexture of leaves interspersed with that of shadows in summer, while the

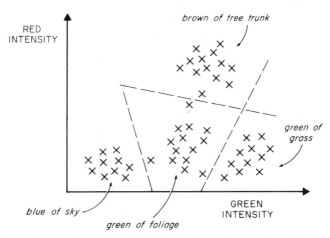

Figure 5.10   An image of a tree in a field is mapped onto feature space. The four microtextures of the blue of sky, green of foliage, green of grass, and brown of a tree trunk define four clusters in feature space. The lines drawn to separate clusters are somewhat arbitrary, and further processing is required to settle "demarcation disputes."

microtextures of branches and sky might characterize its winter appearance.

We extract microtexture first. The goal is to do so without using predefined features. The general method is as follows: Pick n feature parameters (usually $n = 2$), and map each image point into the feature space forming an n-dimensional histogram. Then apply a "clustering" algorithm to segregate the points into a small number of clusters in feature space. Each cluster forms a candidate for microtexture of use in segmenting the original image. For example, while tree foliage and grass may each yield a range of greens, the feature points of the two regions should form two clusters with relatively little overlap. The result of the clustering operation is suggested by the (hypothetical) example of Figure 5.10.

Once clusters have been formed, each may be assigned a distinct label. Returning to the original image, a cluster label may be associated with each point, which thus has a tentative, ad hoc microtexture associated with it. So far, however, no spatial information has been used to bind texture elements together. If N clusters had been formed, spatial information is used to construct an $N \times N$ adjacency matrix, in which the (i, j) element records the number of times a point labeled i is adjacent to a point labeled j (i.e., bearing the microtexture label of the jth cluster). A homogeneous region of points from a single cluster j will yield large values of the (j, j) element of the matrix. A large number of adjacencies between points of two cluster types may signal a cohesive region that has a repetitive mixture of cluster types—in which case it determines a macrotexture. (Note, however, that two microtextures may be interdistributed in different ways to determine macrotextures.) Macrotextures suggested by large (i, j) entries can then be used as labels for the final pass of region-growing on the image.

The contribution from a boundary between two homogeneous regions of types i and j, respectively, would distort the (i, j) entry. To avoid this situation, it pays to remove large connected homogeneous regions and then to form a modified adjacency matrix without these boundary contributions. Another boundary problem is that a cluster may appear due to windows overlapping in two regions. However, if we apply curve-following as well as region-growing algorithms to the cluster types, we can generate boundaries to supplement our region-growing process. The resultant regions, labeled by macrotexture features, can then provide the input to a semantic labeling process of the kind we caricature in Section IV,B (see also Kohler, 1981; Nagin, Hanson, & Riseman, 1982).

IV. COMPETITION AND COOPERATION

IV.A. Competition and Cooperation in Neural Networks

Selfridge (1959) introduced a character recognition system called Pandemonium which behaves as if there were a number of different "demons" sampling the input. Each demon is an expert in recognizing a particular classification and yells out the strength of its conviction. An executive demon then decrees that the input belongs to the class of whichever demon is heard yelling the loudest. In modeling the reticular formation of the brainstem, Kilmer, McCulloch, and Blum (1969) posited a system without executive control. Rather, each of an array of modules in their model, called S-RETIC, samples the input and makes a preliminary decision as to the relative weights of different modes as being appropriate to the overall commitment of the organism. The modules are then coupled in a back-and-forth fashion so that eventually a majority of the modules will agree on the appropriate mode—at which stage the system will be committed to action. A reasonable analogy is a panel of physicians discussing a patient's symptoms and coming to a consensus about a diagnosis.

We say that S-RETIC converges to output mode j if more than 50% of the modules indicate the jth mode with probability $> .5$. In computer simulations, convergence always took place in less than 25 cycles and, once converged, stayed converged for that input. What is important for us

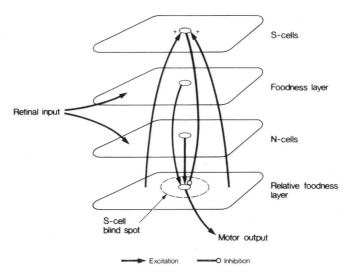

Figure 5.11   Didday's (1976) model of prey selection. Retinal input yields a retinotopic map
of prey location in the "foodness layer." This map is projected on the relative foodness
layer in which different peaks "compete" via S-cell-mediated inhibition. Build-up of inhibition yields diminished responsiveness to changes in the retinal input; N-cells signal such
changes to break through this hysteresis.

here is that S-RETIC provides an early model of how a system might
reach consensus as to a course of action through competition (of modes)
and cooperation (of modules), without the imposition of control by an
executive. To support this analysis, we offer another example of competition and cooperation taken from the analysis of visuomotor coordination
in frog and toad (for a more general survey, see Arbib, 1982).

In 1959, Lettvin, Maturana, McCulloch and Pitts, published a study
entitled, "What the Frog's Eye tells the Frog's Brain." Some 10 years
later, Richard Didday and I sought to understand "what the frog's eye
tells the frog"—what are the plausible networks that can take the retinal
signals and transduce them to yield appropriate behavior? One of the key
experiments for our work was Ingle's (1968) observation that when a frog
was confronted with two flylike stimuli, either of which alone would be
potent enough to release a snapping response, the animal might well
respond to one of them but might also respond to neither, as if there were
"competition" between the stimuli which sometimes resulted in a "stand-
off." The model that we developed (Didday, 1970, 1976) is shown in
Figure 5.11. The "foodness layer" is a retinotopic layer within the tectum. Retinal ganglion cell activity is combined in this layer to provide a
spatial map whose intensity correlates with the presence of foodlike stim-

uli in the environment. The "relative foodness layer" holds a modified form of this map in which, as a result of interactions with other maps, most of the peaks will be suppressed, so that normally only one peak will be able to get through to trigger snapping in the corresponding direction. (The locus of activity in the array, rather than the value of a single scalar, provides the control signal. The need for different control surfaces for different control systems may provide much of the rationale for the "many visual systems.")

The actual competition between the peaks of "foodness" is mediated by another retinotopic array—that of the S-cells. To the extent that there is activity in other regions, it is somewhat less likely that a given region will be the one that should be snapped at. This process is implemented via the S-cells, which are excited by activity in the relative foodness layer outside a certain blind spot, with the S-cells then providing inhibition to the cells within that blind spot on the relative foodness layer. Both computer and mathematical analyses show that the system will normally converge to a pattern of relative foodness activity with a single peak of activity, but there are cases where no peak will survive this process of convergence, as observed experimentally. Moreover, if activity within the network is uniform prior to input, the largest peak will be that which survives the competition. However, the system does exhibit hysteresis: Once a single peak has been established, it may be hard for new activity arriving at the foodness layer to break through. To this end, the N-cells can respond to a sudden change of activity within the foodness layer and on this basis provide excitation to the corresponding locus of the relative foodness layer, thus breaking through the S-cell inhibition and reducing the hysteretic effect.

In the original version of the model, the N-cells were identified with newness cells, and the S-cells were identified with sameness cells, with the entire circuitry being contained within the tectum. However, experiments subsequent to those used as the basis for this model have suggested a somewhat different interpretation. Ewert (1976) has shown that, deprived of the inhibitory influence of pretectum and thalamus, a toad will snap at moving objects of all sizes, without showing the pattern discrimination between small, "snappable" objects and larger objects which are to be avoided. On this basis, the N-cells are still to be interpreted as newness cells within the tectum, but the S-cells are to be viewed as cells in the pretectum–thalamus (Lara & Arbib, 1982).

Of course, this is only part of the story. Ewert and von Seelen (1974) have built on Ewert's experiments to come up with a linear lumped model (not spelled out in terms of detailed neural interactions) of prey–predator discrimination, meeting Ewert's data on the rate of response that toads exhibit to mechanical analogs of worms, to "antiworms" (rectangles elongated orthogonal to the direction of their movement), and to moving squares, as a function of their size. Current modeling within my own laboratory is not only addressing this rapprochement but also coming up with plausible analyses of tectal microcircuitry (Lara, Arbib, & Cromarty, 1982) that could underlie the facilitation effects observed by Ingle (1975), as well as the pretectal–tectal interactions that could underlie the effects studied by Ewert (Lara, Cervantes, & Arbib, 1982).

Amari and Arbib (1977) have placed the Dev model of stereopsis and the Didday model of prey selection in a common mathematical framework. For a less mathematical view of these commonalities (Montalvo, 1975), see Figure 5.12. In the Didday model there is competition between "bug locations"; in the Dev and S-RETIC model we see both a competition and a cooperation dimension (for a recent symposium volume on *Competition and Cooperation in Neural Nets,* see Amari & Arbib, 1982).

IV.B. Competition and Cooperation between Schemas

We regard the structure of the internal representation as a schema assemblage, an assemblage of perceptual schemas, representations of objects. In Section III, we studied the segmentation of visual input. A region that has been "segmented out" in this way can then provide excellent input for a higher-level routine that attempts to determine the object of which this region is a part. It is beyond the scope of this chapter to discuss the status of high-level vision [see, for example, the appropriate chapters in Ballard & Brown (1982) and Nevatia (1982)], but we shall try to offer an intuitive caricature of these processes in the present section.

What should be emphasized in this introductory statement is that the processes of segmentation on low-level features and of input matching to determine the object of which the segment is a part do not proceed in the fixed order of segmentation first and object assignment second. Rather, it is often the case that when one region is segmented, it will provide a cue that greatly increases the activity of a particular schema. The high activation level of this schema will suggest the presence of another region having certain properties, and this hypothesis can then speed up the low-level segmentation processes in that region. And so it goes in a highly cooperative process.

Imagine that a segmentation program has divided a scene into just the two regions common to the top half of Figure 5.13. With only this much information available, two quite different pairs of schemas may be activated to cover this input. In the first interpretation the schemas would represent green ice cream and a brown ice cream cone; in the second

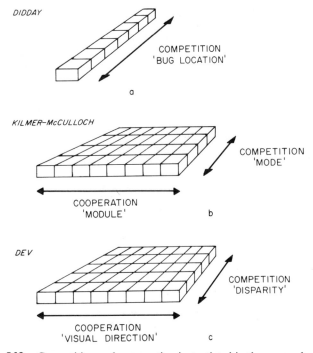

DIDDAY

COMPETITION
'BUG LOCATION'

a

KILMER–McCULLOCH

COMPETITION
'MODE'

COOPERATION
'MODULE'

b

DEV

COMPETITION
'DISPARITY'

COOPERATION
'VISUAL DIRECTION'

c

Figure 5.12   Competition and cooperation instantiated in three neural models.

interpretation, the schemas would represent the foliage and trunk of a tree. There would be competition between the pairs (perhaps mediated as suggested in Figure 5.1), and cooperation between the schemas within each pair. Thus the system of interactions would have two large attractors, corresponding to the two natural interpretations, and very small attractors for the "unreal" pairings—though these could be forced by a trick photograph or a Magritte painting.

As a brain theorist, I view the schemas as being autonomously active. Each one is continually monitoring input from the periphery and from other schemas, trying to increase its own activity and influence the activity of the others. Out of this cooperative and competitive interaction emerges a stable pattern that is in equilibrium with the environmental input and constitutes the representation of the input. Even when one tries to simulate such a system on a serial computer, it is the cooperative computation by autonomously active schemas that is the real logic of perceptual activity, even though any limited system, be it a computer or a brain, must in some way cut down the totality of interactions.

In case of blurred images, the input may start the system close to the

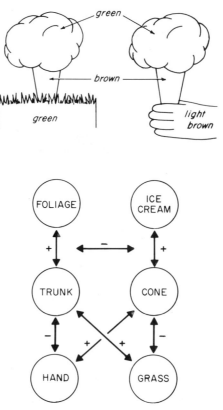

Figure 5.13   The effect of context in resolving ambiguous interpretations of portions of a scene.

boundary between the two attractors. Convergence may be slow and even incorrect. Context can provide a mechanism to speed, and correct, convergence. Thus the two contexts atop Figure 5.13 correspond to the two extra schemas shown at the bottom, and in each case we expect rapid convergence to the correct interpretation. Thus an initial configuration in which the schemas for foliage, trunk, ice cream, and cone have comparable activity will converge rapidly to a state of high activity in foliage and trunk schemas and low activity in ice cream and cone schemas if the grass schema is given a higher activity level than the hand schemas, and vice versa.

As well as schemas for objects, we may also have more abstract schemas, such as one for winter. At the change of seasons, the first fall of snow may be the signal for winter, so that we must posit the activity level

Figure 5.14   A house image.

of the snow schema as providing excitatory input to the winter schema. However, in the normal course of events, the organism *knows* that it is winter and can use this contextual information to favor the hypothesis that a white expanse is snow rather than burnished sand, say, or moonlit water. It is this type of reciprocal activation (whether we regard it as an additional input or as the action of a cooperation routine) that gives the system of schemas its heterarchical character. [Strictly defined, a heterarchy is a system of rule by alien leaders. In artificial intelligence, however, stimulated by McCulloch (1949), it denotes a structure in which a subsystem A may dominate a subsystem B at one time and yet be dominated by B at some other time.]

To exemplify the processes described here, we now outline mechanisms for the interpretation of the scene in Figure 5.14 (see Parma, Hanson, & Riseman, 1981, for a technical discussion of the schema-matching techniques outlined here). We first return to the segmentation problem of Section III by asking the reader to carefully examine Figure 5.14. Despite the coarse quantization, one can delineate the roof quite clearly from this image as something close to a parallelogram. This suggests that we could deliver an image of this kind to a computer system and program it to recognize various things like, "Here is a blue region at the top; that must be sky (assuming a system that works with color photographs as input).

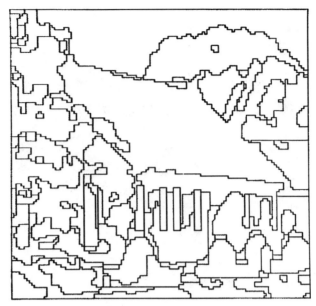

Figure 5.15   An initial segmentation of the house image. Note the "bleeding" of the roof and the subsegmentation of several of the shutters.

Here is a parallelogram beneath it (given that it is an outdoor scene, a parallelogram abutting the sky is probably a roof). Beneath the roof are some rectangles—such rectangles are either windows or shutters or doors." So the process could continue, calling on high-level information to classify all portions of the image.

The previous account was designed to lull you into a false sense of security. To see this effect, try to find the parallelogram in Figure 5.14. We can design algorithms that will smooth over the quantization and report with some confidence the lines at the top and bottom of the roof. The left side, however, will not be well defined, for an algorithm using some gradient in color or texture would not return the roof edge but rather the contour where the foliage occludes the roof. The problem is even worse for an algorithm tracing a gradient of color and texture along the right side of the roof. Halfway up, the gradient "wanders off" into the sky, eventually coming back and going off again to yield a bizarre shape that is nothing like a parallelogram, both because of occlusion and because of spectral problems that wash out boundaries in the image. Figure 5.15 shows the result of running cooperative segmentation algorithms on the image of Figure 5.14. We see that the top and bottom of the roof are fairly well delineated, but the left edge is occluded while the right edge "bleeds" into the sky and foliage. The figure also illustrates that highlighting or variations in texture may lead the algorithm to subdivide a natural region into several segments, as we see for several of the shutters.

The problem, then is to design algorithms that can, on the one hand, take a region and split it into parts that are to be seen as giving us information about different objects and, on the other hand, aggregate regions that together characterize some distinctive portion of the image. This process of image interpretation calls on high-level information about possible objects in the scene. For example, information about houses would, among other things, initiate a search for a parallelogram. However, the program would not fail if there were no parallelogram in the image but might pursue more subtle possibilities, such as, "If you find two approximately parallel lines at top and bottom and portions of approximately parallel lines on the left and right, join up the lines and explore the hypothesis that the resultant parallelogram is a roof." Given a confident roof hypothesis, the system could hypothesize that below the roof the image would contain shutters or windows. If regions there could be aggregated into a rectangle, the program could then follow the hypothesis that there was a rectangle.

How is high-level information to be represented? One approach (Parma et al., 1981) is to provide a three-dimensional schema that gives confidence ranges for the location of different objects in space. Figure 5.16 shows a two-dimensional view of such information. A sphere is not to be thought of as a veridical representation of a tree; rather, it gives a 90% confidence interval for where tree foliage is located. Here we have gone from a specific tree in a specific position to a "stochastic" tree. Ongoing research seeks more general ways of representation which will allow us to recognize very different types of trees or houses. One question is to what extent we can recognize a house from one very general template, and to what extent it is our experience of having seen many kinds of houses that allows us to use the appropriate form from occasion to occasion. It is beyond the scope of this chapter to detail the way in which information is applied, but Figure 5.17 shows how the system analyzes the segmentation of Figure 5.15. The roof is clearly delineated, shutter subregions are aggregated, and most of the image has been characterized correctly.

The overall computation thus involves the interleaving of multiple processes. It is a cooperative computation in which each process is invoked where appropriate, possibly many times, with hypotheses being generated and discarded until the system converges on as good an interpretation as it is able to give using the facilities available to it. We claim that this style characterizes the perceptual mechanisms of the brain and will provide the style for future developments in machine perception. In clos-

Figure 5.16   Two-dimensional graphic representation of a three-dimensional schema for a house scene.

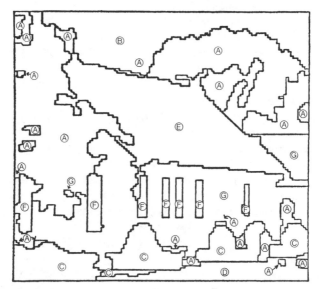

Figure 5.17   Labeled refinement of the segmentation of Figure 5.15 following invocation of the three-dimensional schema of Figure 5.15 (B for sky, C for bushes, E for roof, etc.).

ing this section, let us stress once again the generative nature of the internal representations that we have posited: The representation of the world at any time is an assemblage of active schemas. Consequently, animals or machines can represent situations internally that they have never before encountered because the elements of the situation are familiar, even though the combination of those elements may be completely novel to the organism.

V. EPILOGUE: UNITIES AND DIVERSITIES

My goal in this chapter has been to extract contributions from extant artificial intelligence and brain theory literature and to meld them together in an attempt to sketch a coherent model of cooperative computation subserving perception. To the extent that I have succeeded, the reader may be puzzled to learn that the literatures of artificial intelligence and brain theory hardly overlap at all. While the problems of artificial intelligence can be defined functionally, the problems of brain theory are defined structurally. Most artificial intelligence workers are interested in making computers interpret images, solve problems, plan, play games, understand natural language, and so forth. Few workers in artificial intelligence feel that it is important to relate their research to actual brain mechanisms (but see Marr, 1982, for an important exception). Increasingly many are interested in using artificial intelligence to shed new light on human problem solving, but such studies are psychological rather than neurophysiological—they fall in the new area of "cognitive science." The brain theorist, in contrast, studies neural networks, be they representative of actual brain structures, indicative of a regular geometry conducive to simulation or the proving of theorems, or of interest mainly for the way in which their connections change over time. Most of the functions dominating artifical intelligence work are simply at too high a level for their expression in neural networks to be ripe for study.

It is precisely to bridge this gap that I have urged the interest of a top-down aproach to brain theory (compare Marr & Poggio, 1977a). Artificial intelligence techniques may help us understand how some overall behavior can be caricatured, at least, in terms of a scheme of cooperative computation by subsystems whose function can be ascribed to regions of the brain (for a view of this approach in the context of language, rather than vision, see Arbib & Caplan, 1979). Bottom-up brain theory can then be used to analyze how the neural networks of each brain region might achieve the ascribed function. Of course, the neural modeling may well modify the top-down analysis.

Given the goal of this chapter, the reader will understand that the review of the literature has been highly selective and that many truly excellent contributions to the fields of both artificial intelligence and brain theory have been left out. Unfortunately, it is still the case that both artificial intelligence and brain theory lack a coherent body of theory accepted by the majority of practitioners. Both fields badly need a good dose of systematization. For too long, papers have been written with no attempt to build on the work of others or to contribute to a unification of the achievements of several laboratories. It is my belief—but not at all a widely held one—that this process of systematization can benefit from the type of melding process to which this article is a contribution.

This study points to the emergence of an increasing number of common principles for artifical intelligence and brain theory. However, it would be wrong to infer from this that the two subjects will, or should, merge into one. Artifical intelligence must look from the common principles toward the world of computer science—to the writing of programs with increasing "intelligence" to augment our use of computers by providing them with perceptual capabilities, natural language understanding, automatically reconfigurable databases, goal-oriented comptuter languages, and so forth. Brain theory must look from the common principles toward the world of biology—to the increased understanding of animal behavior and of brain regions and the neural networks that compose them. Thus, no matter how far an artificial intelligence and a brain theory worker travel together on solving a common problem, their paths eventually diverge when the artificial intelligence worker must find the most efficient data structure for currently available computers and the brain theorist must reconcile these theoretical schemes with the reality of neural experiments. Nonetheless, it is my feeling that much work in artificial intelligence and brain theory suffers from a premature casting of ideas into some programming language or neural network formalization, and that both fields could gain insight from a unified perspective.

REFERENCES

Amari, S., & Arbib, M. A. (1977). Competition and cooperation in neural nets. In J. Metzler (Ed.), *Systems neuroscience*, pp. 119–165. New York: Academic Press.
Amari, S., & Arbib, M. A. (Eds.) (1982). *Competition and cooperation in neural nets*. New York: Springer-Verlag.
Arbib, M. A. (1970). Cognition—a cybernetic approach. In P. L. Garvin (Ed.), *Cognition: A multiple view*, pp. 331–348. Washington, DC: Spartan.
Arbib, M. A. (1972). *The metaphorical brain: An introduction to cybernetics as artificial intelligence and brain theory*. New York: Wiley.
Arbib, M. A. (1975a). Artificial intelligence and brain theory: Unities and diversities. *Annals of Biomedical Engineering, 3*, 238–274.
Arbib, M. A. (1975b). Parallelism, slides, schemas and frames. In W. E. Hartnett (Ed.),

Systems: Approaches, theories, applications, pp. 27–43. Dordrecht, The Netherlands: Reidel.

Arbib, M. A. (1978). Segmentation, schemas and cooperative computation. In S. Levin (Ed.), *Studies in mathematical biology. Part I: Cellular behavior and the development of pattern,* pp. 118–155. Mathematical Association of America.

Arbib, M. A. (1979). Local organizing processes and motion schemas in visual perception. In J. E. Hayes, D. Michie, & L. I. Mikulich (Eds.), *Machine intelligence* (Vol. 9), pp. 287–298. Chichester, England: Ellis Horwood.

Arbib, M. A. (1981a). Perceptual structures and distributed motor control. In V. B. Brooks (Ed.), *Handbook of physiology—the nervous system* (Vol. II), pp. 1449–1480. Bethesda, MD: American Physiological Society.

Arbib, M. A. (1981b). Visuomotor coordination: From neural nets to schema theory. *Cognition & Brain Theory,* **4,** 23–39.

Arbib, M. A. (1982). Modelling neural mechanisms of visuomotor coordination in frog and toad. In S. Amari & M. A. Arbib (Eds.), *Competiton and cooperation in neural nets,* pp. 342–370. New York: Springer-Verlag.

Arbib, M. A., & Caplan, D. (1979). Neurolinguisitics must be computational. *Behavioral & Brain Sciences,* **2,** 449–483.

Arbib, M. A., & Hanson, A. R. (Eds.) (1986). *Vision, brain and cooperative computation.* Cambridge, MA: Bradford Books/MIT Press.

Ballard, D. H., & Brown, C. M. (1982). *Computer vision.* Englewood Cliffs, NJ: Prentice-Hall.

Barlow, H. B., Blakemore, C., & Pettigrew, J. D. (1967). The neural mechanism of binocular depth discrimination. *Journal of Physiology,* **193,** 327–342.

Bartlett, F. C. (1932). *Remembering: A study in experimental and social psychology.* Cambridge, England: Cambridge University Press.

Dev, P. (1975). Perception of depth surfaces in random-dot stereograms: A neural model. *International Journal of Man-Machine Studies,* **7,** 511–528.

Didday, R. L. (1970). *The simulation and modelling of distributed information processing in the frog visual system.* Ph.D. dissertation, Stanford University, Stanford, CA.

Didday, R. L. (1976). A model of visuomotor mechanisms in the frog optic tectum. *Mathematical Bioscience,* **30,** 169–180.

Ewert, J. P. (1976). The visual system of the toad: Behavioral and physiological studies in a pattern recognition system. In K. Fite (Ed.), *The amphibian visual system: A multidisciplinary approach,* pp. 142–202. New York: Academic Press.

Ewert, J. P., & von Seelen, W. (1974). Neurobiologie und System-Theorie eines visuellen Muster-Erkennungsmechanismus bei Kroten. *Kybernetik,* **14,** 167–183.

Furth, H. G. (1969). *Piaget and knowledge: Theoretical foundations.* Englewood Cliffs, NJ: Prentice-Hall.

Gibson, J. J. (1955). The optical expansion-pattern in aerial location. *American Journal of Psychology,* **68,** 480–484.

Gibson, J. J. (1966). *The senses considered as perceptual systems.* London: Allen & Unwin.

Gibson, J. J. (1977). The theory of affordances. In R. E. Shaw & J. Bransford (Eds.), *Perceiving, acting and knowing.* Hillsdale, NJ: Erlbaum.

Goffman, E. (1974). *Frame analysis: An essay on the organization of experience.* New York: Harper Colophon Books.

Greene, P. H. (1964). New problems in adaptive control. In J. T. Tou & R. H. Wilcox (Eds.), *Computer and information sciences* Washington, DC: Spartan.

Hanson, A. R., & Riseman, E. M. (Eds.), (1978). *Computer vision systems.* New York: Academic Press.

Hanson, A. R., Riseman, E. M., & Nagin, P. (1975). Region growing in outdoor scenes. In

Proceedings of the Third Milwaukee Symposium on Automatic Computation and Control, pp. 407–417.

Ingle, D. (1968). Visual releasers of prey catching behavior in frogs and toads. *Brain, Behavior, and Evolution,* **1,** 500–518.

Ingle, D. (1975). Focal attention in the frog: Behavioral and physiological correlates. *Science,* **188,** 1033–1035.

Jackson, J. H. (1898). Relations of different divisions of the central nervous system to one another and to parts of the body. *Lancet,* January 8.

Jeannerod, M., & Biguer, B. (1982). Visuomotor mechanisms in reaching within extra-personal space. In D. J. Ingle, M. A. Goodale, & R. J. W. Mansfield (Eds.), *Analysis of visual behavior,* pp. 387–409. Cambridge, MA: MIT Press.

Julesz, B. (1971). *Foundation of cyclopean perception.* Chicago: University of Chicago Press.

Kilmer, W. L., McCulloch, W. S., & Blum, J. (1969). A model of the vertebrate central command system. *International Journal of Man-Machine Studies,* **1,** 279–309.

Kohler, R. (1981). A segmentation system based on thresholding. *Computer Graphics and Image Processing,* **15,** 319–338.

Lara, R., & Arbib, M. A. (1982). A neural model of interaction between tectum and pretectum in prey selection. *Cognition & Brain Theory,* **5,** 149–171.

Lara, R., Arbib, M. A., & Cromarty, A. S. (1982). The role of the tectal column in facilitation of amphibian prey-catching behavior: A neural model. *Journal of Neuroscience,* **2,** 521–530.

Lara, R., Cervantes, F., & Arbib, M. A. (1982). Two-dimensional model of retinal-tectal-pretectal interactions for the control of prey-predator recognition and size preference in amphibia. In S. Amari & M. A. Arbib (Eds.), *Competition and cooperation in neural nets,* pp. 371–393. New York: Springer-Verlag.

Lee, D. N. (1974). Visual information during locomotion. In R. B. McLeod & H. L. Pick, Jr. (Eds.), *Perception: Essays in honor of J. J. Gibson,* pp. 250–267. Ithaca, NY: Cornell University Press.

Lee, D. N., & Lishman, J. R. (1977). Visual control of locomotion. *Scandinavian Journal of Psychology,* **18,** 224–230.

Lettvin, J. Y., Maturana, H., McCulloch, W. S., & Pitts, W. H. (1959). What the frog's eye tells the frog's brain. *Proceedings of the IRE,* **47,** 1940–1951.

Marr, D. (1982). *Vision: A computational investigation into the human representation and processing of visual information.* San Francisco: Freeman.

Marr, D., & Poggio, T. (1977a). From understanding computation to understanding neural circuitry. *Neurosciences Research Program Bulletin,* **15,** 470–488.

Marr, D., & Poggio, T. (1977b). Cooperative computation of stereo disparity. *Science,* **194,** 283–287.

Marr, D., & Poggio, T. (1979). A theory of human stereopsis. *Proceedings of the Royal Society,* **204,** 301–328.

McCulloch, W. S. (1949). A heterarchy of values determined by the topology of nervous nets. *Bulletin of Mathematical Biophysics,* **11,** 89–93.

McCulloch, W. S. (1965). *Embodiments of mind.* Cambridge, MA: MIT Press.

Miller, G. A., Galanter, E., & Pribram, K. H. (1960). *Plans and the structure of behavior.* New York: Henry Holt.

Minsky, M. L. (1975). A framework for representing knowledge. In P. H. Winston (Ed.), *The psychology of computer vision,* pp. 211–277. New York: McGraw-Hill.

Montalvo, F. S. (1975). Consensus vs. competition in neural networks: A cooperative analysis of three models. *International Journal of Man–Machine Studies,* **7,** 333–346.

Nagin, P. A., Hanson, A. R., & Riseman, E. M. (1982). Studies in global and local histogram-guided relaxation algorithms. *IEEE Transactions on Pattern Analysis and Machine Intelligence*, **4**, 263–277.

Nelson, J. I. (1975). Globality and stereoscopic fusion in binocular vision. *Journal of Theoretical Biology*, **49**, 1–88.

Nevatia, R. (1982). *Machine perception*. New York: Prentice-Hall.

Newell, A., & Simon, H. A. (1972). *Human problem solving*. New York: Prentice-Hall.

Newell, A., Shaw, J. C., & Simon, H. A. (1960). Report on a general problem-solving program for a computer. In *Proceedings of the International Conference on Information Processing*, pp. 256–264. New York: UNESCO.

Parma, C. C., Hanson, A. R., & Riseman, E. M. (1981). Experiments in schema-driven interpretation of a natural scene. In J. C. Simon & R. M. Haralick (Eds.), *Digital image processing*, pp. 449–509. Dordrecht, The Netherlands: Reidel.

Pettigrew, J. D., Nikara, T., & Bishop, P. O. (1968). Binocular interaction on single units in cat striate cortex. *Experimental Brain Research*, **6**, 391–410.

Prager, J. M. (1979). *Segmentation of static and dynamic scenes*. Ph.D. dissertation, University of Massachusetts at Amherst, Computer and Information Science Department.

Prager, J. M., & Arbib, M. A. (1983). Computing the optic flow: The MATCH algorithm and prediction. *Computer Vision Graphics and Image Processing*, **24**, 271–304.

Schank, R. C., & Abelson, R. P. (1975). Scripts, plans and knowledge. In *Proceedings of the 4th International Joint Conference on Artificial Intelligence*. Cambridge, MA: MIT, Artificial Intelligence Laboratory.

Schmidt, C. F. (1975). Understanding human action. In *Proceedings of the Workshop on Theoretical Issues in National Language Processing*, pp. 196–200. Washington, DC: Association for Computational Linguistics.

Searle, J. R. (1959). What is a speech act? In M. Black (Ed.), *Philosophy in America*, pp. 221–239. London: Allen & Unwin.

Selfridge, O. G. (Ed.) (1959). Pandemonium: A paradigm for learning. In *Mechanization of thought processes*, pp. 513–526. London: HMSO.

Singer, W. (1977). Control of thalamic transmission by corticofugal and ascending reticular pathways in the visual system. *Physiological Review*, **57**, 386–420.

Sperling, G. (1970). Binocular vision: A physical and neural theory. *American Journal of Psychology*, **83**, 463–534.

CHAPTER 6

Visual Routines: Where Bottom-Up and Top-Down Processing Meet

Shimon Ullman

The Artificial Intelligence Laboratory,
Massachusetts Institute of Technology,
Cambridge, Massachusetts 02139

I. THE PERCEPTION OF SPATIAL RELATIONS

I.A. Introduction

Visual perception requires the capacity to extract shape properties and spatial relations among objects and objects' parts. This capacity is fundamental to visual recognition, since objects are often defined visually by abstract shape properties and spatial relations among their components. A simple example is illustrated in Figure 6.1a, which is readily perceived as representing a face. The shapes of the individual constituents—the eyes, nose, and mouth—in this drawing are highly schematized; it is primarily the spatial arrangement of the constituents that defines the face. In Figure 6.1b, the same components have been rearranged, and the figure is no longer interpreted as a face. Clearly, the recognition of objects depends not only on the presence of certain features but also on their spatial arrangement.

The role of establishing properties and relations visually is not confined to the task of visual recognition. In the course of manipulating objects, we often rely on our visual perception to obtain answers to such questions as, "Is *A* longer than *B*?" and "Does *A* fit inside *B*?" Problems of this type can be solved without necessarily implicating object recognition. However, they do require the visual analysis of shape and spatial relations

PATTERN RECOGNITION BY HUMANS
AND MACHINES: Visual Perception
Volume 2

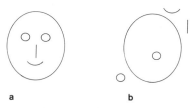

a   b

Figure 6.1 Schematic drawings of normally arranged (a) and scrambled (b) faces. (a) Readily recognizable as representing a face, although the individual features are meaningless. (b) The same constituents have been rearranged, and the figure is no longer perceived as a face.

among parts.[1] Spatial relations in three-dimensional space therefore play an important role in visual perception.

In view of the fundamental importance of the task, it is not surprising that our visual system is remarkably adept at establishing a variety of spatial relations among items in the visual input. This proficiency is evidenced by the fact that the perception of spatial properties and relations that are complex from a computational standpoint nevertheless often appears immediate and effortless. It also appears that some of the capacity to establish spatial relations is manifested by the visual system from a very early age. For example, infants of 1–15 weeks of age are reported to respond preferentially to schematic facelike figures and to prefer normally arranged face figures over "scrambled" face patterns (Fantz, 1961).

The apparent immediateness and ease of perceiving spatial relations is deceiving. As we shall see, it conceals a complex array of processes that have evolved to establish certain spatial relations with considerable efficiency. The processes underlying the perception of spatial relations are still unknown, even in the case of simple, elementary relations. Consider, for instance, the task of comparing the length of two line segments. Faced with this simple task, a drafter may measure the length of the first line, record the result, measure the second line, and compare the resulting measurements. Of course, when the two lines are present simultaneously in the field of view, it is often possible to compare their lengths by merely looking at them. This capacity raises the problem of how the drafter "in our head" operates, without the benefit of a ruler and scratchpad. More generally, a theory of the perception of spatial relations should aim at unraveling the processes that take place within our visual system when we establish shape properties of objects and their spatial relations by merely looking at them.

---

[1] Shape properties (overall orientation, area, etc.) refer to a single item, while spatial relations (above, inside, longer than, etc.) involve two or more items. For brevity, the term "spatial relations" used in this discussion refers to both shape properties and spatial relations.

The perception of abstract shape properties and spatial relations raises fundamental difficulties with major implications for the overall processing of visual information. The purpose of this chapter is to examine these problems and implications. Briefly, it is argued that the computation of spatial relations divides the analysis of visual information into two main stages. The first is the bottom-up creation of certain representations of the visible environment. Examples of such representations are the primal sketch (Marr, 1976) and the 2½-dimensional sketch (Marr & Nishihara, 1978). The second stage involves the top-down application of visual routines to the representations constructed in the first stage. These routines can establish properties and relations that cannot be represented explicitly in the initial base representations. Underlying the visual routines, there exists a fixed set of elemental operations that constitute the basic "instruction set" for more complicated processes. The perception of a large variety of properties and relations is obtained by assembling appropriate routines based on this set of elemental operations.

The chapter is divided into three parts. The first introduces the notion of visual routines. The second examines the role of visual routines within the overall scheme of processing visual information. The third (Sections III and IV) examines the elemental operations out of which visual routines are constructed. In the remainder of this section, the need for visual routines is introduced first through an example—the perception of "inside" and "outside" relationships. We then examine the general requirements that lead to the use of visual routines. Finally, we summarize the conclusions and list the main problems associated with the use of visual routines.

I.B. The Perception of Inside/Outside Relations

The perception of inside/outside relationships is performed by the human perceptual system with intriguing efficiency. To take a concrete example, suppose that the visual input consists of a single closed curve and a small X figure (see Figure 6.2), and that one is required to determine visually whether the X lies inside or outside the closed curve. The correct answers in Figure 6.2a and b appear to be immediate and effortless, and the response fast and accurate.[2]

---

[2] For simple figures such as 6.2a, viewing time of less than 50 ms with moderate intensity, followed by effective masking, is sufficient. This is well within the limit of what is considered immediate, effortless perception (e.g., Julesz, 1975). Reaction time of about 500 ms can be obtained with such figures.

Shimon Ullman

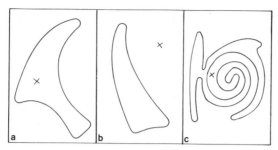

Figure 6.2 Perceiving inside and outside. In a and b, the perception is immediate and effortless; in c, it is not.

One possible reason for our proficiency in establishing inside/outside relations is their potential value in visual recognition based on their stability with respect to the viewing position. That is, inside/outside relations tend to remain invariant over considerable variations in viewing position. When viewing a face, for instance, the eyes remain within the head boundary as long as they are visible, regardless of the viewing position.

The immediate perception of the inside/outside relation is subject to some limitations (Figure 6.2c). These limitations are not very restrictive, however, and the computations performed by the visual system in distinguishing "inside" from "outside" exhibit considerable flexibility: The curve can have a variety of shapes, and the positions of the X and the curve do not have to be known in advance.

The processes underlying the perception of inside/outside relations are entirely unknown. In the following Section I examine two methods for computing "insideness" and compare them with human perception. The comparison then serves to introduce the general discussion concerning the notion of visual routines and their role in visual perception.

I.B.1. Computing Inside and Outside

I.B.1.a. The Ray-Intersection Method

Shape perception and recognition is often described in terms of a hierarchy of "feature detectors" (Barlow, 1972; Milner, 1974; Sutherland, 1968). According to these hierarchical models, simple feature-detecting units such as edge detectors are combined to produce higher-order units such as, say, triangle detectors, leading eventually to the detection and recognition of objects. It does not seem possible, however, to construct an "inside/outside detector" from a combination of elementary feature

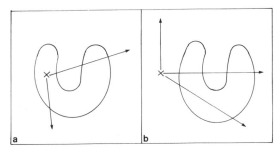

Figure 6.3   The ray-intersection method for establishing inside/outside relations. When the point lies inside the closed curve, the number of intersections is odd (a); when it lies outside, the number of intersections is even (b).

detectors. Approaches that are more procedural in nature have therefore been suggested instead. A simple procedure that can establish whether a given point lies inside or outside a closed curve is the method of ray intersections. To use this method, a ray is drawn, emanating from the point in question and extending to "infinity". For practical purposes, infinity is a region that is guaranteed somehow to lie outside the curve. The number of intersections made by the ray with the curve is recorded. (The ray may also happen to be tangent to the curve, without crossing it at one or more points. In this case, each tangent point is counted as two intersection points.) If the resulting intersection number is odd, the origin point of the ray lies inside the closed curve. If it is even (including zero), then it must be outside (see Figure 6.3).

This procedure has been implemented in computer programs (Evans, 1968; Winston, 1977, chap. 2), and it may appear rather simple and straightforward. The success of the ray-intersection method is guaranteed, however, only if rather restrictive constraints are met. First, it must be assumed that the curve is closed; otherwise, an odd number of intersections would not be indicative of an "inside" relation (see Figure 6.4a). Second, it must be assumed that the curve is isolated: In Figure 6.4b and c, point p lies within the region bounded by the closed curve c, but the number of intersections is even.[3]

These limitations on the ray-intersection method are not shared by the

---

[3] In Figure 6.4c, region p can also be interpreted as lying inside a hole cut in a planar figure. Under this interpretation, the result of the ray-intersection method can be accepted as correct. For the original task, however, which is to determine whether p lies within the region bounded by c, the answer provided by the ray-intersection method is incorrect.

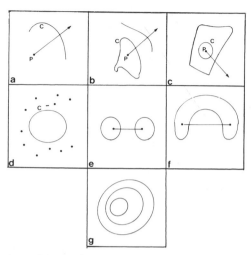

Figure 6.4   Limitations of the ray-intersection method: (a) An open curve. The number of intersections is odd, but p does not lie inside C. (b, c) Additional curves may change the number of intersections, leading to errors. (d–g) Variations of the inside/outside problem that render the ray-intersection method ineffective. In d, the task is to determine visually whether any of the dots lie inside C; in e and f, whether the two dots lie inside the same curve. In g the task is to find a point that lies inside all three curves.

human visual system. In all of the above examples, the correct relation is easily established. In addition, some variations of the inside/outside problem pose almost insurmountable difficulties to the ray-intersection procedure but not to human vision. Suppose that in Figure 6.4d, the problem is to determine whether any of the points lie inside the curve c. Using the ray-intersection procedure, rays must be constructed from all points, adding significantly to the complexity of the solution. In Figure 6.4e and 6.4f, the problem is to determine whether the two points marked by Xs lie inside the same curve. In this case, the number of intersections of the connecting line is not helpful in establishing the desired relation. In Figure 6.4g, the task is to find an innermost point—a point that lies inside all three curves. The task is again straightforward, but it poses serious difficulties for the ray-intersection method. It can be concluded from such considerations that the computations employed by our perceptual system are different from and often superior to the ray-intersection method.

I.B.1.b. The "Coloring" Method

An alternative procedure that avoids some of the limitations inherent in the ray-intersection method uses the operation of activating, or "color-

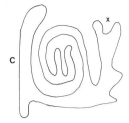

Figure 6.5   That the x does not lie inside the curve *C* can be established without a detailed analysis of the curve.

ing,'' an area. Starting from a given point, the area around it in the internal representation is somehow activated. This activation spreads outward until a boundary is reached, but it is not allowed to cross the boundary. Depending on the starting point, either the inside or the outside of the curve, but not both, will be activated. This can provide a basis for separating inside from outside. An additional stage is still required, however, to complete the procedure, and this additional stage will depend on the specific problem at hand. One can test, for example, whether the region surrounding a "point at infinity" has been activated. Since this point lies outside the curve in question, it will thereby be established whether the activated area constitutes the curve's inside or outside. In this manner, a point can sometimes be determined to lie outside the curve without requiring a detailed analysis of the curve itself. In Figure 6.5, most of the curve can be ignored, since activation that starts at the X will soon "leak out" of the enclosing corridor and spread to infinity. It will thus be determined that the X cannot lie inside the curve, but without analyzing the curve and without attempting to separate its inside from the outside.[4]

Alternatively, one may start at an infinity point, using, for instance, the

---

[4] In practical applications, "infinity points" can be located if the curve is known in advance not to extend beyond a limited region. In human vision, it is not clear what may constitute an infinity point, but it seems that we have little difficulty in finding such points. Even for a complex shape that may not have a well-defined inside and outside, it is easy to determine visually a location that clearly lies outside the region occupied by the shape. An empirical finding that bears on the perceptual ability to determine infinity points is the "distance from boundary principle" reported by Podgorny and Shepard (1978). Their task required the discrimination of whether a test point lay on or off a black figure. They found that in immediate memory and imagery tasks, response time decreased significantly when the test point was distant from the figure's boundary. An infinity point that lies far off the figure is thus easy to locate.

following procedure: (1) move toward the curve until a boundary is met; (2) mark this meeting point; (3) start to track the boundary, in a clockwise direction, activating the area on the right; (4) stop when the marked position is reached. If a termination of the curve is encountered before the marked position is reached again and the activation spread stops, the inside of the curve will be activated. Both routines are possible, but depending on the shape of the curve and the location of the X, one or the other may become more efficient.

The coloring method avoids some of the main difficulties with the ray-intersection method, but it also falls short of accounting for the performance of human perception in similar tasks. It seems, for example, that for human perception, the computation time is to a large extent scale-independent. That is, the size of the figures can be increased considerably with only a small effect on the computation time.[5] In contrast, in the activation scheme outlined here, computation time should increase with the size of the figures.

The basic coloring scheme can be modified to increase its efficiency and endow it with scale independence—for example, by performing the computation simultaneously at a number of resolution scales. Even the modified scheme will have difficulties. However, competing with the performance of the human perceptual system. Evidently, elaborate computations will be required to match the efficiency and flexibility exhibited by the human perceptual system in establishing inside/outside relationships.

The goal of the previous discussion was not to examine the perception of inside/outside relations in detail but to introduce the problems associated with the seemingly effortless and immediate perception of spatial relations. We turn now to a more general discussion of the difficulties associated with the perception of spatial relations and shape properties, and of the implications of these difficulties for the processing of visual information.

I.C. Spatial Analysis by Visual Routines

In this section we examine the general requirements imposed by the visual analysis of shape properties and spatial relations. The difficulties involved in the analysis of spatial properties and relations are summarized

---

[5] The dependency of inside/outside judgments on the size of the figure is currently under empirical investigation by P. Jolicoeur at the University of Saskatchewan. There seems to be a slight increase in reaction time as a function of figure size.

below in terms of three requirements that must be faced by the "visual processor" that performs such analysis. The three requirements are (1) the capacity to establish abstract properties and relations (abstractness), (2) the capacity to establish a variety of relations and properties, including newly defined ones (open-endedness), and (3) the capacity to cope efficiently with the complexity involved in the computation of spatial relations (complexity).

I.C.1. Abstractness

The perception of inside/outside relations provides an example of the visual system's capacity to analyze abstract spatial relations. In this section the notion of abstract properties and relations and the difficulties raised by their perception is discussed briefly.

Formally, a shape property P defines a set S of shapes that share this property. The property of closure, for example, divides the set of all curves into the set of closed curves that share this property and the complementary set of open curves. (Similarly, a relation such as "inside" defines a set of configurations that satisfy this relation.) Clearly, in many cases the set of shapes S that satisfy a property P can be large and unwieldly. It therefore becomes impossible to test a shape for property P by comparing it against all the members of S stored in memory. The problem lies not simply in the size of the set S, but in what may be called the size of the *support* of S. To illustrate this distinction, suppose that given a plane with a coordinate system drawn on it, we wish to consider all the black figures containing the origin. This set of figures is large, but it is nevertheless simple to test whether any given figure belongs to it. Only a single point (the origin) need be inspected. In this case, the relevant part of the figure, or its support, consists of a single point. In contrast, the set of supports for the property of closure, or the inside/outside relation, is unmanageably large.

When the set of supports is small, the recognition of even a large set of objects can be accomplished by simple template matching. This means that a small number of patterns is stored and later matched against the figure in question.[6] When the set of supports is prohibitively large, a

---

[6] For the present discussion, template matching between plane figures can be defined as their cross-correlation. This definition can be extended to symbolic descriptions in the plane. In this case, at each location in a plane a number of symbols can be activated, and a pattern is then a subset of activated symbols. Given a pattern P and a template T, their degree of match m is a function that is increasing in $P \cap T$ and decreasing in $P \cup T - P \cap T$ (when P is "positioned over" T so as to maximize m).

template-matching decision scheme becomes impossible. The classification task may nevertheless be feasible if the set contains certain regularities. This means roughly that the recognition of a property P can be
broken down into a set of operations in such a manner that the overall
computation required for establishing P is substantially less demanding
than the storing of all the shapes in S. The set of all closed curves, for
example, is not just a random collection of shapes, and there are obviously more efficient methods for establishing closure than simple template
matching. For a completely random set of shapes containing no regularities, simplified recognition procedures will not be possible. In this case,
the minimal program required for the recognition of the set would be
essentially as large as the set itself.

The previous discussion can now serve to define what is meant here by
"abstract" shape properties and spatial relations. This notion refers to
properties and relations with a prohibitively large set of supports that can
nevertheless be established efficiently by a computation that captures the
regularities in the set. Our visual system can clearly establish abstract
properties and relations. The implication is that it should employ sets of
processes for establishing shape properties and spatial relations. The perception of abstract properties such as insideness or closure would then be
explained in terms of the computations employed by the visual system to
capture the regularities underlying different properties and relations.
These computations would be described in terms of their constituent
operations and how they are combined to establish different properties
and relations.

Earlier we saw examples of possible computations for the analysis of
inside/outside relations. It is suggested that processes of this general type
are performed by the human visual system in perceiving inside/outside
relations. The operations employed by the visual system may prove, however, to be different from those considered previously. To explain the
perception of inside/outside relations, it would be necessary to unravel
the constituent operations employed by the visual system and to discover
how they are used in different inside/outside judgments.

I.C.2. Open-endedness

As we have seen the perception of an abstract relation is quite a remarkable feat even for a single relation, such as insideness. Additional
complications arise from the requirement to recognize not only one but
many different properties and relations. A reasonable approach to the
problem would be to assume that the computations that establish different
properties and relations share their underlying elemental operations. In

this manner, a variety of abstract shape properties and spatial relations can be established by different processes assembled from a fixed set of elemental operations. The term "visual routines" will be used to refer to the processes composed out of the set of elemental operations to establish shape properties and spatial relations.

A further implication of the open-endedness constraint is that a mechanism is required which assembles new combinations of basic operations to meet new computational goals. One can impose goals for visual analysis, such as "determine whether the green and red elements lie on the same side of the vertical line." That the visual system can cope effectively with such goals suggests that it has the capacity to create new processes out of the basic set of elemental operations.

I.C.3. Complexity

The last requirement implied that different processes should share elemental operations. The same conclusion is also suggested by complexity considerations. The complexity of basic operations such as the bounded activation (discussed in more detail in Section III,D) implies that different routines that establish different properties and relations and use the bounded activation operation would have to share the same machinery rather than have their own separate machineries.

A special case of the complexity consideration arises from the need to apply the same computation at different spatial locations. The ability to perform a given computation at different spatial positions can be obtained by having an independent processing module at each location. For example, the orientation of a line segment at a given location seems to be performed in the primary visual cortex, largely independent of other locations. In constrast, the computations of more complex relations, such as inside/outside, independent of location cannot be explained by assuming a large number of independent "inside/outside modules," one for each location. Routines that establish a given property or relation at different positions are likely to share some of their machinery, similar to the sharing of elemental operations by different routines.

Certain constraints will be imposed on the computation of spatial relations by the sharing of elemental operations. For example, the sharing of operations by different routines will restrict the simultaneous perception of different spatial relations. The application of a given routine to different spatial locations will be similarly restricted. In applying visual routines, the need will consequently arise for the sequencing of elemental operations, and for selecting the location at which a given operation is applied.

In summary, the three requirements discussed earlier suggest the following implications:

1. Spatial properties and relations are established by the application of visual routines to early visual representations.
2. Visual routines are assembled from a fixed set of elemental operations.
3. New routines can be assembled to meet newly specified processing goals.
4. Different routines share elemental operations.
5. A routine can be applied to different spatial locations; the processes that perform the same routine at different locations are not independent.
6. In applying visual routines, mechanisms are required for sequencing elemental operations and for selecting the locations at which they are applied.

I.D. Conclusions and Open Problems

The immediate perception of seeminly simple spatial relations requires complex computations that are difficult to unravel and difficult to imitate. These computations are examples of what were earlier termed "visual routines." The general proposal is that using a fixed set of basic operations, the visual system can assemble routines that are then applied to the visual representations to extract abstract shape properties and spatial relations.

The use of visual routines to establish shape properties and spatial relations raises fundamental problems at the levels of computational theory, algorithms, and the underlying mechanisms. A general problem on the computational level is which spatial properties and relations are important for object recognition and manipulation. On the algorithmic level, the problem is how these relations are computed. This is a challenging issue, since the processing of spatial relations and properties by the visual system is remarkably flexible and efficient. On the mechanism level, the problem is how visual routines are implemented in neural networks within the visual system.

In concluding this section, major problems raised by the notion of visual routines are listed under four main categories:

1. *The elemental operations.* In the examples discussed earlier, the computation of inside/outside relations employed operations such as drawing a ray, counting intersections, boundary tracking, and area activation. The same basic operations can also be used in establishing other

properties and relations. In this manner, a variety of spatial relations can be computed using a fixed and powerful set of basic operations, together with means for combining them into different routines that are then applied to the base representation. The first problem that arises is therefore the identification of the elemental operations that constitute the basic "instruction set" in the composition of visual routines.

2. *Integration.* The second problem that arises is how the elemental operations are integrated into meaningful routines. This problem has two aspects. First, the general principles of the integration process—for example, whether different elemental operations can be applied simultaneously. Second, there is the question of how specific routines are composed in terms of the elemental operations. For example, an account of our perception of inside/outside relations should include a description of the routines that are employed in this particular task and the composition of each of these routines in terms of the elemental operations.

3. *Control.* The questions in this category are how visual routines are selected and controlled—for example, what triggers the execution of different routines during visual recognition and other visual tasks, and how the order of their execution is determined.

4. *Compilation.* How new routines are generated to meet specific needs, and how they are stored and modified with practice.

The remainder of this chapter is organized as follows: In Section II I discuss the role of visual routines within the overall processing of visual information. Section III examines the first of the problems listed above— the basic operations problem. Section IV offers a few brief comments pertaining to the other problems.

II. VISUAL ROUTINES AND THEIR ROLE IN THE PROCESSING OF VISUAL INFORMATION

The purpose of this section is to examine how the application of visual routines fits within the overall processing of visual information. The main goal is to elaborate the relations between the initial creation of the early visual representations and the subsequent application of visual routines. The discussion is structured along the following lines: The first half of this section examines the relation between visual routines and the creation of visual representations. Section II,A describes the distinction between the stage of creating the earliest visual representations (called the "base representations") and the subsequent stage of applying visual routines to these representations. Section II,B discusses the so-called "incremental representations" that are produced by the visual routines. The second half of Section II examines two general problems raised by the nature of visual routines as described in the first half. Section II,C examines the problem of the initial selection of appropriate routines to be applied, while Section II,D examines the problem of visual routines and the parallel processing of visual information.

II.A. Base Representations and Visual Routines

In the scheme suggested earlier, the processing of visual information can be divided into two main stages. The first is the bottom-up creation of some base representations by the early visual processes (Marr, 1980). The second stage is the application of visual routines. At this stage, procedures are applied to the base representations to define distinct entities within these representations, establish their shape properties, and extract spatial relations among them. In this section we examine more closely the distinctions between these two stages.

II.A.1. The Base Representations

The first stage in the analysis of visual information can usefully be described as the creation of certain representations to be used by subsequent visual processes. Marr (1976) and Marr and Nishihara (1978) suggest a division of these early representations into two types: the primal sketch, which is a representation of the incoming image, and the 2½-dimensional sketch, which is a representation of the visible surfaces in three-dimensional space. The early visual representations share a number of fundamental characteristics: They are unarticulated, viewer-centered, uniform, and bottom-up driven. By unarticulated, I mean that they are essentially pointwise descriptions that represent properties such as depth, orientation, color, and direction of motion at a point. The definition of larger, more complicated units, and the extraction and description of spatial relationships among their parts, is not achieved at this level.

The base representations are spatially uniform in the sense that, with the exception of a scaling factor, the same properties are extracted and represented across the visual field (or throughout large parts of it). The descriptions of different points (e.g., the depth at a point) in the early representations are all with respect to the viewer, not with respect to one another. Finally, the construction of the base representations proceeds in a bottom-up fashion. This means that the base representations depend on the visual input alone.[7] If the same image is viewed twice, at two different times, the base representations associated with it will be identical.

II.A.2. Visual Routines

Beyond the construction of base representations, the processing of visual information requires the definition of objects and parts in the scene, and the analysis of spatial properties and relations. The discussion in Section I,C concluded that for these tasks, the uniform bottom-up computation is no longer possible, and suggested instead the application of visual routines. In contrast with the construction of base representations, the properties and relations to be extracted are not determined by the input alone. For the same visual input, different aspects will be made explicit at different times, depending on the goals of the computation. Unlike the base representations, the computations by visual routines are not applied uniformly over the visual field (e.g., not all of the possible inside/outside relations in the scene are computed) but only to selected objects.

The objects and parts to which these computations apply are also not determined uniquely by the input alone; that is, there does not seem to be a universal set of primitive elements and relations that can be used for all possible perceptual tasks. The definition of objects and distinct parts in the input, and the relations to be computed among them, may change with the situation. I may recognize a particular cat, for instance, using the shape of the white patch on its forehead. However, this does not imply that the shapes of all the white patches in every possible scene and all the spatial relations in which such patches participate are universally made explicit in some internal representation. More generally, the definition of what constitutes a distinct part (and the relations to be established) often depends on the particular object to be recognized. It is therefore unlikely that a fixed set of operations applied uniformly over the base representations would be sufficient to capture all of the properties and relations that may be relevant for subsequent visual analysis.[8] A final distinction between the two stages is that the construction of the base representations is

---

[7] Physiologically, various mechanisms that are likely to be involved in the creation of the base representation appear to be bottom-up driven; their responses can be predicted from the parameters of the stimulus alone. They also show a strong similarity in their responses in the awake, anesthetized, and naturally sleeping animal (e.g., Livingston & Hubel, 1981).

[8] This argument does not preclude the possibility that some grouping processes that help to define distinct parts, as well as some local shape descriptions, take place within the basic representations.

fixed and unchanging, while visual routines are open-ended and permit the extraction of newly defined properties and relations.

In conclusion, it is suggested that the analysis of visual information begins with the construction of base representations that are uniform, bottom-up, unchanging, and unarticulated. Their subsequent use requires the analysis of shape properties and spatial relations among objects and parts within them. Such analysis requires the application of visual routines. At this stage, the processing is no longer a function of the input alone, nor is it applied uniformly everywhere within the base representations. The overall computation therefore divides naturally into two distinct, successive stages—the creation of the base representations, followed by the application of visual routines to them. The visual routines can define objects within the base representations and establish properties and spatial relations that cannot be established within them.

Finally, it should be noted that many of the relations established at this stage are defined not in the image but in three-dimensional space. Since the base representations already contain three-dimensional information, the visual routines applied to them can also establish properties and relations in three-dimensional space.[9]

II.B. The Incremental Representations

The creation of visual representations does not stop at the base representations level. It is reasonable to expect that results established by visual routines are retained temporarily for further use. This means that in addition to the base representations to which routines are applied initially, representations are also being created and modified in the course of executing visual routines. I shall refer to these additional structures as "incremental representations," since their content is modified incrementally in the course of applying visual routines. Unlike base representations, incremental representations are not created in a uniform and unguided manner; the same input can give rise to different incremental representations, depending on the routines that have been applied.

The role of incremental representations can be illustrated using the inside/outside judgments considered in Section I. Suppose that following

---

[9] Many of the spatial judgments we make depend primarily on three-dimensional relations rather than on projected, two-dimensional ones (see, for example, Joynson & Kirk, 1960; Pinker, 1980). The suggested implication is that visual routines that can be used in comparing distances and shapes operate on a three-dimensional representation rather than one that resembles the two-dimensional image.

the response to an inside/outside display using a fairly complex figure, an additional point is lit up. The task is now to determine whether this second point lies inside or outside the closed figure. If the results of previous computations are already summarized in the incremental representation of the figure in question, it is expected that the judgment in the second task would be considerably faster than the first, and the effects of the figure's complexity may thus be reduced.[10] Such facilitation effects would provide evidence for the creation of some internal structure in the course of reaching a decision in the first task that is subsequently used to reach a faster decision in the second task. For example, if area activation or "coloring" is used to separate inside from outside, then following the first task, the inside of the figure would be already "colored." If, in addition, this coloring is preserved in the incremental representation, then subsequent inside/outside judgments with respect to the same figure would require considerably less processing and may depend less on the complexity of the figure.

This example also serves to illustrate the distinction between base representations and incremental representations. The "coloring" of the curve in question will depend on the particular routines that happens to be employed. Given the same visual input but a different visual task, or the same task but applied to a different part of the input, the same curve will not be "colored" and a similar saving in computation time will not be obtained. The general point illustrated by this example is that for a given visual stimulus (but different computational goals), the base representations would remain the same, while the incremental representations would vary.

Various other perceptual phenomena can be interpreted in a similar manner in light of the distinction between base and incremental representations. I mention here only one recent example from a study by Rock and Gutman (1981). In this study, subjects were presented with pairs of overlapping red and green figures. When they were instructed to attend selectively to the green or red member of the pair, they were later able to recognize the "attended" but not the "unattended" figure. This result can be interpreted in terms of the base and incremental representations. The creation of the base representations is assumed to be a bottom-up process, unaffected by the goal of the computation. Consequently, the two figures are not expected to be treated differently within these representations. Attempts to attend selectively to one subfigure resulted in visual routines being applied preferentially to it. A detailed description of

---

[10] This example is due to Steve Kosslyn. It is currently under empirical investigation.

this subfigure is consequently created in the incremental representations. This detailed description can then be used by subsequent routines subserving comparison and recognition tasks.

The creation and use of incremental representations imply that visual routines should not be thought of merely as predicates or decision processes that supply "yes" or "no" answers. For example, an inside/outside routine does not merely signal "yes" if an inside relation is established, and "no" otherwise. In addition to the decision process, certain structures are created during the execution of the routine. These structures are maintained in the incremental representation and can be used in subsequent visual tasks. The study of a given routine is therefore not confined to the problem of how a certain decision is reached but also includes the structures constructed in the incremental representations by the routine in question.

In summary, the use of visual routines introduces a distinction between two different types of visual representations: base representations and incremental representations. The base representations provide the initial data structures on which the routines operate, and the incremental representations maintain the results obtained by the application of visual routines.

The second half of Section II examines two general issues raised by the nature of visual routines as introduced so far. Visual routines have been described here as sequences of elementary operations that are assembled to meet specific computational goals. A major problem that arises from this view is the initial selection of routines to be applied. This problem is examined briefly in Section II,C. Finally, the sequential application of elementary operations seems to stand in contrast with the notion of parallel processing in visual perception (Biederman, Glass, & Stacy, 1973; Donneri & Zelnicker, 1969; Egeth, Jonides, & Wall, 1972; Jonides & Gleitman, 1972, Neisser, Novick, & Lazar, 1963). To analyze this problem, Section II,C examines the distinction between sequential and parallel processing, its significance to the processing of visual information, and its relation to visual routines.

II.C. Universal Routines

The act of perception requires more than the passive existence of a set of representations. Beyond the creation of base representations, the perceptual process depends on the current computational goal. At the level of applying visual routines, perceptual activity is required to provide answers to queries, generated either externally or internally, such as: "Is this my cat?" or, at a lower level, "Is A longer than B"? Such queries arise naturally in the course of using visual information in recognition, manipulation, and more abstract visual thinking. In response to these queries, routines are executed to provide the answers. The process of applying the appropriate routines is apparently efficient and smooth, thereby contributing to the impression that we perceive the entire image at a glance when in fact we process only limited aspects of it at any given time. We may not be aware of the restricted processing, since whenever we wish to establish new facts about the scene—that is, whenever an internal query is posed—an answer is made available by the execution of an appropriate routine.

Such application of visual routines raises the problem of guiding the perceptual activity and selecting the appropriate routines at any given instant. In dealing with this problem, several theories of perception have used the notion of schemata (Bartlett, 1932; Biederman et al., 1973; Neisser, 1967) or frames (Minsky, 1975) to emphasize the role of expectations in guiding perceptual activity. According to these theories, at any given instant we maintain detailed expectations regarding the objects in view. Our perceptual activity can be viewed according to such theories as hypothesizing a specific object and then using detailed prior knowledge about the object in an attempt to confirm or refute the current hypothesis.

The emphasis on detailed expectations does not seem to me to provide a satisfactory answer to the problem of guiding perceptual activity and selecting appropriate routines. Consider, for example, the "slide show" situation in which an observer is presented with a sequence of unrelated pictures flashed briefly on a screen. The sequence may contain arbitrary ordinary objects, say, a horse, a beachball, a printed letter, or the like. Although the observer can have no expectations regarding the next picture in the sequence, he or she will experience little difficulty in identifying the viewed objects. Furthermore, suppose that an observer does have some clear expectations (e.g., opening a door expecting to find a familiar office but finding an ocean beach instead). The contradiction to the expected scene will surely cause a surprise, but no major perceptual difficulties. Although expectations can under some conditions facilitate perceptual processes significantly (e.g., Potter, 1975), their role is not indispensable. Perception can usually proceed in the absence of prior specific expectations and even when expectations are contradicted.

The selection of appropriate routines therefore raises a difficult problem. On one hand, routines that establish properties and relations are situation-dependent. For example, the white patch on the cat's forehead is analyzed in the course of recognizing the cat, but white patches are not analyzed invariably in every scene. On the other hand, the recognition process should not depend entirely on prior knowledge or detailed expectations about the scene being viewed. How, then, are the appropriate routines selected?

It seems to me that this problem can best be approached by dividing the process of routine selection into two stages. The first stage is the application of what may be called "universal routines. These are routines that can be usefully applied to any scene to provide some initial analysis. For instance, they may be able to isolate some prominent parts in the scene and describe, though perhaps crudely, some general aspects of their shape, motion, color, the spatial relations among them, and so forth. These universal routines provide sufficient information to allow initial indexing to a recognition memory, which then serves to guide the application of more specialized routines.

To make the notion of universal routines even more concrete, I cite one example in which universal routines probably play a role. Studying the comparison of shapes presented sequentially, Rock, Halper, and Clayton (1972) found that some parts of the presented shapes could be compared reliably, while others could not. Suppose that a shape is composed, for example, of a combination of a bounding contour and internal lines. In the absence of any specific instructions, only the boundary contour could be used in the successive comparison task, even if the first figure presented was viewed for a long period (5 sec). This result would be surprising if only base representations were used in the comparison task, since there is no reason to assume that in these representations the bounding contours of such line drawings enjoy a special status. It seems reasonable, however, that the bounding contour is special from the point of view of the universal routines and is therefore analyzed first.

If successive comparisons used the incremental representation as suggested earlier, then performance would be superior on those parts that have been already analyzed by the visual routines. It is suggested, therefore, that in the absence of specific instructions, universal routines are applied first to the bounding contour. Furthermore, it appears that in the absence of specific goals, no detailed descriptions of the entire figure are generated, even under long viewing periods. Only those aspects analyzed by the universal routines are summarized in the incremental representation. As a result, a description of the outside boundary alone has been created in the incremental representation. This description can then be compared with the second figure presented. It is of interest to note that the description generated in this task appears to be more than just a coarse structural description of the figure. Rather, it has a templatelike quality that enables fine judgments of shape similarity.

These results can be contrasted with the study mentioned earlier by Rock and Gutman (1981) using pairs of overlapping red and green figures.

When subjects were instructed to attend selectively to one of the sub-figures, they were subsequently able to make reliable shape comparisons to this, but not the other, subfigure. Specific requirements can therefore bias the selection and application of visual routines. Universal routines are meant to fill the void when no specific requirements are set. They are intended to acquire sufficient information to then determine the application of more specific routines.

For such a scheme to be of value in visual recognition, two interrelated requirements must be met. The first is that with universal routines alone, it should be possible to gather sufficiently useful information to allow initial classification. The second requirement has to do with the organization of the memory used in visual recognition. It should contain categories that are accessible using the information gathered by the universal routines, and accessing one of these categories should provide the means for selecting specialized routines for refining the recognition process. The first requirement raises the question of whether universal routines, un-aided by specific knowledge regarding the viewed objects, can reasonably be expected to supply sufficiently useful information about any viewed scene. The question is difficult to address in detail, since it is intimately related to problems regarding the structure of the memory used in visual recognition. It nonetheless seems plausible that universal routines may be sufficient to analyze a scene in enough detail to allow the application of specialized routines.

The usefulness of universal routines can be motivated in part by what Richards (1982) has called ''the perceptual 20 questions game.'' In this game, as in the ordinary version, one player chooses an object, and a second player attempts to discover the selected object by a series of questions. The only difference is that all the questions must be ''perceptual''—that is, questions that can be answered easily and immediately based on the visual perception of the object in question. Examples of such perceptual questions are if the object moves and in which direction, what color it is, whether it is supported from below, and so forth. The game can serve to illustrate the fact that a small fixed set of questions is usually sufficient to form a good idea of what the object is (e.g., a walking person), although the guessing of a specific object (e.g., who the person is) may be considerably more difficult (see Milner, 1974). Of course, this informal game does not supply direct support for the applicability of universal routines. However, it serves to illustrate the distinction in visual recognition between universal and specific stages. In the former, universal routines can supply sufficient information for accessing a useful general category. In the latter, specific routines associated with this category can be applied.

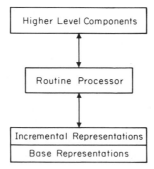

Figure 6.6   The routine processor acts as an intermediary between the visual representations and higher-level components of the system.

The relations between the different representations and routines can be summarized as follows: The first stage in the analysis of incoming visual input is the creation of base representations. Next, visual routines are applied to the base representations. In the absence of specific expectations or prior knowledge, universal routines are applied first, followed by the selective application of specific routines. Intermediate results obtained by visual routines are summarized in the incremental representation and can be used by subsequent routines.

II.C.1. Routines as Intermediaries between Base Representations and Higher-Level Components

The general role of visual routines in the overall processing of visual information as discussed so far is illustrated schematically in Figure 6.6. The processes that assemble and execute visual routines (the "routines processor" module in the figure) serve as an intermediary between the visual representations and higher-level components of the system, such as recognition memory. Communication required between the higher-level components and the visual representations for the analysis of shape and spatial relations are channeled via the routine processor.[11]

Visual routines operate in the middle ground that, unlike the bottom-up

---

[11] Responses to certain visual stimuli that do not require the extraction of abstract spatial analysis could bypass the routine processor. For example, a looming object may initiate an immediate avoidance response (Regan & Beverly, 1978). Such "visual reflexes" do not require the application of visual routines. The visual system of lower animals such as insects or the frog, although remarkably sophisticated, probably lack routine mechanisms and can be described as collections of visual reflexes.

creation of the base representations, is a part of the top-down processing and yet independent of object-specific knowledge. Their study therefore provides the advantage of going beyond the base representations while avoiding many of the additional complications associated with higher-level components of the system. The recognition of familiar objects, for example, often requires the use of knowledge specific to these objects. What we know about telephones or elephants can enter into the recognition process of these objects.

Such knowledge can determine the routine to be applied. For instance, the recognition of a particular object may require the application of inside/outside routines. When a routine is selected and applied, however, the processing is no longer dependent on object-specific knowledge. It is suggested, therefore, that in studying the processing of visual information beyond the creation of early representations, a useful distinction can be drawn between two problem areas. One can approach first the study of visual routines almost independently of the higher-level components of the system. A full understanding of problems such as visually guided manipulation and object recognition would require, in addition, the study of higher-level components, including how they determine the application of visual routines and how they are affected by the results of applying visual routines.

II.D. Routines and the Parallel Processing of Visual Information

A popular controversy in theories of visual perception is whether the processing of visual information proceeds in parallel or sequentially. Since visual routines are composed of sequences of elementary operations, they may seem to indicate sequential processing in perception. In this section I examine two related questions that bear on this issue. First, does the application of visual routines imply sequential processing? Second, what is the significance of the distinction between the parallel and sequential processing of visual information?

II.D.1. Three Types of Parallelism

The notion of processing visual information "in parallel" does not have a unique, well-defined meaning. At least three types of parallelism can be distinguished: spatial, functional, and temporal. Spatial parallelism means that the same or similar operations are applied simultaneously to different spatial locations. The operations performed by the retina and the primary visual cortex, for example, fall under this category. Functional parallelism means that different computations are applied simultaneously to the same location. Current views of the visual cortex (e.g., Zeki, 1978a,b) suggest that different visual areas in the extrastriate cortex process different aspects of the input (such as color, motion, and stereoscopic disparity) at the same location simultaneously, thereby achieving functional parallelism.[12] Temporal parallelism is the simultaneous application of different processing stages to different inputs (McClelland, 1979). This type of parallelism is also called "pipelining."[13]

In principle, visual routines can employ all three types of parallelism. Suppose that a given routine is composed of a sequence of operations O_1, O_2, . . . O_n. Spatial parallelism can be obtained if a given operation O_i is applied simultaneously to various locations. Temporal parallelism can be obtained by applying different operations O_i simultaneously to successive inputs. Finally, functional parallelism can be obtained by the concurrent application of different routines. The application of visual routines is thus compatible in principle with all three notions of parallelism. It seems, however, that in visual routines the use of spatial parallelism is more restricted than in the construction of base representations.[14] At least some of the basic operations do not employ extensive spatial parallelism. For instance, the internal tracking of a discontinuity boundary in the base representation is sequential in nature and does not apply to all locations simultaneously. Possible reasons for the limited spatial parallelism in visual routines are discussed in the next section.

II.D.2. Essential and Nonessential Sequential Processing

When considering sequential versus spatially parallel processing, it is useful to distinguish between essential and nonessential sequentiality. Suppose, for example, that O_1 and O_2 are two independent operations that can, in principle, be applied simultaneously. It is possible to apply them in sequence, but such sequentiality would be nonessential. The total compu-

---

[12] Disagreements exist regarding this view, particularly the role of area V4 in the rhesus monkey in processing color (Schein, Marrocco, & De Monasterio, 1982). Although the notion of one cortical area for each function is probably too simplistic, in general the physiological data support the notion of functional parallelism.

[13] Suppose that a sequence of operations O_1, O_2 . . . O_k is applied to each input in a temporal sequence I_1, I_2, I_3 . . . . . First, O_1 is applied to I_1. Next, as O_2 is applied to I_1, O_1 can be applied to I_2. In general, O_i, $1 \le i \le k$ can be applied simultaneously to I_{n-i}. Such a simultaneous application constitutes temporal parallelism.

[14] The general notion of an extensively parallel stage followed by a more sequential one is in agreement with various findings and theories of visual perception (e.g., Estes, 1972; Neisser, 1967; Shiffrin, McKay, & Shaffer, 1976).

tation required in this case will be the same regardless of whether the operations are performed in parallel or sequentially. Essential sequentiality, on the other hand, arises when the nature of the task makes parallel processing impossible or highly wasteful in terms of the overall computation required.

Problems pertaining to the use of spatial parallelism in the computation of spatial properties and relations have been studied extensively by Minsky and Papert (1969) within the perceptrons model.[15] These authors have established that certain relations, including the inside/outside relation, cannot be computed at all in parallel by any diameter-limited or order-limited perceptrons. This limitation does not seem to depend critically on the perceptronlike decision scheme. It may be conjectured, therefore, that certain relations (of which inside/outside is an example) are inherently sequential in the sense that it is impossible or highly wasteful to employ extensive spatial parallelism in their computation. In this case, sequentiality is essential, as it is imposed by the nature of the task, not by particular properties of the underlying mechanisms. Essential sequentiality is theoretically more interesting and has more significant ramifications than nonessential sequential ordering. In nonessential processing, the ordering has no particular importance, and no fundamentally new problems are introduced. Essential sequentiality, on the other hand, requires mechanisms for controlling the appropriate sequencing of the computation.

It has been suggested by various theories of visual attention that sequential ordering in perception is nonessential, arising primarily from a capacity limitation of the system (see, e.g., Holtzman & Gazzaniga, 1982; Kahneman, 1973; Rumelhart, 1970). In this view (see, e.g., Eriksen & Hoffman, 1972; see also Humphreys, 1981; Mackworth, 1965) only a limited region of the visual scene is processed at any given time because the system is capacity-limited and would be overloaded by excessive information unless a spatial restriction were employed. The discussion above suggests, in contrast, that sequential ordering may in fact be essen-

---

[15] In the perceptron scheme, the computation is performed in parallel by a large number of units ϕ_i. Each unit examines a restricted part of the "retina" R. In a diameter-limited perceptron, for instance, the region examined by each unit is restricted to lie within a circle whose diameter is small compared to the size of R. The computation performed by each unit is a predicate of its inputs (i.e., $\phi_i = 0$ or $\phi_i - 1$). For example, a unit may be a "corner detector" at a particular location, signaling 1 in the presence of a corner and 0 otherwise. All the local units then feed a final decision stage, assumed to be a linear threshold device. That is, it tests whether the weighted sum of the inputs $\Sigma_i w_i \phi_i$ exceeds a predetermined threshold θ.

tial, imposed by the inherently sequential nature of various visual tasks. This sequential ordering has substantial implications since it requires perceptual mechanisms for directing the processing and for concatenating and controlling the sequences of basic operations.

Although the elemental operations are sequences, some of them, such as bounded activation, employ spatial parallelism and are not confined to a limited region. This spatial parallelism plays an important role in the inside/outside routines. To appreciate the difficulties in computing inside/outside relations without the benefit of spatial parallelism, consider solving a tactile version of the same problem by moving a cane or a fingertip over a relief surface. Clearly, when the processing is always limited to a small region of space, the task becomes considerably more difficult. Spatial parallelism must therefore play an important role in visual routines.

In summary, visual routines are compatible in principle with spatial, temporal, and functional parallelism. Nevertheless, the degree of spatial parallelism employed by the basic operations seems limited. It is conjectured that this limitation reflects primarily essential sequentiality, imposed by the nature of the computations.

III. THE ELEMENTAL OPERATIONS

III.A. Methodological Considerations

In this section, we examine the set of basic operations that may be used in the construction of visual routines. In trying to explore this set of internal operations, at least two types of approaches can be followed. The first is the use of empirical psychological and physiological evidence. The second is computational. One can examine, for instance, the types of basic operations that would be useful in principle for establishing a large variety of relevant properties and relations. In particular, it would be useful to examine complex tasks in which we exhibit a high degree of proficiency. For such tasks, processes that match the human system in performance are difficult to devise. Consequently, their examination is likely to provide useful constraints on the nature of the underlying computations.

In exploring such tasks, the examples I use employ schematic drawings rather than natural scenes. The reason is that simplified artificial stimuli allow more flexibility in adapting the stimulus to the operation under investigation. It seems to me that insofar as we examine visual tasks for which our proficiency is difficult to explain, we are likely to be exploring useful basic operations even if the stimuli employed are artificially constructed. In fact, this ability to cope efficiently with artificially imposed visual tasks underscores two essential capacities in the computation of spatial relations. First, the computation of spatial relations is flexible and open-ended; new relations can be defined and computed efficiently. Second, such computation demonstrates our capacity to accept the nonvisual specification of a task and immediately produce a visual routine to meet that specification.

Empirical and computational studies can then be combined. For example, the complexity of various visual tasks can be compared. That is, theoretical studies can be used to predict how different tasks should vary in complexity, and the predicted complexity measure can be gauged against human performance. We have seen in Section I,B an example along this line in the discussion of the inside/outside computation. Predictions regarding relative complexity, success, and failure based on the ray-intersection method have proven largely incompatible with human performance. Consequently the employment of this method by the human perceptual system can be ruled out. In this case, the refutation is also supported by theoretical considerations exposing the inherent limitations of the ray-intersection method.

In this section, only initial steps toward examining the basic operations problem will be taken. I examine a number of plausible candidates for basic operations, discuss the available evidence, and raise problems for further study. Only a few operations will be examined; they are not intended to form a comprehensive list. Since the available empirical evidence is scant, the emphasis will be on computational considerations of usefulness. Finally, some of the problems associated with the assembly of basic operations into visual routines are discussed briefly.

III.B. Shifting the Processing Focus

A fundamental requirement for the execution of visual routines is the capacity to control the locations at which certain operations take place. For example, the operation of area activation suggested in Section I,B will be of little use if the activation starts simultaneously everywhere. Rather, it must start at a selected location or along a selected contour. More generally, in applying visual routines it would be useful to have a directing mechanism that would allow the application of the same operation at different spatial locations. It is natural, therefore, to start the discussion of elemental operations by examining the processes that control the locations at which these operations are applied.

Directing the processing focus (i.e., the location to which an operation is applied) may be achieved in part by moving the eyes (Norton & Stark, 1971). However, this approach is clearly insufficient: Many relations, including the inside/outside relation examined in Section I,B, can be established without eye movements. A capacity to shift the processing focus internally is therefore required.

Problems related to a possible shift of internal operations have been studied empirically, both psychophysically and physiologically. Unfortunately, these diverse studies do not provide a complete picture of the shift operations and their use in the analysis of visual information. However, they do provide, strong support for the notion that shifts of the processing focus play an important role in visual information processing, starting from the early processing stages. The main directions of psychological studies that bear on the shift operation are reviewed briefly in the next section. The physiological evidence will not be reviewed in this chapter.[16]

III.B.1. Psychological Evidence

A number of psychological studies have suggested that the focus of visual processing can be directed either voluntarily or by manipulating the visual stimulus to different spatial locations in the visual input. They are listed here under three main categories.

The first line of evidence comes from reaction time studies suggesting that it takes some measurable time to shift the processing focus from one location to another. In a study by Eriksen and Schultz (1977), for instance, it was found that the time required to identify a letter increased linearly with the eccentricity of the target letter, with the difference being on the order of 100 msec at 3° from the fovea center. Such a result may reflect the effect of shift time, but as pointed out by Eriksen and Schultz, alternative explanations are possible.

More direct evidence comes from a study by Posner, Nissen, & Ogden (1978). In this study, a target was presented 7° to the left or right of fixation. It was shown that if the subjects correctly anticipated the location at which the target would appear, using prior cuing (an arrow at

---

[16] Shift-related mechanisms have been explored physiologically in the monkey in a number of different visual areas: the superior colliculus, the posterior parietal lobe (area 7), the frontal eye fields (areas V1, V2, V4, MT, and MST), and the inferior temporal lobe. For relevant studies in the superior colliculus, see Goldberg and Wurtz (1972), Wurtz and Mohler (1976a), Wurtz, Goldberg, and Robinson (1982); in area 7 see Mountcastle, Lynch, Georgopoulos, Sakata, and Acuna (1975), Mountcastle (1976), Robinson, Goldberg, and Stanton (1978); in area TE, see Fuster and Jervey (1981), Richmond and Sato (1982); in areas 8, V1, V2, V4, MT, and MST, see Wurtz and Mohler (1976b), Fischer and Boch (1981), Wurtz et al., 1982, Newsome and Wurtz (1982). Related work has also been performed in the pulvinar (e.g., Gattas, Oswaldo-Cruz, & Sousa, 1979). The physiological evidence and their implications will be discussed elsewhere.

fixation), their reaction time to the target in both detection and identification tasks was consistently lower (without eye movements). For simple detection tasks, the gain in detection time for a target at 7° eccentricity was on the order of 30 msec.

A related study by Tsal (1983) employed peripheral rather than central cuing. In this study, a target letter could appear at different eccentricities, preceded by the brief presentation of a dot at the same location. The results were consistent with the assumption that the dot initiated a shift toward the cued location. If a shift to the location of the letter is required for its identification, it is expected that the cue will reduce the time between the letter presentation and its identification. If the cue precedes the target letter by k msec, then by the time the letter appears, the shift operation is already k msec under way, and the response time should decrease by this amount. The facilitation should therefore increase linearly with the temporal delay between the cue and target until the delay equals the total shift time. Further increase of the delay should have no additional effect. This is exactly what the experimental results indicated. It was further found that the delay at which facilitation saturates (presumably the total shift time) increases with eccentricity by about 8 msec on the average per one degree of visual angle.

A second line of evidence comes from experiments suggesting that visual sensitivity at different locations can be somewhat modified with a fixed eye position. Experiments by Shulman, Remington, and Mclean (1979) can be interpreted as indicating that a region of somewhat increased sensitivity can be shifted across the visual field. A related experiment by Remington (described in Posner, 1980) showed an increase in sensitivity at a distance of 8° from the fixation point 50–100 msec after the location has been cued.

A third line of evidence that may bear on the internal shift operations comes from experiments exploring the selective readout from some form of short-term visual memory (e.g., Shiffrin et al., 1976; Sperling, 1960). These experiments suggest that some internal scanning can be directed to different locations a short time after the presentation of a visual stimulus.

III.B.2. The Shift Operation and Selective Visual Attention

Many of the experiments mentioned previously were aimed at exploring the concept of "selective attention." This concept has a variety of meanings and connotations (see Estes 1972), many of which are not directly related to the proposed shift of processing focus in visual routines. The notion of selective visual attention often implies that the processing of visual information is restricted to a small region of space, in order to avoid overloading the system with excessive information. According to this description, certain processing stages have a limited total capacity to invest in the processing, and this capacity can be concentrated in a spatially restricted region. Attempts to process additional information would detract from this capacity, causing interference effects and the deterioration of performance. Processes that do not draw on this general capacity are, by definition, preattentive. In contrast, the notion of processing shift discussed earlier stems from the need for spatially structured processes; it does not necessarily imply such notions as general capacity or protection from overload. For example, the coloring operation used in Section I,B for separating inside from outside started from a selected point or contour. Even with no capacity limitations, such coloring would not start simultaneously everywhere, since a simultaneous activation would defy the purpose of the coloring operation. The main problem in this case is in coordinating the process, rather than excessive capacity demands. As a result, the process is spatially structured, though not necessarily in a simple manner, as it is in the "spotlight model" of selective attention.

Many of the results mentioned previously are nevertheless in general agreement with the possible existence of a directable processing focus. They suggest that the redirection of the processing focus to a new location may be achieved in two ways. The experiments of Posner (1980) and of Shulman et al. (1979) suggest that it can be "programmed" to move along a straight path using central cuing. In other experiments, such as Remington's (Posner, 1980) and Tsal's (1983), the processing focus is shifted by being attracted to a peripheral cue.

III.B.3. Indexing

Computational considerations strongly suggest the use of internal shifts of the processing focus. This notion is supported by psychological evidence, and to some degree by physiological data. The next issue to be considered is the selection problem—how specific locations are selected for further processing. There are various manners in which such a selection process can be realized. On a digital computer, for instance, the selection can take place by providing the coordinates of the next location to be processed. The content of the specified address can then be inspected and processed. Of course, this is probably not how locations are selected for processing in the human visual system. What determines, then, the next location to be processed, and how is the processing focus moved from one location to the next?

In this section, we consider one operation that seems to be used by the visual system in shifting the processing focus. This operation is called "indexing." It can be described as a shift of the processing focus to special "odd-man-out" locations. These locations are detected in parallel across the base representations and can serve as "anchor points" for the application of visual routines.

As an example of indexing, suppose that a page of printed text is to be inspected for the occurrence of the letter A. In a background of similar letters, the A will not stand out, and considerable scanning will be required for its detection (Nickerson, 1966). If, however, all the letters remain stationary with the exception of one that is jiggled, or if all the letters are red with the exception of one green letter, the odd-man-out will be identified immediately. The identification of the odd-man-out item proceeds in several stages.[17] First, the odd-man-out location is detected on the basis of its unique motion or color properties. Next, the processing focus is shifted to this odd-man-out location. This is the indexing stage. As a result of this stage, visual routines can be applied to the figure. By applying the appropriate routines, the figure is identified.

Indexing also played a role in the inside/outside example examined in Section I,B. It was noted that one plausible strategy is to start the processing at the location marked by the X figure. This approach raises a problem, since the location of the X and of the closed curve were not known in advance. If the X can define an indexable location (i.e., if it can serve to attract the processing focus), then the execution of the routine can start at that location. More generally, indexable locations can serve as starting points, or "anchors," for visual routines. In a novel scene, it would be possible to direct the processing focus immediately to a salient, indexable item and start the processing at that location. This technique will be particularly valuable in the execution of universal routines that are to be applied prior to any analysis of the viewed objects.

In conclusion, certain special locations that are sufficiently different from their surroundings can attract the processing focus directly and eliminate the need for lengthy scanning. These indexable locations can thereby serve as starting points for the application of visual routines.

The indexing operation can be further subdivided into three successive stages. First, properties used for indexing, such as motion, orientation, and color, must be computed across the base representations. Second, an odd-man-out operation is required to define locations that are sufficiently different from their surroundings. The third and final stage is the shift of

---

[17] The reasons for assuming several stages are both theoretical and empirical. On the empirical side, the experiments by Posner (1980), Treisman (1977), and Tsal (1983) provide support for this view.

the processing focus to the indexed location. These three stages are examined in the next three subsections.

III.B.3.a. Indexable Properties

Certain odd-man-out items can serve for immediate indexing, while others cannot. For example, the orientation and direction of motion are indexable, while a single occurrence of the letter A among similar letters does not define an indexable location. This situation is to be expected, since the recognition of letters requires the application of visual routines, while indexing must precede their application. The first question that arises, therefore, concerns the set of elemental properties that can be computed everywhere across the base representations prior to the application of visual routines.

One method of exploring indexable properties empirically is by employing an odd-man-out test. If an item is singled out in the visual field by an indexable property, then its detection is expected to be immediate. For instance, the ability to index an item by its color implies that a red item in a field of green items should be detected in roughly constant time, independent of the number of green distractors. Using this and other techniques, Treisman and her collaborators (Treisman, 1977; Treisman & Gelade, 1980; see also Beck & Ambler, 1972, 1973; Pomerantz, Sager, & Stoever, 1977) have shown that color and simple shape parameters can serve for immediate indexing. For example, the time to detect a target blue X in a field of brown T's and green X's does not change significantly as the number of distractors is increased (up to 30 in these experiments). The target is immediately indexable by its unique color. Similarly, a target green S letter is detectable in a field of brown T's and green X's in constant time. In this case, it is probably indexable by certain shape parameters, although it cannot be determined from the experiments what the relevant parameters are. Possible candidates include curvature, orientation (since the S contains some orientations that are missing in the X and T), and the number of terminators, which is two for the S but higher for the X and T. It would be of interest to explore the indexability of these and other properties in an attempt to discover the complete set of indexable properties.

The notion of a severely limited set of properties that can be processed preattentively agrees with Julesz's studies of texture perception (see Julesz, 1981, for a review). In detailed studies, Julesz and his collaborators have found that only a limited set of features, which he terms "textons," can mediate immediate texture discrimination. Textons include color, elongated blobs of specific sizes, orientations, and aspect ratios, as well as the terminations of the elongated blobs. These psychological studies are also in general agreement with physiological evidence. Properties such as motion, orientation, and color were found to be extracted in parallel by units that cover the visual field. On physiological grounds, these properties are suitable, therefore, for immediate indexing.

In conclusion, the emerging picture is that a small number of properties are computed in parallel over the base representations prior to the application of visual routines, and that they are represented in ordered retinotopic maps. Several of these properties are known, but a complete list has yet to be established. The results are then used in a number of visual tasks, including texture discrimination, motion correspondence, stereo, and indexing.

III.B.3.b. Defining an Indexable Location

Following the initial computation of elementary properties, the next stage in the indexing operation requires comparisons among properties computed at different locations to define the odd-man-out indexable locations. Psychological evidence suggests that only simple comparisons are used at this stage. Several studies by Treisman and her collaborators have examined the problem of whether different properties measured at a given location can be combined prior to the indexing operation.[18] They have tested, for instance, whether a green T could be detected in a field of brown T's and green X's. The target in this case matches half the distractors in color, and the other half in shape. It is the combination of shape and color that makes it distinct. Earlier experiments have established that such a target is indexable if it has a unique color or shape. The question now was whether the conjunction of two indexable properties was also immediately indexable. The empirical evidence indicates that items cannot be indexed by a conjunction of properties: The time to detect the target increases linearly in the conjunction task with the number of distractors. The results obtained by Treisman were consistent with a serial self-terminating search in which the items were examined sequentially until the target was reached.

The difference between single and double indexing supports the view that computations performed in parallel by the distributed local units are severely limited. In particular, these units cannot combine two indexable properties to define a new indexable property. In a scheme where most of the computation is performed by a directable central processor, these

---

[18] Treisman and her colleagues' (1977; Treisman & Gelade, 1980) approach to the problem was somewhat different from the one discussed here.

results also place constraints on communication between the local units and the central processor. The central unit is assumed to be computationally powerful; consequently, it can also be assumed that if the signals relayed to it from the local units contained sufficient information for double indexing, this information could be put to use by the central processor. Since it is not, the information relayed to the central processor must be limited.

The results regarding single and double indexing can be explained by assuming that the local computation that precedes indexing is limited to simple local comparisons. For example, the color in a small neighborhood may be compared with the color in a surrounding area, perhaps employing lateral inhibition between similar detectors (Estes, 1972; Pomerantz et al., 1977). If the item differs significantly from its surround, the difference signal can be used in shifting the processing focus to that location. If an item is distinguishable from its surround by the conjunction of two properties such as color and orientation, then no difference signal will be generated by either the color or the orientation comparisons, and direct indexing will not be possible. Such a local comparison will also allow the indexing of a local, rather than a global, odd man out. Suppose, for example, that the visual field contains green and red elements in equal numbers, but one and only one of the green elements is completely surrounded by a large region of red elements. If the local elements signaled not their colors but the results of local color comparisons, the odd man out alone would produce a difference signal and would therefore be indexable. To explore the computations performed at the distributed stage, it would therefore be of interest to examine the indexability of local odd men out. Various properties can be tested while manipulating the size and shape of the surrounding region.

III.B.3.c. Shifting the Processing Focus to an Indexable Location

The discussion so far suggests the following indexing scheme: A number of elementary properties are computed in parallel across the visual field. For each property, local comparisons are performed everywhere. The resulting difference signals are somehow combined to produce a final odd-man-out signal at each location. The processing focus then shifts to the location of the strongest signal. This final shift operation is examined next.

Several studies of selective visual attention have likened the internal shift operation to the directing of a spotlight. A directable spotlight is used to "illuminate" a restricted region of the visual field, and only the infor-

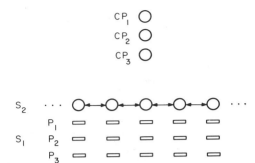

Figure 6.7   A simplified scheme that can serve as a basis for the indexing operation. In the first stage (S_1), a number of properties (P_1, P_2, P_3) are detected everywhere. In the subsequent stage (S_2), local comparisons generate difference signals. The element generating the strongest signal is mapped onto the central common representations (CP_1, CP_2, CP_3).

mation within this region can be inspected. Of course, this is a metaphor that still requires an agent to direct the spotlight and observe the illuminated region. The goal of this section is to give a more concrete notion of the shift in processing focus and, using a simple example, to show what it means and how it may be implemented.

The example we examine here is a version of the property conjunction problem mentioned in the previous section. Supposed that small colored bars are scattered over the visual field. One of them is red, all the others green. The task is to report the orientation of the red bar. We would therefore like to shift the processing focus to the red bar and "read out" its orientation. A simplified scheme for handling this task is illustrated schematically in Figure 6.7. This scheme incorporates the first two stages in the indexing operation discussed previously. In the first stage ($S1$ in the figure), a number of different properties (denoted by P_1, P_2, P_3 in the figure) are detected at each location. For example, the existence of a horizontal green bar at a given location is reflected by the activity of the color and orientation detecting units at that location. In addition to these local units, there is also a central common representation of the various properties, denoted by CP_1, CP_2, CP_3 in the figure. For simplicity, we shall assume that all of the local detectors are connected to the corresponding unit in the central representation. That is, a common central unit exists to which all of the local units that signal vertical orientation are connected.

It has been suggested that to perform the task just defined and to determine the orientation of the red bar, this orientation must be represented in the central common representation. Subsequent processing stages have access to this common representation, but not to all of the local detectors.

To answer the question, What is the orientation of the red element?, this orientation alone must therefore be mapped into the common representation.

In Section III,2 it was suggested that the initial detection of the various local properties is followed by local comparisons that generate difference signals. These comparisons take place in stage $S2$ in Figure 6.7, in which the odd-man-out item ends up with the strongest signal. Following these two initial stages, it is not difficult to conceive of mechanisms by which the most active unit in $S2$ would inhibit all of the others. As a result the properties of all but the odd-man-out location would be inhibited from reaching the central representation.[19] The central representations would then represent faithfully the properties of the odd-man-out item (the red bar in our example). At this stage, the processing is focused on the red element. Consequently, its properties are represented explicitly in the central representation, accessible to subsequent processing stages. The initial question is thereby answered, without the use of a specialized vertical red line detector.

In this scheme, only the properties of the odd-man-out item can be detected immediately. Other items must await additional processing stages. This scheme can be easily extended to generate successive shifts of the processing focus from one element to another in an order that depends on the strength of their signals in $S2$. These successive shifts mean that the properties of different elements will be mapped successively onto the common representations.

Possible mechanisms for performing indexing and processing focus shifts are not considered here beyond the simple scheme discussed so far. However, even this simplified scheme illustrates a number of points regarding shift and indexing. First, it provides an example of what it means to shift the processing focus to a given location. In this case, the shift entailed a selective readout to the central common representations. Second, it illustrates that a shift of the processing focus can be achieved in a simple manner without physical shifts or an internal spotlight. Third, it raises the point that the shift of the processing focus is not a single, elementary operation but a family of operations, only some of which were discussed. There is, for example, some evidence for the use of "similarity enhancement"—that is, when the processing focus is centered on an

---

[19] Models for this stage are being tested by C. Koch at the MIT AI Laboratory. One interesting result from this modeling is that a realization of the inhibition among units leads naturally to the processing focus being shifted continuously from item to item rather than "leaping" (disappearing at one location and reappearing at another).

item, similar items nearby become more likely to be processed next. There is also some degree of central control over the processing focus. Although the shift appears to be determined primarily by the visual input, there is also a possibility of directing the processing focus voluntarily— for example, to the right or the left of fixation (van Voorhis & Hillyard, 1977). Finally, this scheme suggests that psychophysical experiments of the type used by Julesz, Treisman, and others, combined with physiological studies of the kind described in Section III,B, can provide guidance for developing detailed testable models for the shift operations and their implementation in the visual system.

In summary, the execution of visual routines requires a capacity to control the locations at which elemental operations are applied. Psychological evidence and, to some degree, physiological evidence are in agreement with the general notion of an internal shift of the processing focus which is obtained by a family of related processes. One of these is the indexing operation, which directs the processing focus toward certain odd-man-out locations. Indexing requires three successive stages. First, a set of properties that can be used for indexing, such as orientation, motion, and color, are computed in parallel across the base represetation. Second, a location that differs significantly from its surroundings in one of these properties (but not their combinations) can be singled out as an indexed location. Finally, the processing focus is redirected toward the indexed location. This redirection can be achieved by simple schemes of interaction among the initial detecting units and by central common representations that lead to a selective mapping from the initial detectors to the common representations.

III.B.4. Bounded Activation (Coloring)

The bounded activation, or "coloring," operation was suggested in Section I,B in examining the inside/outside relation. It consisted of the spread of activation over a surface in the base representation emanating from a given location or contour and stopping at discontinuity boundaries. The results of the coloring operation may be retained in the incremental representation for further use by additional routines. In this manner, coloring provides one method for defining larger units in the unarticulated base representations: The colored region becomes a unit to which routines can be applied selectively. A simple example of this role of the coloring operation was mentioned in Section II,B, in which the initial coloring facilitated subsequent inside/outside judgments.

A more complicated example along the same line is illustrated in Figure 6.8. The visual task here is to identify the subfigure marked by the black

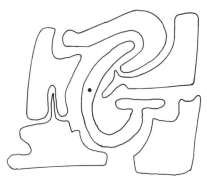

Figure 6.8   The visual task here is to identify the subfigure containing the black dot. This figure (the letter G) can be recognized despite the presence of confounding features in close proximity to its contours. The capacity to "pull out" the figure from the irrelevant background may involve the bounded activation operation.

dot. One may have the subjective feeling of being able to concentrate on this subfigure, and to pull it out from its complicated background. This capacity to "pull out" the figure of interest can also be tested objectively—for example, by testing how well the subfigure can be identified. It is easily seen in Figure 6.8 that the marked subfigure has the shape of the letter G. The area surrounding the subfigure in close proximity contains myriad irrelevant features, and therefore identification would be difficult unless processing could be directed to the subfigure.

The subfigure of interest in Figure 6.8 is the region inside which the black dot resides. This region could be defined and separated from its surroundings by using the area activation operation. Recognition routines could then concentrate on the activated region, ignoring the irrelevant contours.

III.B.4.a. Discontinuity Boundaries for the Coloring Operation

The activation operation is supposed to spread until a discontinuity boundary is reached. This condition raises the question of what constitutes a discontinuity boundary for the activation operation. In Figure 6.8, lines in the two-dimensional drawing served for this task. If activation is applied to the base representations discussed in Section II, it is expected that discontinuities in depth, surface orientation, and texture will all serve a similar role. Clearly, the use of boundaries to check the activation spread is not straightforward. It appears that in certain situations the boundaries do not have to be entirely continuous in order to block the

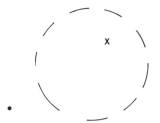

Figure 6.9   Fragmented boundaries. The curve is defined by a dashed line, but inside/ outside judgments are still immediate.

coloring spread. In Figure 6.9 a curve is defined by a fragmented line, but it is still apparent that the X lies inside and the black dot outside this curve.[20] If activation is to be used in this situation as well, then incomplete boundaries should have the capacity to block the activation spread. Finally, the activation is sometimes required to spread across certain boundaries. For example, in Figure 6.10, which is similar to Figure 6.8, the letter G is still recognizable, in spite of the internal bounding contours. To allow the coloring of the entire subfigure in this case, the activation must spread across internal boundaries.

---

[20] Empirical results (Varanese, 1983) show that inside/outside judgments using dashed boundaries require somewhat longer times compared with continuous curves, suggesting that fragmented boundaries may require additional processing. The extra cost associated with fragmented boundaries is small. In a series of experiments performed by Varanese at Harvard University, this cost averaged about 20 msec. The mean response time was about 540 msec (see also Pomerantz, Goldberg, Golder, & Tetewsky, 1981, on the use of subjective contours in inside/outside judgements).

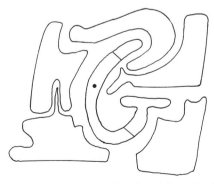

Figure 6.10   Additional internal lines are introduced into the G-shaped subfigure. If bounded activation is used to color this figure, it must spread across the internal contours.

In conclusion, the bounded activation, and particularly its interactions with different contours, is a complicated process. It is possible that as far as the activation operation is concerned, boundaries are not defined universally but may be defined somewhat differently in different routines.

III.B.4.b. A Mechanism for Bounded Activation and Its Implications

The coloring spread can be realized by using only simple, local operations. The activation can spread in a network in which each element excites all of its neighbors. (The neighbors of an element are not necessarily all adjacent to it; they may also be more remote, connected via long-range connections.) A second network containing a map of the discontinuity boundaries is used to check the activation spread. An element in the activation network will be activated if any of its neighbors is turned on, provided that the corresponding location in the second, control network does not contain a boundary. The turning on of a single element in the activation network will thus initiate an activation spread from the selected point outward, that will fill the area bounded by the surrounding contours.

In this scheme, an "activity layer" serves for the execution of the basic operation, subject to the constraints in a second "control layer." The control layer may receive its content (the discontinuity boundaries) from a variety of sources, which thereby affect the execution of the operation. An interesting question to consider is whether the visual system incorporates mechanisms of this general sort. If this were the case, the interconnected network of cells in cortical visual areas may contain distinct subnetworks for carrying out the different elementary operations. Some layers of cells within the retinotopically organized visual areas would then be best understood as serving for the execution of basic operations. Other layers receiving their inputs from different visual areas may serve in this scheme for the control of these operations.

If such networks for executing and controlling basic operations are incorporated in the visual system, they will have important implications for the interpretation of physiological data. In exploring such networks, physiological studies that attempted to characterize units in terms of their optimal stimuli would run into difficulties. The activity of units in such networks could be better understood not in terms of high-order features extracted by the units but in terms of the basic operations performed by the networks. Elucidating the basic operations would therefore provide clues for understanding the activity in such networks and their patterns of interconnection.

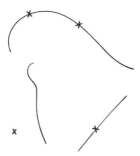

Figure 6.11   The task here is to determine visually whether there are two X's lying on a common curve. This simple task requires complex processing that will benefit from the use of a contour-tracing operation.

III.B.5. Boundary Tracing and Activation

Since contours and boundaries of different types are fundamental entities in visual perception, a basic operation that could serve a useful role in visual routines is the tracking of contours in the base representation. This section examines the tracing operation in two parts. The first shows examples of boundary tracing and activation and their use in visual routines. The second examines the requirements imposed by the goal of having a useful, flexible tracing operation.

III.B.5.a. Examples of Tracing and Activation

A simple example that will benefit from the operation of contour tracing is the problem of determining whether a contour is open or closed. If the contour is isolated in the visual field, an answer can be obtained by detecting the presence or absence of contour terminators. This strategy would not apply, however, in the presence of additional contours. This is an example of the "figure in a context" problem (Minsky & Papert, 1969): Figural properties are often substantially more difficult to establish in the presence of additional context. In the case of open and closed curves, it becomes necessary to relate the terminations to the contour in question. The problem can be solved by tracing the contour and testing for the presence of termination points on that contour.

Another simple example which illustrates the role of boundary tracing is shown in Figure 6.11. The question here is whether there are two X's lying on a common curve. The answer seems immediate and effortless, but how is it achieved? Unlike the detection of single indexable items, it cannot be mediated by a fixed array of two-X's-on-a-curve detectors. Instead, I suggest that this simple perception conceals an elaborate chain

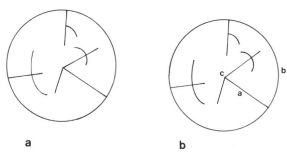

a   **b**

Figure 6.12   The task in a is to determine visually whether there is a path connecting the center of the figure to the surrounding circle. In b, the solution is labeled. The interpretation of such labels relies on a set of common, natural visual routines.

of events. In response to the question, a routine has been compiled and executed. An appropriate routine can be constructed if the repertoire of basic operations includes the indexing of the X's and the tracking of curves. The tracking provides an identity, or "sameness" operator in this task. It serves to verify that the two X figures are marked on the same curve, and not on two disconnected curves.[21]

Boundary tracking can also be used in conjunction with the area activation operation to establish inside/outside relations. As mentioned in Section I,B, it is possible to separate inside from outside by moving along a boundary, coloring only one side. If the curve is closed, its inside and outside will be separated. Otherwise, the fact that the curve is open will be established by the coloring spread, and by reaching a termination point while tracking the boundary.

These examples employed the tracking of a single contour. In other cases, it would be advantageous to activate a number of contours simultaneously. In Figure 6.12a, for instance, the task is to establish visually whether there is a path connecting the center of the figure to the surrounding contour. The solution can be obtained effortlessly by looking at the figure, but again, it must involve a complicated chain of processing. To cope with this seemingly simple problem, visual routines must (1) identify the location referred to as "the center of the figure," (2) identify the outside contour, and (3) determine whether there is a path connecting the

---

[21] Jolicoeur, Ullman, and Mackay (1986) of the University of Saskatchewan have examined this problem. The time to detect that the two Xs were lying on the same curve increased monotonically with the length of the connecting curve (the separation of the two Xs in the visual field was held constant).

two. (It is also possible to proceed from the outside inward.) In analogy with the area activation, the solution can be found by activating contours at the center point and examining the activation spread to the periphery. In Figure 6.12b, the solution is labeled; the center is marked by the letter c, the surrounding boundary by b, and the connecting path by a. Labeling of this kind is common in describing graphs and figures. A point worth noting is that to be unambiguous, such notations must rely on the use of common, natural visual routines. The label b, for example, is detached from the figure and does not explicitly identify a complete contour. Rather, the labeling notation implicitly assumes that there is a common procedure for identifying a distinct contour associated with the label.[22]

In searching for a connecting contour in Figure 6.12, the contours could be activated in parallel in a manner analogous to area coloring. It seems likely that at least in certain situations, the search for a connecting path is not just an unguided sequential tracking and exploration of all possible paths. However, a definite answer would require an empirical investigation—for example, by manipulating the number of distracting cul-de-sac paths connected to the center and the surrounding contour. In a sequential search, the detection of the connecting path should be strongly affected by the addition of distracting paths. However, if activation can spread along many paths simultaneously, detection will be little affected by the additional paths.

III.B.5.a.i. Tracking Boundaries in the Base Representations. The examples mentioned here used contours in schematic line drawings. If boundary tracking is indeed a basic operation in establishing properties and spatial relations, it is expected to be applicable not only to such lines but also to the different types of contours and discontinuity boundaries in the base representations. Experiments with textures, for instance, have demonstrated that texture boundaries can be effective for defining shapes in visual recognition. Figure 6.13a (reproduced from Riley, 1981) illustrates an easily recognizable Z shape defined by texture boundaries. However, not all types of discontinuity can be used for rapid recognition. In Figure 6.13b, for example, recognition is difficult. The boundaries defined by a transition between small k-like figures and triangles cannot be used in immediate recognition, although the textures generated by these micropatterns are early discriminable (Figure 6.13c).

What makes some discontinuities considerably more efficient than

---

[22] It is also of interest to consider how we locate the center of figures. In Norton and Stark's (1971) study of eye movements, there are indications of an ability to start the scanning of a figure approximately at its center.

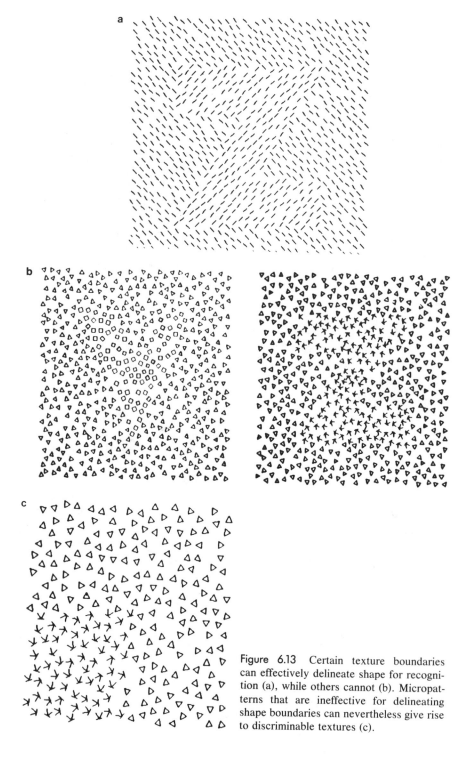

Figure 6.13 Certain texture boundaries can effectively delineate shape for recognition (a), while others cannot (b). Micropatterns that are ineffective for delineating shape boundaries can nevertheless give rise to discriminable textures (c).

others in facilitating recognition? Recognition requires the establishment of spatial properties and relations. It can therefore be expected that recognition is facilitated if the defining boundaries are already represented in the base representations, so that operations such as activation and tracking may be applied to them. Other discontinuities that are not represented in the base representations can be detected by applying appropriate visual routines, but recognition based on these contours is considerably slower.[23]

III.B.5.b. Requirements on Boundary Tracing

The tracing of a contour is a simple operation when the contour is continuous, isolated, and well defined. When these conditions are not met, however, the tracing operation must cope with a number of challenging requirements. These requirements and their implications for the tracing operation are examined in this section.

III.B.5.b.i. Tracing Incomplete Boundaries. The incompleteness of boundaries and contours is a well-known difficulty in image processing systems. Edges and contours produced by such systems often suffer from gaps due to noise, insufficient contrast, and other problems. This difficulty is probably not confined to man-made systems alone; boundaries detected by the early processes in the human visual system are also unlikely to be perfect. The boundary-tracing operation should not be limited, therefore, to continuous boundaries only. As noted earlier with respect to inside/outside routines for human perception, fragmented contours can often replace continuous ones.

III.B.5.b.ii. Tracking across Intersections and Branches. In tracing a boundary, crossings and branching points may be encountered. It then becomes necessary to decide which branch is the natural continuation of the curve. Similarity of color, contrast, motion, and so on may affect this decision. For similar contours, collinearity, or a minimal change in direction (and perhaps curvature), seems to be the main criterion for preferring one branch over another.

Tracking a contour through an intersection can often be useful in ob-

---

[23] Riley (1981) has found a close agreement between texture boundaries that can be used in immediate recognition and boundaries that can be used in long-range apparent motion (Ullman, 1979). Boundaries participating in motion correspondence must be made explicit within the base representations so that they can be matched over discrete frames. The implication is that the boundaries involved in immediate recognition also preexist in the base representations.

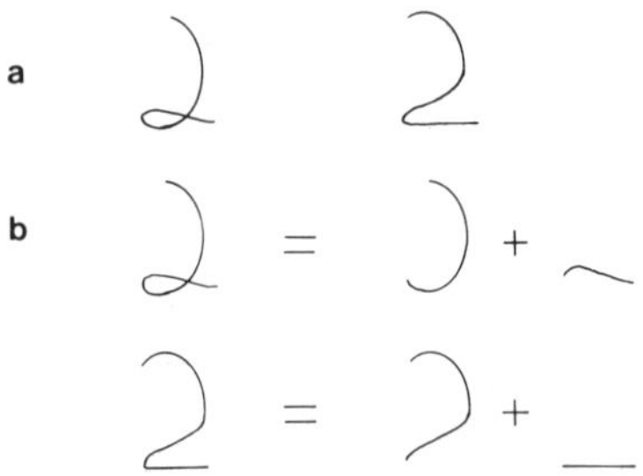

Figure 6.14   The tracking of a contour through an intersection is used here in generating a stable description of the contour. (a) Two instances of the numeral 2. (b) In spite of the marked difference in their shape, their eventual decomposition and description are very similar.

taining a stable description of the contour for recognition purposes. Consider, for example, the two different instances of the numeral 2 in Figure 6.14a. There are considerable differences between these two shapes. For example, one contains a hole, while the other does not. Suppose, however, that the contours are traced and decomposed at places of maxima in curvature. This process leads to the decomposition shown in Figure 6.14b. In the resulting descriptions, the decomposition into strokes and the shapes of the underlying strokes are very similar.

III.B.5.b.iii. Tracking at Different Resolutions.   Tracking can proceed along the main skeleton of a contour without tracing its individual components. An example is illustrated in Figure 6.15, in which a figure is constructed from a collection of individual tokens. The overall figure can be traced and recognized without tracing and identifying its components. Examples similar to Figure 6.15 have been used to argue that "global" or "wholistic" perception precedes the extraction of local features. According to the visual routines scheme, the constituent line elements are in fact extracted by the earliest visual processes and represented in the base

```
        I   S   I
      H           S
    T               T
                      H
                    E
                  N
              M   U
          B
          E   R   T   W   O
```

Figure 6.15   Tracing a skeleton. The overall figure can be traced and recognized without first recognizing all of the individual components.

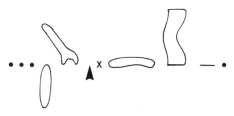

Figure 6.16   The collinearity of tokens (items and endpoints) can easily be perceived. This perception may be related to a routine that traces collinear arrangements rather than to sophisticated grouping processes within the base representations.

representations. The constituents are not recognized, since their recognition requires the application of visual routines. The "forest before the trees" phenomenon (Navon, 1977) is the result of applying appropriate routines that can trace and analyze aggregates without analyzing their individual components, thereby leading to the recognition of the overall figure prior to the recognition of its constituents.

The ability to trace collections of tokens and extract properties of their arrangement raises a question regarding the role of grouping processes in early vision. Our ability to perceive the collinear arrangement of different tokens, as illustrated in Figure 6.16, has been used to argue for the existence of sophisticated grouping processes within the early visual representations that detect such arrangements and make them explicit (Marr, 1976). In this view, these grouping processes participate in the construction of the base representations. Consequently, collinear arrangements of tokens are detected and represented throughout the base representation prior to the application of visual routines. An alternative possibility is that such arrangements are identified as a result of applying the appropriate routine. This is not to deny the existence of certain grouping processes within the base representations. There is, in fact, strong evidence in support of the existence of such processes.[24] Nevertheless, the more complicated and abstract grouping phenomena such as in Figure 6.16 may be the result of applying the appropriate routines, rather than being explicitly represented in the base representations.

Finally, from the point of view of the underlying mechanism, one obvious possibility is that the operation of tracing an overall skeleton is the

[24] For evidence supporting the existence of grouping processes within the early creation of the base representations using dot-interference patterns, see Glass (1969), Glass and Perez (1973), Marroquin (1976), and Stevens (1978). See also a discussion of grouping in early visual processing in Barlow (1981).

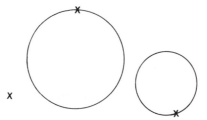

Figure 6.17   The task here is to determine visually whether there are two X's on a common curve. The task could be accomplished by employing marking and tracing operations.

result of applying tracing routines to a low-resolution copy of the image, mediated by low-frequency channels within the visual system. This is not the only possibility, however, and in attempting to investigate this operation further, alternative methods for tracing the overall skeleton of figures should also be considered.

In summary, the tracing and activation of boundaries are useful operations in the analysis of shape and the establishment of spatial relations. This is a complicated operation, since flexible, reliable tracing should be able to cope with breaks, crossings, and branching, and with different resolution requirements.

III.B.6. Marking

In the course of applying a visual routine, the processing shifts across the base representations from one location to another. To control and coordinate the routine, it would be useful to have the capability to keep at least a partial track of the locations already processed. A simple operation of this type is the marking of a single location for future reference. This operation can be used, for instance, in establishing the closure of a contour. As noted in the preceding section, closure cannot be tested in general by the presence or absence of terminators, but it can be established using a combination of tracing and marking. The starting point of the tracing operation is marked, and if the marked location is reached again, the tracing is completed and the contour is known to be closed.

Figure 6.17 shows a similar problem, which is a version of a problem examined in the previous section. The task here is to determine visually whether there are two X's on the same curve. Once again, the correct answer is perceived immediately. To establish that only a single X lies on the closed curve, one can use the previous strategy of marking the X and tracking the curve. It has been suggested that the perceptual system has marking and tracing in its repertoire of basic operations, and that the simple perception of the X on the curve involves the application of visual routines that employ such operations.

Other tasks may benefit from the marking of more than a single location. A simple example is visual counting—that is, the problem of determining as quickly as possible the number of distinct items in view (Atkinson, Campbell, & Francis, 1969; Kowler & Steinman, 1979). For a small number of items, visual counting is fast and reliable. When the number of items is four or less, the perception of their number is so immediate that it has given rise to conjectures regarding special Gestalt mechanisms that can somehow respond directly to the number of items in view, provided that this number does not exceed four (Atkinson et al., 1969). In the following section, we see that although such mechanisms are possible in principle, they are unlikely to be incorporated in the human visual system. It is suggested instead that even the perception of a small number of items involves the execution of visual routines in which marking plays an important role.

III.B.6.a. Comparing Schemes for Visual Counting

III.B.6.a.i. Perceptronlike Counting Networks. In their book, *Perceptrons,* Minsky and Papert (1969, Chap. 1) describe parallel networks that can count the number of elements in their input (see also Milner, 1974). Counting is based on computing the predicates "the input has exactly M points" and "the input has between M and N points" for different values of M and N. For any given value of M, it is thereby possible to construct a special network that will respond only when the number of items in view is exactly M. Unlike visual routines composed of elementary operations, such a network can adequately be described as an elementary mechanism responding directly to the presence of M items in view. Unlike the shifting and marking operations, the computation is performed by these networks uniformly and in parallel over the entire field.

III.B.6.a.ii. Counting by Visual Routines. Counting can also be performed by simple visual routines that employ elementary operations such as shifting and marking. For example, the indexing operation described in Section III,C can be used to perform the counting task, provided that it is extended somewhat to include marking operations. Section III,C illustrates how a simple shifting scheme can be used to move the processing focus to an indexable item. In the counting problem, there is more than a single indexable item to be considered. To use the same scheme for counting, the processing focus is required to travel among all of the indexable items, without visiting an item more than once.

A straightforward extension that will allow the shifting scheme in Section III,C to travel among different items is to allow it to mark the elements already visited. Simple marking can be obtained in this case by "switching off" the element at the current location of the processing focus. The shifting scheme described earlier is always attracted to the location producing the strongest signal. If this signal is turned off, the shift will automatically continue to the next strong signal. The processing focus can now continue its tour until all the items have been visited and their number counted.

A simple example of this counting routine is the "single point detection" task. In this problem, it is assumed that one or more points can be lit up in the visual field. The task is to say "yes" if a single point is lit up and "no" otherwise. Following the counting procedure just outlined, the first point will soon be reached and masked. If there are no remaining signals, the point is unique and the correct answer is "yes"; otherwise, it is "no."

In this scheme, counting is achieved by shifting the processing focus among the items of interest without scanning the entire image systematically. Alternatively, shifting and marking can be used for visual counting by scanning the entire scene in a predetermined pattern. As the number of items increases, programmed scanning may become the more efficient strategy. The two alternative schemes will behave differently for different numbers of items. The fixed scanning scheme is largely independent of the number of items, whereas in the traveling scheme the computation time depends on the number of items, as well as on their spatial configuration.

There are two main differences between counting by visual routines of one type or another, on one hand, and by specialized counting networks on the other. First, unlike the perceptronlike networks, the process of determining the number of items by visual routines can be decomposed into a sequence of elementary operations. This decomposition process holds true for the perception of a small number of items and even for single-item detection. Second, in contrast with a counting network, which is specially constructed for the task of detecting a prescribed number of items, the same elementary operations employed in the counting routine also participate in other visual routines.

This difference makes counting by visual routines more attractive than the counting networks. It does not seem plausible to assume that visual counting is essential enough to justify specialized networks dedicated to this task alone. In other words, visual counting is simple unlikely to be an elementary operation. In my view, it is more plausible that visual count-

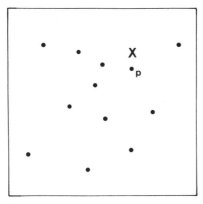

Figure 6.18   The use of an external reference. The position of point p can be defined and retained relative to the predominant X nearby.

ing can be performed efficiently as a result of our general capacity to generate and execute visual routines, and of the availability of the appropriate elementary operations that can be harnessed for the task.

III.B.6.b. Reference Frames in Marking

The marking of a location for later reference requires a coordinate system, or frame of reference, with respect to which the location is defined. Thus one general question regarding marking concerns the referencing scheme in which locations are defined and remembered for subsequent use by visual routines. One possibility is to maintain an internal, "egocentric" spatial map that can be used in directing the processing focus. The use of marking would then be analogous to reaching in the dark: The location of one or more objects can be remembered so that they can be reached (approximately) in the dark without external reference cues. It is also possible to use an internal map in combination with external referencing. For example, the position of point p in Figure 6.18 can be defined and remembered using the prominent X figure nearby. In such a scheme, it becomes possible to maintain a crude map with which prominent features can be located and a more detailed local map in which the position of the marked item is defined with respect to the prominent feature.

The referencing problem can also be approached empirically—for example, by making a point in figures such as Figure 6.18 disappear and then reappear (possibly in a slightly displaced location), and then testing the accuracy at which the two locations can be compared (care has to be taken to avoid apparent motion). One can test the effect of potential reference markers on accuracy, and marking accuracy can be tested across eye movements.

III.B.6.c. Marking and the Integration of Information in a Scene

To be useful in the natural analysis of visual scenes, the marking map should be preserved across eye motions. This means that if a certain location in space is marked prior to an eye movement, the marking should point to the same spatial location following the eye movement. Such a marking operation, combined with the incremental representation, can play a valuable role in integrating the information across eye movements and from different regions in the course of viewing a complete scene.[25] Suppose, for example, that a scene contains several objects, such as a man at one location and a dog at another, and that following the visual analysis of the man figure, we shift our gaze and processing focus to the dog. The visual analysis of the man figure has been summarized in the incremental representation, and this information is still available, at least in part, as the gaze is shifted to the dog. In addition to this information, we keep a spatial map, comprising a set of spatial pointers, which tell us that the dog is at one direction and the man at another. Although we no longer see the man clearly, we have a strong notion of what exists where. The "what" is supplied by the incremental representations, and the "where" by the marking map.

In such a scheme, we do not maintain a full panoramic representation of the scene. After looking at various parts of the scene, our representation of it will have the following structure: There will be a retinotopic representation of the scene in the current viewing direction. To this representation we can apply visual routines to analyze the properties of and relations among the items in view. In addition, we will have markers for the spatial locations of items in the scene already analyzed. These markers can point to peripheral objects, and perhaps even to locations outside the field of view (Attneave & Pierce, 1978). If we are currently looking at the dog, we will see it in fine detail and be able to apply visual routines to extract information regarding the dog's shape. At the same time, we know the locations of the other objects in the scene (from the marking map) and what they are (from the incremental representation). We know, for exam-

---

[25] The problem considered here is not limited to the integration of views across saccadic eye motions, for which an "integrative visual buffer" has been proposed by Rayner (1978) and by Jonides, Irwin, and Yantis (1982).

ple, the location of the man in the scene. We also know various aspects of his shape, although it may now appear only as a blurred blob, since these aspects are summarized in the incremental representation. To obtain new information, however, we would have to shift our gaze back to the man figure and apply additional visual routines.

III.B.6.c.i. The Hidden Complexities in Perceiving Spatial Relationships. We have examined a number of plausible elemental operations, including shift, indexing, bounded activation, boundary tracing and activation, and marking. These operations are valuable in establishing abstract shape properties and spatial relations, and some of them are partially supported by empirical data. (However, they certainly do not constitute a comprehensive set.) The examination of these basic operations and their use reveals that in perceiving spatial relations, the visual system accomplishes highly complex tasks with intriguing efficiency. There are two main sources for these complexities. First, as illustrated earlier, from a computational standpoint the efficient and reliable implementation of each of the elemental operations poses challenging problems. It is evident, for instance, that a sophisticated, specialized processer would be required for an efficient and flexible bounded activation operation, or for the tracing of contours and collinear arrangements of tokens.

In addition to the complications involved in the realization of the different elemental operations, new complications are introduced when the elemental operations are assembled into meaningful visual routines. As illustrated by the inside/outside example, in perceiving a given spatial relation, different strategies may be employed, depending on the various parameters of the stimuli (such as the complexity of the boundary, or the distance of the X from the bounding contour). Therefore, the immediate perception of seemingly simple relations often requires decision processes and selection among possible routines, followed by the coordinated application of the elemental operations that make up the visual routines. Some of the problems involved in the assembly of these operations into visual routines are discussed briefly in the next section.

IV. THE ASSEMBLY, COMPILATION, AND STORAGE OF VISUAL ROUTINES

The use of visual routines allows a variety of properties and relations to be established using a fixed set of basic operations. According to this view, the establishment of relations requires the application of a coordinated sequence of basic operations. We have discussed a number of plausible basic operations. In this section I raise some of the general problems associated with the construction of useful routines from combinations of basic operations.

The appropriate routine to be applied in a given situation depends on the goal of the computation, and on various parameters of the configuration to be analyzed. We have seen, for example, that the routine for establishing inside/ouside relations may depend on various properties of the configuration. In some cases, it would be efficient to start at the location of the X figure; in other situations, it may be more efficient to start at some distant location. Similarly, in Treisman's (1977, 1980) experiments on indexing by two properties (e.g., a vertical red item in a field of vertical green and horizontal red distracters), there are at least two alternative strategies for detecting the target. Since direct indexing by two properties is impossible, one may either scan the red items, testing for orientation, or scan the vertical items, testing for color. The distribution of distracters in the field determines the relative efficiency of these alternative strategies. In such cases it may therefore prove useful to precede the application of a particular routine with a stage in which certain relevant properties of the configuration to be analyzed are sampled and inspected. It would be of interest to examine whether, in the double indexing task, for example, the human visual system tends to employ the more efficient search strategy.

The previous discussion introduces what may be called the "assembly problem"—that is, the problem of how routines are constructed in response to specific goals, and how this generation is controlled by aspects of the configuration to be analyzed. In earlier examples, a goal for the computation is set up externally, and an appropriate routine is applied in response. In the course of recognizing and manipulating objects, routines are usually invoked in response to internally generated queries. Some of these routines may be stored in memory rather than assembled anew each time they are needed. The recognition of a specific object may then use preassembled routines for inspecting relevant features and the relations among them. Since routines can also be generated efficiently by the assembly mechanism in response to specific goals, it would probably be sufficient to store routines in memory in a skeletonized form. The assembly mechanism would then fill in details and generate intermediate routines when necessary. In such a scheme, the perceptual activity during recognition would be guided by setting prestored goals that the assembly process would then expand into detailed visual routines.

The application of prestored routines rather then assembling them again each time they are required can lead to improvements in performance and the speedup of performing familiar perceptual tasks. These improvements can come from two different sources. First, assembly time will be saved if the routine is already "compiled" in memory. The time savings can increase if stored routines for familiar tasks, which may be skeletonized at first, become more detailed, thereby requiring less assembly time. Second, stored routines may be improved with practice (e.g., as a result of either external instruction or by modifying routines when they fail to accomplish their tasks efficiently).

V. SUMMARY

1. Visual perception requires the capacity to extract abstract shape properties and spatial relations. This requirement divides the overall processing of visual information into two distinct stages. The first is the creation of base representations (such as the primal sketch and the 2½-dimensional sketch). The second is the application of visual routines to the base representations.

2. The creation of the base representations is a bottom-up and spatially uniform process. The representations it produces are unarticulated and viewer-centered.

3. The application of visual routines is no longer bottom-up, spatially uniform, and viewer-centered. It is at this stage that objects and parts are defined, and their shape properties and spatial relations are established.

4. The perception of abstract shape properties and spatial relations raises two major difficulties. First, the perception of even seemingly simple, immediate properties and relations requires complex computation. Second, visual perception requires the capacity to establish a variety of different properties and relations.

5. It has been suggested that the perception of spatial relations is achieved by application to the base representations of visual routines composed of sequences of elemental operations. Routines for different properties and relations share elemental operations. Using a fixed set of basic operations, the visual system can assemble different routines to extract an unbounded variety of shape properties and spatial relations.

6. Unlike the construction of the base representation, the application of visual routines is not determined by visual input alone. Routines are selected or created to meet specific computational goals.

7. Results obtained by the application of visual routines are retained in the incremental representation and can be used by subsequent processes.

8. Some of the elemental operations employed by visual routines are

applied to restricted locations in the visual field, rather than to the entire field in parallel. It is suggested that this apparent limitation on spatial parallelism reflects in part essential limitations, inherent in the nature of the computation, rather than nonessential capacity limitations.

9. At a more detailed level, a number of plausible basic operations have been suggested, based primarily on their potential usefulness and supported in part by empirical evidence. These operations include:

   A. *Shift of the Processing Focus.* This is a family of operations that allow the application of the same basic operation to different locations across base representations.

   B. *Indexing.* This is a shift operation toward special odd-man-out locations. A location can be indexed if it is sufficiently different from its surroundings in an indexable property. Indexable properties, which are computed in parallel by early visual processes, include contrast, orientation, color, motion, and also, size, binocular disparity, curvature, and the existence of terminators, corners, and intersections.

   C. *Bounded Activation.* This operation consists of the spread of activation over a surface in the base representation, emanating from a given location or contour and stopping at discontinuity boundaries. This is not a simple operation, since it must cope with difficult problems that arise from the existence of internal contours and fragmented boundaries. A discussion of the mechanisms that may be implicated in this operation suggests that specialized networks may exist within the visual system for executing and controlling the application of visual routines.

   D. *Boundary Tracing.* This operation consists of either the tracing of a single contour or the simultaneous activation of a number of contours. This operation must be able to cope with the difficulties raised by the tracing of incomplete boundaries, tracing across intersections and branching points, and tracing contours defined at different resolution scales.

   E. *Marking.* The operation of marking a location means that this location is remembered, and processing can return to it whenever necessary. Such an operation would be useful in the integration of information in the processing of different parts of a complete scene.

10. It has been suggested that the seemingly simple and immediate perception of spatial relations conceals a complex array of processes involved in the selection, assembly, and execution of visual routines.

REFERENCES

Atkinson, J., Campbell, F. W., & Francis, M. R. (1969). The magic number 4 ± 0: A new look at visual numerosity judgments. *Perception,* **5,** 327–334.

Attneave, F., & Pierce, C. R. (1978). The accuracy of extrapolating a pointer into perceived and imagined space. *American Journal of Psychology,* **91,(3),** 371–387.

Barlow, H. B. (1972). Single units and sensation: A neuron doctrine for perceptual psychology? *Perception,* **1,** 371–394.

Barlow, H. B. (1981). Critical limiting factors in the design of the eye and the visual cortex: The Ferrier Lecture, 1980. *Proceedings of the Royal Society (London),* **212,** 1–34.

Bartlett, F. C. (1932). *Remembering.* Cambridge: Cambridge University Press.

Beck, J., & Ambler, B. (1972). Discriminability of differences in line slope and in line arrangement as a function of mask delay. *Perception & Psychophysics,* **12(1A),** 33–38.

Beck, J., & Ambler, B. (1973). The effects of concentrated and distributed attention on peripheral acuity. *Perception & Psychophysics,* **14(2),** 225–230.

Biederman, I., Glass, A. L., & Stacy, E. W. (1973). Searching for objects in real-world scenes. *Journal of Experimental Psychology,* **97(1),** 22–27.

Donneri, D. C., & Zelnicker, D. (1969). Parallel processing in visual same-different decisions. *Perception & Psychophysics,* **5(4),** 197–200.

Egeth, H., Jonides, J., & Wall, S. (1972). Parallel processing of multielement displays. *Cognitive Psychology,* **3,** 674–698.

Eriksen, C. W., & Hoffman, J. E. (1972). Temporal and spatial characteristics of selective encoding from visual displays. *Perception & Psychophysics,* **12,** 201–204.

Eriksen, C. W., & Schultz, D. W. (1977). Retinal locus and acuity in visual information processing. *Bulletin of the Psychonomic Society,* **9(2),** 81–84.

Estes, W. K. (1972). Interactions of signal and background variables in visual processing. *Perception & Psychophysics,* **12(3),** 278–286.

Evans, T. G. (1968). A heuristic program to solve geometric analogy problems. In M. Minsky (Ed.), *Semantic information processing,* pp. 271–353. Cambridge, MA: MIT Press.

Fantz, R. L. (1961). The origin of form perception. *Scientific American,* **204(5),** 66–72.

Fischer, B., & Boch, R. (1981). Enhanced activation of neurons in prelunate cortex before visually guided saccades of trained rhesus monkey. *Experimental Brain Research,* **44,** 129–137.

Fuster, J. M., & Jervey, J. P. (1981). Inferotemporal neurons distinguish and retain behaviorally relevant features of visual stimuli. *Science,* **212,** 952–955.

Gattas, R., Oswaldo-Cruz, E., & Sousa, A. P. B. (1979). Visual receptive fields of units in the pulvinar of cebus monkey. *Brain Research,* **160,** 413–430.

Glass, L. (1969). Moire effect from random dots. *Nature,* **243,** 578–580.

Glass, L., & Perez, R. (1973). Perception of random dot interference patterns. *Nature,* **246,** 360–362.

Goldberg, M. E., & Wurtz, R. H. (1972). Activity of superior colliculus in behaving monkey, II: Effect of attention of neural responses. *Journal of Neurophysiology,* **35,** 560–574.

Holtzman, J. D., & Gazzaniga, M. S. (1982). Dual task interactions due exclusively to limits in processing resources. *Science,* **218,** 1325–1327.

Humphreys, G. W. (1981). On varying the span of visual attention: Evidence for two modes of spatial attention. *Quarterly Journal of Experimental Psychology,* **33A,** 17–31.

Jolicoeur, P., Ullman, S., and Mackay, M. E. (1986). Curve tracing: A possible basic operation in the perception of spatial relation. *Memory and Cognition,* in press.

Jonides, J., & Gleitman, H. (1972). A conceptual category effect in visual search: O as a letter or as digit. *Perception & Psychophysics,* **12(6),** 457–460.

Jonides, J., Irwin, D. E., & Yantis, S. (1982). Integrating visual information from successive fixations. *Science*, **215**, 192–194.

Joynson, R. B., & Kirk, N. S. (1960). The perception of size: An experimental synthesis of the associationist and Gestalt accounts of the perception of size. *Quarterly Journal of Experimental Psychology*, **12**, 221–230.

Julesz, B. (1975). Experiments in the visual perception of texture. *Scientific American*, **232(4)**, 34–43.

Julesz, B. (1981). Textons, the elements of texture perception, and their interactions. *Nature*, **290**, 91–97.

Kahneman, D. (1973). *Attention and effort*. Englewood Cliffs, NJ: Prentice-Hall.

Kowler, E., & Steinman, R. M. (1979). Miniature saccades: Eye movements that do not count. *Vision Research*, **19**, 105–108.

Livingston, M. L., & Hubel, D. H. (1981). Effects of sleep and arousal on the processing of visual information in the cat. *Nature*, **291**, 554–561.

Mackworth, N. H. (1965). Visual noise causes tunnel vision. *Psychonomic Science* **3**, 67–68.

Marr, D. (1976). Early processing of visual information. *Philosophical Transactions of the Royal Society (London)*, **275**, 483–524.

Marr, D. (1980). Visual information processing: The structure and creation of visual representations. *Philosophical Transactions of the Royal Society (London)*, **290**, 199–218.

Marr, D., & Nishihara, H. K. (1978). Representation and recognition of the spatial organization of three-dimensional shapes. *Proceedings of the Royal Society (London)*, **200**, 269–294.

Marroquin, J. L. (1976). *Human visual perception of structure*. Unpublished M. Sc. thesis, MIT. Department of Electrical Engineering and Computer Science, Cambridge, MA.

McClelland, J. L. (1979). On the time relations of mental processes: An examination of systems of processes in cascade. *Psychological Review*, **86(4)**, 287–330.

Milner, P. M. (1974). A model for visual shape recognition. *Psychological Review* **81(6)**, 521–535.

Minsky, M. (1975). A framework for representing knowledge. In P. H. Winston (Ed.), *The psychology of computer vision*, pp. 211–277. New York: Prentice-Hall.

Minsky, M., & Papert, S. (1969). *Perceptrons*. Cambridge, MA: MIT Press.

Mountcastle, V. B. (1976). The world around us: Neural command functions for selective attention: The F. O. Schmitt Lecture in Neuroscience. *Neuroscience Research Program Bulletin*, **14**, Suppl. 1–47.

Mountcastle, V. B., Lynch, J. C., Georgopoulos, A., Sakata, H., & Acuna, A. (1975). Posterior parietal association cortex of the monkey: Command functions for operations within extrapersonal space. *Journal of Neurophysiology*, **38**, 871–908.

Navon, D. (1977). Forest before trees: The precedence of global features in visual perception. *Cognitive Psychology* **9**, 353–383.

Neisser, U. (1967). *Cognitive psychology*. New York: Prentice-Hall.

Neisser, U., Novick, R., & Lazar, R. (1963). Searching for ten targets simultaneously. *Perception & Motor Skills*, **17**, 955–961.

Newsome, W. T., & Wurtz, R. H. (1982). Identification of architectonic zones containing visual tracking cells in the superior temporal sulcus of macaque monkeys. *Investigative Ophthalmology & Visual Science*, **22**, 238.

Nickerson, R. S. (1966). Response times with memory-dependent decision task. *Journal of Experimental Psychology*, **72(5)**, 761–769.

Norton, D., & Stark, L. (1971). Eye movements and visual perception. *Scientific American*, **224(6)**, 34–43.

Pinker, S. (1980). Mental imagery and the third dimension. *Journal of Experimental Psychology General*, **109(3)**, 354–371.

Podgorny, P., & Shepard, R. N. (1978). Functional representation common to visual perception and imagination. *Journal of Experimental Psychology, Human Perception & Performance*, **4(1)**, 21–35.

Pomerantz, J. R., Goldberg, D. M., Golder, P. S., & Tetewsky, S. (1981). Subjective contours can facilitate performance in a reaction-time task. *Perception & Psychophysics*, **29(6)**, 605–611.

Pomerantz, J. R., Sager, L. C., & Stoever, R. J. (1977). Perception of wholes and of their component parts: Some configural superiority effects. *Journal of Experimental Psychology, Human Perception & Performance* **3(3)**, 422–435.

Posner, M. I. (1980). Orienting of attention. *Quarterly Journal of Experimental Psychology*, **32**, 3–25.

Posner, M. I., Nissen, M. J., & Ogden, W. C. (1978). Attended and unattended processing modes: The role of set for spatial location. In H. L. Pick & I. J. Saltzman (Eds.), *Modes of perceiving and processing information*, pp. 137–157. Hillsdale, NJ: Erlbaum.

Potter, M. C. (1975). Meaning in visual search. *Science*, **187**, 965–966.

Rayner, K. (1978). Eye movements in reading and information processing. *Psychological Bulletin*, **85(3)**, 618–660.

Regan, D., & Beverly, K. I. (1978). Looming detectors in the human visual pathway. *Vision Research*, **18**, 209–212.

Richards, W. (1982). *How to play twenty questions with nature and win* (MIT AI Laboratory Memo No. 660). Cambridge, MA: MIT.

Richmond, B. J., & Sato, T. (1982). Visual responses of inferior temporal neurons are modified by attention to different stimuli dimensions. *Society of Neuroscience*, **8**, 812.

Riley, M. D. (1981). *The representation of image texture*. Unpublished M. Sc. thesis, MIT, Department of Electrical Engineering and Computer Science, Cambridge, MA.

Robinson, D. L., Goldberg, M. G., & Stanton, G. B. (1978). Parietal association cortex in the primate: Sensory mechanisms and behavioral modulations. *Journal of Neurophysiology*, **41(4)**, 910–932.

Rock, I., & Gutman, D. (1981). The effect of inattention on form perception. *Journal of Experimental Psychology, Human Perception & Performance*, **7(2)**, 275–285.

Rock, I., Halper, F., & Clayton, T. (1972). The perception and recognition of complex figures. *Cognitive Psychology*, **3**, 655–673.

Rumelhart, D. E. (1970). A multicomponent theory of the perception of briefly exposed visual displays. *J. Mathematical Psychology*, **7**, 191–218.

Schein, S. J., Marrocco, R. T., & De Monasterio, F. M. (1982). Is there a high concentration of color-selective cells in area V4 of monkey visual cortex? *Journal of Neurophysiology*, **47(2)**, 193–213.

Shiffrin, R. M., McKay, D. P., & Shaffer, W. O. (1976). Attending to forty-nine spatial positions at once. *Journal of Experimental Psychology, Human Perception & Performance*, **2(1)**, 14–22.

Shulman, G. L., Remington, R. W., & McLean, I. P. (1979). Moving attention through visual space. *Journal of Experimental Psychology, Human Perception & Performance*, **5**, 522–526.

Sperling, G. (1960). The information available in brief visual presentations. *Psychological Monographs*, **74** (11, Whole No. 498).

Stevens, K. A. (1978). Computation of locally parallel structure. *Biological Cybernetics*, **29**, 19–28.

Sutherland, N. S. (1968). Outline of a theory of the visual pattern recognition in animal and man. *Proceedings of the Royal Society (London)* **171**, 297–317.

Treisman, A. (1977). Focused attention in the perception and retrieval of multidimensional stimuli. *Perception & Psychophysics,* **22**, 1–11.

Treisman, A., & Gelade, G. (1980). A feature integration theory of attention. *Cognitive Psychology,* **12**, 97–136.

Tsal, Y. (1983). Movements of attention across the visual field. *Journal of Experimental Psychology: Human Perception & Performance,* **9**, 523–530.

Ullman, S. (1979). *The interpretation of visual motion.* Cambridge, MA: MIT Press.

van Voorhis, S., & Hillyard, S. A. (1977). Visual evoked potentials and selective attention to points in space. *Perception & Psychophysics,* **22(1)**, 54–62.

Varanese, J. (1983). *Abstracting spatial relations from the visual world.* Unpublished thesis, Harvard University, Boston, MA.

Winston, P. H. (1977). *Artificial intelligence.* New York: Addison-Wesley.

Wurtz, R. H., Goldberg, M. E., & Robinson, D. L. (1982). Brain mechanisms of visual attention. *Scientific American,* **246(6)**, 124–135.

Wurtz, R. H., & Mohler, C. W. (1976a). Enhancement of visual response in monkey striate cortex and frontal eye fields. *Journal of Neurophysiology,* **39**, 766–772.

Wurtz, R. H., & Mohler, C. W. (1976b). Organization of monkey superior colliculus: Enhanced visual response of superficial layer cells. *Journal of Neurophysiology,* **39(4)**, 745–765.

Zeki, S. M. (1978a). Functional specialization in the visual cortex of the rhesus monkey. *Nature,* **274**, 423–428.

Zeki, S. M. (1978b). Uniformity and diversity of structure and function in rhesus monkey prestriate visual cortex. *Journal of Physiology,* **277**, 273–290.

CHAPTER 7

Knowledge-Mediated Perception

Eugene C. Freuder

*Department of Computer Science, University of
New Hampshire, Durham, New Hampshire 03824*

I. INTRODUCTION

"It is easier to see something when you know what you are looking for." Knowledge-mediated machine vision seeks to implement this crude aphorism in its literal application to visual perception. Other forms of perception, such as speech understanding, are subject to similar approaches.

Much work in artificial intelligence is concerned with providing an analysis of such "common sense" insights, an analysis that is sufficiently detailed to permit specific application to the computer realization of intelligent behavior. The primary focus of this chapter is on the use of contextual knowledge or hypotheses to guide a computer's perceptual processing. For example, knowledge of the shape of a brick might lead a program to find an edge between interior surfaces which otherwise could easily be lost between surfaces that were "noisy" with extraneous markings or very similar in reflectance properties.

Distinctions may be made in perceptual processing between model-driven and data-driven processing, between semantics and syntax, between active and passive knowledge. Model-driven, semantic, and active knowledge processing all suggest knowledge mediation.

Model-driven processing uses expectations to guide perception. ACRONYM (Brooks, 1981) uses models of expected objects to build a prediction graph in which vertices predict image features and edges predict expected relations between features. ACRONYM has been applied to airplane identification in aerial photographs.

Semantics can reduce the space of possible interpretations permitted by syntax. Feldman and Yakimovsky (1974) used semantic model criteria to segment a scene into regions. The system iterates toward a final analysis by repeatedly erasing boundary lines; semantic knowledge is used to

219

judge which lines to remove. The system was structured so as to be able to utilize semantic expectations the system might have about e.g. the nature of the boundary between tree and sky. The system was tested on outdoor scenes and X-ray images.

Active knowledge requires knowledge to direct control. Particular knowledge obtained from partial processing interacts with general knowledge to guide further processing. The SEER system (Freuder, 1977) advocates active knowledge for visual recognition. Looking at hammers, SEER is able to use the identification of a hammer handle to suggest looking for a hammer, which in turn leads to identification of the hammer head.

We do not need high-level models like "hammer" to make the distinction between active and passive processing. Consider the following two approaches to line finding. Both operate on an image array which has been processed to reveal feature points, or suspected edge points. The first algorithm applies a function to each entry in the array, assigning it a new "strength factor" dependent on the adjoining points. This function is applied conceptually in parallel at every array element. The process is repeated several times. Lines are then defined as connected sets of feature points above a strength threshold. The idea is that the function can encourage or discourage based on the local context, and this effect can propagate (see Zucker, Hummel, & Rosenfeld, 1975). The second algorithm tracks lines through the array. Tracking along a line, it examines feature points at the end and uses the best to extend the line if it suggests the same type of edge with sufficient strength, where the strength required depends on the length of the line segment found so far. When tracking stops, the beginning of a new line is sought. Thus, the same general knowledge may be used in both models. However, only in the first does it affect the flow of control. Partial results and a general knowledge of edge models affect what happens next.

In the rest of this chapter I outline some of the issues and techniques involved in knowledge mediation, illustrating them with examples from the literature—primarily the artificial intelligence literature on computer vision. The SEER system (Freuder, 1977) is used for a disproportionate number of examples simply because I am most familiar with this work.

Note that I am not attempting a comprehensive survey of the work in this field. There are several general sources which I would like to acknowledge at the outset and suggest as good starting points for those interested in further exploration. Ballard and Brown's (1982) text on computer vision pays considerable attention to knowledge mediation. Binford (1982) surveys model-based vision systems. A good collection of workshop papers on computer vision can be found in Hanson and Riseman (1978). The proceedings (Haralick, 1982) provides an additional workshop collection. The vision papers in the Proceedings of the International Joint Conferences on Artificial Intelligence should also be consulted. The journal *Artificial Intelligence* has devoted a special issue to computer vision (Brady, 1981b), while Volume 3 of the *Handbook of Artificial Intelligence* (Barr & Feigenbaum, 1982) provides a survey of artificial intelligence work on vision, and Volume 1 (Barr & Feigenbaum, 1981) a survey of artificial intelligence work on speech understanding. The collection in Winston (1975) should also be noted. Rosenfeld (1981) provides an extensive bibliography of later work in computer picture processing.

In Section II, I discuss how the flow of control and information can permit knowledge mediation in computer perception. In Section III, I indicate how artificial intelligence knowledge structures can facilitate that flow. Section IV is a mock debate on the pros and cons of knowledge mediation, while Section V illustrates how knowledge mediation can be put to use.

II. CONTROL FLOW

The obvious flow of control and information in perceptual processing proceeds bottom-up. This type of processing is associated with data-driven, rather than model-driven, perception. The light intensity values are resolved into lines and regions, which are grouped into bodies and recognized as chairs, tables, or whatever. Roberts's (1965) pioneering vision system exhibits such a bottom-up structure. His program finds edge elements, then lines, and then matches these against stored models of polyhedral objects.

The opposite approach is, of course, top-down processing. Looking for a chair, we observe an appropriate shape and confirm the details. This type of processing clearly allows for knowledge mediation. Bolles (1977) implemented a "verification vision" system intended to operate in a highly constrained environment (e.g., an industrial assembly operation). The system has a top-down, task-oriented flavor. Training pictures were used to provide knowledge for a task such as locating a screw dispenser.

In section IV we debate the relative merits of top-down versus bottom-up—to mediate or not to mediate. We now provide some motivation by noting that as a practical matter, bottom-up processing seems to rely on success at each level. What happens if we are unable to produce a line finder guaranteed to find all the right lines? Can we avoid the "garbage in, garbage out" phenomenon? Will incorrect lines throw off a body finder and in turn invalidate recognition? Early efforts in machine vision confronted these questions, and one response was a departure from the strict bottom-up chain.

Bottom-up and top-down processing can be mixed in one system. Ballard (1976) describes a system that alternates top-down and bottom-up passes. The system detects tumors in chest radiographs, operating top-down to find lung boundaries, bottom-up to find candidate nodule sites and large tumors, and then top-down to find nodule boundaries.

Of course, the strict top-down mode begs a question: How do we get the top-level hypothesis? While we may consider special purpose, strictly top-down tasks, compromise is clearly called for. Some bottom-up processing can lead to a hypothesis which can then be pursued top-down.

Perhaps the earliest and most obvious introduction of top-down knowledge mediation involves criticizing the output of an earlier stage of processing. If the line-finder misses an interior line of a brick, a knowledge of bricks, or more generally of parallelepipeds, could lead to a suspicion that a line is indeed missing. Furthermore, this knowledge may lead to a proposal as to the presence and location of the missing line. A verifier could then proceed to try to confirm the proposal of the missing line.

Rather than searching for the "perfect" lowest-level line-finder, we might find it preferable to think in terms of a multistage process that utilizes imperfect results in conjunction with higher-level expectations to guide a second stage. Minsky and Papert (1970) report early work by Manuel Blum in recognizing how the outer profile of a blocks configuration suggests interior lines, and by Arnold Griffith in programming a system that finds some edges in a first-stage line-finding process and then uses cues such as parallelism to propose and verify further lines.

As opposed to the "fall back" mode of criticism, partial results can be used to "jump ahead" to higher-level hypotheses which can then be explored top-down. The recognition of furniture legs, for example, can suggest competing hypotheses of tables and chairs. On a smaller scale, higher-level knowledge may provide guidance for lower-level processing. Lines already found in a parallelepiped may suggest where to look next, thus short-cutting the criticize–propose–verify process.

In SEER (Freuder, 1977), a hammer handle can suggest a hammer, which can in turn lead to a search for the head. If fact, we get a kind of zig-zag processing as the system works its way up from low-level properties to high-level recognition by hypothesizing, verifying, leading to a higher-level hypothesis, and so forth.

Since individual components can both hypothesize upward when established and explore downward to become established, I regard the system as having a "middle-out" flavor (Hewitt, Bishop, & Steiger, 1973). However, a better candidate for the middle-out characterization might be the "island-driven" approach used by some speech understanding systems.

Woods (1978) describes the use of islands in SPEECHLIS and HWIM and speculates on the application of such a strategy to vision. Words can be added at the ends of an island of contiguous words, and islands can collide and combine, thus developing theories that account for portions of the utterance.

A planning process such as Kelly's (1971) generates its own contextual knowledge to guide further lower-level processing. Kelly "defocuses" to find crude edges at a coarser resolution and then uses these as a guide to finer processing to describe the edges more precisely. In contrast, a boot-strapping system such as Tenenbaum and Barrow's (1976) iterates the process of using a partial segmentation into regions as a context for further refining the segmentation.

Mackworth (1978) presents an elegant cyclic model: Cue discovery leads to model invocation, which leads to model verification, which leads to model elaboration, which leads back to cue discovery. He suggests that the top-down/bottom-up controversy may be finessed by an ongoing cyclic equilibrium. MAPSEE is presented as an implementation of that cycle (Mulder & Mackworth, 1978) It interprets sketches of geographic maps by proceeding around this cycle. Initial picture fragment cues in a tentative segmentation into chains and regions lead to interpretations which can lead to a refined segmentation.

Heterarchy removes us further from the linear bottom-up/top-down axis. Here, a community of interacting experts cooperate to accomplish a task. Minsky and Papert (1972) were early proponents of heterarchy for machine vision. The HEARSAY-II speech understanding system (Erman, Hayes-Roth, Lesser, & Reddy, 1980) has a heterarchical flavor, with its independent knowledge sources (phrase, word, segment, etc.) communicating via a "blackboard" on which hypotheses can be posted. Reddy (1978) suggests how this model can be adapted to vision.

Constraint relaxation provides a means of integrating distributed knowledge. It seeks consistency among a network of related elements by propagating adjustments throughout the network. Zucker (1978) describes a multilevel relaxation scheme that makes local line segment assertions at one level and joins the segments into lines and curves at another level. Information can flow both horizontally and vertically. Interest in relaxation was sparked by the work of Waltz (1975), who applied three-dimensional labels (e.g. convex and concave) to the lines in a line drawing. Junctions in the line drawings had a limited number of physical interpretations corresponding to line labelings circumscribed by assumptions about the physical domain being viewed, and the manner in which it was viewed. Choices for interpreting adjacent juctions had to agree along their common edge. This simple constraint propagated throughout the scene to remove interpretations unable to find consistent neighboring interpretations.

The preceding should provide some indication of how control flow can facilitate and be affected by knowledge mediation. Of course, any one system may exhibit a combination of control mechanisms.

III. KNOWLEDGE REPRESENTATION

Hierarchical structure and the lines of communication within that structure can clearly facilitate knowledge mediation. This section briefly introduces two knowledge representations which exhibit both features.

Networks are graph structures in which knowledge is attached to vertices and linked by edges. There are various useful types of networks. SEER (Freuder, 1977) uses networks to represent visual knowledge. The vertices represent objects, properties, and the like, and the edges indicate how these items help establish each other. For example, "bar-shaped region" would be linked to both "handle region" and "head region" (SEER recognizes hammers). The edges provide a natural hierarchy, from hammer down to handle and head, to bar-shaped, and so on. These edges indicate how to exploit a result (establishing bar-shaped region 17 or hypothesizing handle region 17) and how to explore a hypothesis (the handle region 17 hypothesis suggests investigating a long-and-thin region 17).

SEER employs a general knowledge network that contains abstractions such as "handle region" and a particular knowledge network that contains items related to a specific scene, such as handle region 17. The particular knowledge instantiates portions of the general knowledge network. In turn, particular results guide the investigation of appropriate portions of the general network of possibilities.

The HARPY speech understanding system (Lowerre & Reddy, 1980) employs a network that compiles phonetic, syntactic, and semantic knowledge into a single structure. A node is a template of allophones, while a sentence corresponds to a path through the network. Different allowable combinations of words, or different pronunciations of a word, lead to different paths. HARPY was able to achieve 97% accuracy in word identification in its domain, with only 42% accuracy in the phonetic segmentation of input, demonstrating the advantage of high-level knowledge about allowable word sequences.

Frames provide structured "chunks" of knowledge with slots that may be filled with "default" expectations or that may link frames together in a hierarchy. Minsky (1975) uses the example of a "room frame" in which expectations aid our visual processing on entering a room and in which subframes provide detail. Frames provide a mechanism for expressing expectations about both features (slots) and their appearance (default values). For example, a door frame might have a slot for a doorknob, with the usual mushroom-shaped default value. A cursory verification would satisfactorily recognize the doorknob in an instance of the door frame for a door opening robot, unless the presence of one of those unusual lever-shaped knobs alerted the robot to the need for a closer look.

Kuipers (1975) applied frames to blocks world recognition. As an example, he considers a scenario in which a wedge is recognized. Early evidence suggests a parallelepiped frame which can predict expected faces and junctions. A specialist looking for one type of junction on this basis complains when it finds another kind. However, the parallelepiped frame knows how to deal with this problem, causing a transition to the wedge frame.

Havens (1978) utilizes schemas linked into hierarchical network structures utilizing "composition hierarchies" to build complex concepts out of more primitive ones. Havens utilizes procedural attachment to link appropriate recognition methods to the schemes. Havens combines top-down and bottom-up processing. Top-down methods seeking recognition of a schema instance can invoke subschema efforts as subgoals.

Other representation schemes which might be of interest to psychologists include the embedding of semantic knowledge in long-term memory (Levine & Shaheen, 1981) and in "production rules" (Tsuji & Nakano, 1981).

IV. TO MEDIATE OR NOT TO MEDIATE

I now attempt to illustrate some of the issues surrounding knowledge mediation by presenting a debate between a proponent (PRO) and opponent (CON) of knowledge mediation.

PRO: Low-level processes cannot in general obtain results sufficient for proper high-level processing merely from light intensities. Higher-level guidance is needed at the lower levels.

CON: Maybe your lower level, for example, your line-finder, needs help, but that is no reason to say that the job cannot be done. Rather than looking to high-level knowledge for help, you should look harder at the low-level problem. Decisions should not be based on the deficiencies of any particular system, but on fundamental features of the visual process.

PRO: That is all very nice, but suppose I am less concerned with the fundamental nature of vision than I am with building a working vision system. What is wrong with using high-level help to bridge a current impasse, even if it may ultimately prove possible to bridge without high-level intervention? And is it possible? Of course, you put me in a difficult position, trying to prove a negative. How can I say that you will not discover a suitable line-finder? On the other hand, let us take an extreme case: Consider a brick whose surface and illumination properties are such as to leave no actual sensory cues to the presence of one of the interior lines. A vision system should still be able to recognize the brick.

CON: Yes, but the high-level recognizer can match the imperfect line drawing without directing low-level efforts, which in any event would be fruitless here.

PRO: Suppose that high-level knowledge about parallelepipeds led to insertion of the missing line?

CON: What? Are you making a psychological distinction now in the "mental state" of the machine? Are you asking whether it "sees" the missing line, or merely copes with its absence? You know, there is a story that an early line-finder was subject to the Müller–Lyer illusion. It was a line-*follower* and got confused by the "barbs" when following a line into an arrow head configuration, causing it to stop and fix the end point sooner than when following a line into a Y-shaped junction. No higher-level explanations needed.

PRO: Well, we are getting a bit far afield. Suppose that the line in question is present in the sensory data, but faint. A line-finder that looks . . . hard enough . . . might find all sorts of other faint scratches and artifacts as lines." Is this not a basic dilemma?

CON: A higher-level routine might still make sense of this input without needing to influence low-level processing, even supposing that a suitably clever lower level could not be made to distinguish. But let me raise a more fundamental issue. Suppose that line finding cannot be accomplished in a satisfactory fashion based on the changes in light intensity in a general image. Has it occurred to you that asking for lines and objects at this point may be a case of asking the wrong questions at the wrong time? Perhaps what we need to ask for at this stage is some form of intermediate surface representation like Marr's 2½-dimensional sketch.

PRO: You accuse me of machine psychoanalysis, but you give me machine philosophy. Asking the wrong questions, am I? Are you not just postponing the inevitable?

CON: The point is to avoid doing things that may later have to be undone—Marr's "principal of least commitment" (1976). At the right time, we may have sufficient information available to make the decision properly, based on the output of the previous level, without making large leaps across levels that later have to be backtracked.

PRO: But why not make those leaps? Commitment can be an advantage. The conservative comprehensive processing at each level can be too exhausting. By not committing, we are forced to carry along and further process the information needed for every alternative. Marr (1978) uses general constraints implied by the nature of three-dimensional space. Why not utilize constraints imposed by a more specific context, if one exists or can be hypothesized?

CON: That is an intrusion on the nature of the visual process. I want to study the true computational nature of vision and its interplay with real-world constraints.

PRO: There you go again. Let us concentrate for the moment on building a computer vision system. My way is more flexible and efficient. Specialized processes can be used where needed and when appropriate, and context can indicate how thorough an investigation needs to be or how best to conduct it.

CON: Yes, but all of this hypothesizing and potential backtracking can be expensive too. How do you efficiently control this process in a general context? Can you show me any extensive computer implementations of knowledge-directed processing in a rich environment involving a great variety of possible objects? Fancy systems can be cumbersome.

PRO: Problems of appropriate representation, retrieval, and control of large-scale bodies of knowledge are central to artificial intelligence. In fact, you're making my point for me. These are the problems we should be attacking, rather than devoting all our attention to understanding specific visual processes. You may also depend on something you do not really have yet—namely, special purpose parallel visual hardware.

CON: If we are studying perceptual processing, why should we be denied a natural hardware context? You're trying to get something for nothing. You can't understand basic perceptual issues, so you present a grand "system" control structure to finesse your basic ignorance. It's one thing to provide subtle means of communication and control, and to provide an example or two; it's another matter to actually have substantial visual knowledge to communicate or control. Systems are not panaceas. You shouldn't start with a system architecture and then try to fit in the pieces. You should begin with a deep understanding of individual aspects of the visual process and develop appropriate representations for your knowledge. Artificial intelligence sometimes starts with a solution that is sophisticated in its control structure, then discovers that greater knowledge of the domain can substitute for search and control. Witness Moses' (1967) work on symbolic integration, as compared with Slagle's (1963).

PRO: There is room for abuse in your approach as well. There is a danger in concentrating on individual modules of the visual system: The interactions may be nonlinear. When it comes time to put the results together into a system, you may experience a revival of ideas like heterarchy. The framework is not enough; we need the pieces to flesh it out.

But the parts without the means to integrate them into a whole will not do either. I seem to remember a story about an installation where they constructed the building and the equipment to run in it separately and then discovered that the equipment would not fit in the building. Furthermore, it may be important to take interaction and mediation into account when studying the modules. They may not be best understood in isolation. In particular, they may be designed to work within a high-level context. Imagine pulling a single piston out of an engine and saying, "What does this do? It goes up and down fast. Well, to build a good one must involve simply building the fastest one we can; then we'll stick it back in the engine and get improved performance.

CON: Well, machine philosophy is better than auto mechanics! What evidence do you have that we can't get along without all that?

PRO: There you go asking me to prove a negative again. Isn't it obvious that some degree of high-level intervention occurs in the perceptual process? Context, expectations, and goals influence what we perceive and how we perceive it—where we focus our attention. Knowledge influences how well we perceive. Nusbaum (1982) provides an amusing and practical example: He wrote to a popular computing magazine to caution potential purchasers of computer speech synthesizers that simply typing in text and listening to the result was not a fair test. The device will sound intelligible when you know its "script" beforehand, but without prior expectation, intelligibility may suffer. Woods (1978) cites evidence for the ambiguity and insufficiency of acoustic evidence alone for speech understanding. The HEARSAY-I speech understanding system was run utilizing different combinations of its knowledge sources. Adding syntax knowledge to phonetics and lexicon knowledge improved performance 25%, while adding semantics knowledge led to another 25% improvement (Lea, 1980). Indeed, I dare say that the typist who produced the manuscript for this chapter would have had considerable difficulty recognizing the letters to type had it not been for context. My unscientific observations suggest that unfamiliar technical jargon is more prone to secretarial typing problems.

CON: Marr (1976) has shown that a good deal of initial visual processing can be carried out with higher-level knowledge playing only a very restricted role; downward-flowing information does not affect his computation of a "primal sketch" at all. You can't just "see what you expect to see," or you will hallucinate. Surely you will admit that some amount of initial sensory processing is domain-independent, free of . . . semantic . . . intervention.

PRO: Perhaps, but as little as possible, and even then semantic considerations might then go back and modify even these levels, or else direct additional processing. We must be very willing to use the partial results we obtain to influence further processing. To use those results, we must be willing to see what they suggest when allowed to interact with semantic knowledge that describes or constrains the completed contexts into which these partial results may fit. Verification will avoid hallucination.

CON: Are you saying that general knowledge about types of surfaces can guide our development of surface descriptors, or are you saying that we find a horse's leg and speculate that a horse must be attached to it? I find the former more plausible, but is it knowledge mediation or just old-fashioned knowledge use?

PRO: I am not sure it is fair for you to deny me the satisfaction of knowledge mediation as soon as the model being applied becomes sufficiently general, but let us go in the other direction. Suppose that we know we are looking at horses, or at pictures of forest formations in aerial photographs. Surely we can use context in such specific applications to provide more efficient or successful processing?

CON: Well, you're not going to like this, but I find an extremely specific single given context difficult to appreciate as knowledge mediation either. It may be knowledge-directed, but there is really no need to "mediate" in a foregone conclusion. At any rate, this sort of example can cut both ways. A very specific situation may simply a bottom-up approach—for example, a highly constrained industrial environment. The higher-level expectations may be "compiled" into the lower-level processing. It is not a matter of consulting alternatives but of utilizing a given. The extreme would be template matching. Would you call that knowledge-mediated?

PRO: The highly constrained approach that you're describing is inflexible and insensitive to variations, subtleties, or errors.

CON: But it might work in situations sufficiently constrained, naturally or artificially. Were you not the one who was interested in just building a working system?

PRO: Well, I am interested in generality, and in the robustness that knowledge mediation can provide over a blind lockstep approach. Also, I am interested in exploring advanced representation and control structures. Vision provides a useful domain. Why, then, can't these structures model human visual processing?

CON: The problem is that you start with an axe to grind, a new toy like "heterarchy" or "frames" to use, and try to fit vision into it rather than determining what the real visual constraints are.

PRO: Well, I admit there may have been excesses. It is possible to have a top-heavy system with a lot of control machinery and not enough to control. But you should not give up on knowledge mediation too early, any more than I should give up on low-level competence too soon. I grant people have come back for another look, as it were, at basic visual processing and description, and have made great strides at enriching our understanding at that level. But we should also look deeper into the use of knowledge mediation. The growing interest in three-dimensional representations may help. At any rate, how can we say that the potential for knowledge mediation has been fully tapped?

Moderator: Of course, the classic method of moderating a dispute is through compromise. In SEER (Freuder, 1977), I point out that control is neither top-down or bottom-up, but zigzag. A result suggested an hypothesis from below, which sought verification by proceeding back down. Individual modules could suggest further work in either direction, to verify or exploit themselves. I regard this as a compromise between a bottom-up system that could not take advantage of context and a top-down one that could direct computations efficiently in accord with a top-level hypothesis but that begged the question of how to arrive at that hypothesis in a general system. Of course, SEER would not look like a compromise to an opponent of top-down knowledge mediation. The program SEER attempted to explore the usefulness of knowledge mediation rather than the extent to which visual processing could proceed without it.

Mackworth (1978) refers to the "chicken and egg" problems of scene analysis. How can we segment a scene without interpreting it, or interpret it without segmenting it? Again, the obvious approach is to try to integrate bottom-up and top-down, data-driven and model-driven processing. If we do so cleverly enough the distinctions between top-down and bottom-up may even begin to blur. Mackworths's "cyclic" model, discussed briefly earlier, is one such approach. SEER treated its combination of exploration and exploitation knowledge as neither purely top-down nor bottom-up, but more "middle-out."

Binford (1982) emphasizes that prediction–hypothesis–verification need not involve great leaps from extreme ends of the visual process. Rather, hypothesis–prediction–verification "loops" can relate primarily nearby levels in a multilevel hierarchy of rich geometric description. Such loops are viewed as both bottom-up and top-down. The relative strength of contextual information versus visual data can affect the top-down versus bottom-up aspect of the system.

I seem to recall some years ago Patrick Winston at MIT pointing to an unfortunate "hourglass" shape in vision systems. I have felt it important to work on expanding that interface between high- and low-level processing. The current work on intermediate levels of representation may overcome the bottle neck, not by dropping better communication lines through it, but by interposing wide, rich layers of intermediate description to produce more of a "cylindrical" system. Nevertheless, especially when sensory data are weak or context strong, we may want to allow the higher echelons to communicate directly with the lower orders, hence cutting out some of the intermediate levels of bureaucracy.

I have touted SEER as a "community of interacting experts," after ideas of Minksy, Papert, and Hewitt. This "bureaucratic" model, motivated by Marr and Binford, is less exciting but perhaps more realistic. In this model, processing proceeds in comprehensive, parallel fashion, establishing a series of rich descriptive layers and utilizing conservative contextual hypotheses when required.

On the other hand, while additional descriptive richness is rather an "apple pie and motherhood" issue, one might still argue that a fundamental problem in vision is that there is too much redundant information available. Visual input is two-dimensional, unlike speech, so that the focus of attention becomes an issue. We can compute all features uniformly across the image at successive homogeneous levels, perhaps adducing massive parallelism. However, possibly some mechanism, such as active knowledge, can still prove appropriate for combing partial results with general knowledge to selectively guide processing through this rich domain. Indeed, the work by Hrechanyk and Ballard (1982) seems to me to be reintroducing active knowledge network ideas to focus sequential attention within an overall "connectionist" context of massive parallelism.

Well, the moderator is beginning to show his bias . . . .

V. KNOWLEDGE MEDIATION PUT TO USE

I once posed the question (Freuder, 1976) of where to use passive knowledge versus active knowledge. I argued for the extensive use of active knowledge but by no means considered the issue resolved. In editing a compendium of work on computer vision, Brady (1981a) lists as a still unresolved issue the nature of the involvement of domain-specific knowledge in visual processing.

While I cannot pretend to resolve such questions here, I can suggest some of the ways in which knowledge mediation may be of use in perceptual processing.

I have presented rather a paean to the potential of knowledge mediation in the context of the SEER active knowledge system (Freuder, 1976). Of course, given the limited practical application and testing of the SEER system, these advantages could best be regarded as something of a "shopping list" of hoped-for benefits: Knowledge mediation can take advantage of useful interactions in our knowledge base that can then guide processing. It permits a flexible response, appropriate to a specific scene. Phe-

nomena can be established in different ways—specifically, how hard we
look and how easily we are convinced may depend on context. Special
techniques can be applied within hypothesized contexts, given previous
results; multiple cases can be handled with multiple methods; and suggestions and advice can be provided by general and particular acquired
knowledge.

Filtering upward, seeking the "winning line," we can avoid unneces-
sary observations, focusing on success. Success-driven priorities can decide in which order we should tackle tasks. Flexibility in processing sequences permits the system to respond to the variety of reality. Aspects
of a scene which are easy to recognize, which stand out in some way, can
be identified first and quickly and can help to avoid or facilitate some
further processing. Combinatorial explosion can be ameliorated, since we
are not always computing all possibilities at all levels. In some sense, a
program can be tailored to the context. Rather than trying to develop
perfect methods sufficiently general as to encompass the great variety of
sensory input, we can direct the application of special purpose, special
case techniques.

Now let us see some more specific examples. Knowledge mediation can
help us answer basic "what" and "how" questions.

The HEARSAY-I speech understanding system (Reddy, Erman, Fennell, & Neely, 1976), in determining *what* to look for, operating in a
machine versus human chess playing environment, went so far as to use
the legal move generator of its chess program to suggest likely moves by
the human player, so that they could be looked for in the player's statement of his move.

In Shirai's line-finding system (Shirai, 1975), general knowledge of
polyhedral shapes combines with partial results to suggest *how* to look,
including *where* to look. Contour and boundary lines, generally easier to
find than internal edges, are sought first. There are ten heuristic line-
proposing steps. For example, consider a point along a boundary at which
two lines form a concave junction, expect that one body may be occluding
another. Look for straight extensions of the two lines into the bounded
region. If only one such extension is found, track along it, using a line-
tracker. In another example, a "circular search" technique is used to
cope with an internal line that does not connect at one end to any other
line. The circular search is used to seek lines leading on from the end
which can then be tracked.

Related questions can involve how hard to look, how much evidence to
require in a given context, when to be suspicious and propose looking
again, how to interpret or disambiguate results, how to proceed, which
questions to ask (in which order), what to ignore, and what to deduce.

The line-labeling scheme proposed in (1980) is an interesting case. To determine the three-dimensional interpretation of lines corresponding to edges in a scene, it is suggested that sensory probes (e.g., with a range-finder) alternate with deduction based on knowledge of which three-dimensional label combinations are possible in a specified domain. Thus, determining that a given edge is convex may allow us to deduce the convexity or concavity of a number of other edges, "without looking." When the deductive process is stuck, an appropriate "peek" at the scene can get it rolling again. By compiling all possible legitimate utterances in its domain into a network, the HARPY speech understanding system (Lowerre & Reddy, 1980), constrains the search process, in a sense telling the system what *not* to look for.

SEER (Freuder, 1976) provides a specific implementation of "what" and "how" in the form of mechanisms to provide "suggestions" and "advice." The links in the general knowledge network described earlier allow an established fact to construct and initiate conjectures like "hammer-handle region 17." Conjectures can be encouraged by "resuggestion" from other sources. Hypotheses can also initiate conjectures in attempting to establish themselves. "What to look for" and "what to look at" correspond to the predicate and arguments in a suggestion. Advice is implemented by suggesting a specific method for doing something. For example, finding a hammer head proposes a specific method for finding the handle.

I conclude with my original inspiration—that it is easier to see something if you know what you are looking for. Working down in context to verify knowledge-based hypotheses, we can employ special methods. We can ask, "Is x this shape?" rather than "What shape is x?" If the shape is symmetric we can take advantage of that fact. Region segmentation can be guided by interpretation, and we can generate regions that meet our hypothesized requirements. We can see only what we "need" to see. Extraneous details need not be "perceived."

SEER has several methods for finding hammer handles. When the hammer head has been found already, it suggests a method based on a program developed by Lozano-Perez (1975) which looks for regions with specified intensity profiles. This program needs to be told where to look and what to look for; it requires a starting point, a direction in which to look, and a specification of the type of light intensity profile to look for. Having found the hammer head, and knowing the expected relationship between head and handle, SEER can suggest where to look. Knowing that it is looking for a hammer handle, and knowing the characteristic curved profile across the width of a hammer handle, SEER can suggest what to look for. This specialized technique is thus able to return a region that a few additional checks can ensure will serve as the hammer handle.

Knowledge mediation can answer many questions. However, it poses many questions as well—intriguing questions about its proper role in the perceptual process. This chapter ends on that questioning note.

REFERENCES

Ballard, D. H. (1976). *Hierarchic recognition of tumors in chest radiographs.* Basel, Switzerland: Birkhauser-Verlag (ISR-16).

Ballard, D. H., & Brown, C. M. (1982). *Computer vision.* Englewood Cliffs, NJ: Prentice-Hall.

Barr, B. A., & Feigenbaum, E. A. (1981). *The handbook of artificial intelligence* (Vol. 1). Los Altos, CA: William Kaufman.

Barr, A., & Feigenbaum, E. A. (1982). *The handbook of artificial intelligence* (Vol. 3). Los Altos, CA: William Kaufman.

Binford, T. O. (1982). Survey of model-based image analysis systems. *The International Journal of Robotics Research, 1* (1).

Bolles, R. C. (1977). Verification vision for programmable assembly. *Proceedings of the Fifth International Joint Conference on Artificial Intelligence, 2,* 569–575.

Brady, J. M. (1981a). Preface—The changing shape of computer vision. *Artificial Intelligence, 17,* 1–15.

Brady, J. M. (Ed.), (1981b). Special volume on computer vision. *Artificial Intelligence, 17.*

Brooks, R. A. (1981). Model-based three-dimensional interpretations of two-dimensional images. *Proceedings of the Seventh International Joint Conference on Artificial Intelligence, 2,* 619–624.

Erman, L. D., Hayes-Roth, F., Lesser, V. R., & Reddy, D. R. (1980). The HEARSAY-II speech understanding system: Integrating knowledge to resolve uncertainty. *Computing Surveys, 12,* 213–253.

Feldman, J. A., & Yakimovsky, Y. (1974). Decision theory and artificial intelligence: I. A semantics-based region analyzer. *Artificial Intelligence, 5,* 349–371.

Freuder, E. C. (1976). *A computer system for visual recognition using active knowledge* (Research Rep. No. AI-TR-345). Cambridge, MA: MIT AI Laboratory.

Freuder, E. C. (1977). A computer system for visual recognition using active knowledge. *Proceedings of the Fifth International Joint Conference on Artificial Intelligence, 2,* 671–677.

Freuder, E. C. (1980). On the knowledge required to label a picture graph. *Artificial Intelligence, 15,* 1–17.

Hanson, A. R., & Riseman, E. M. (Eds.), (1978). *Computer vision systems.* New York: Academic Press.

Haralick, R. M. (Ed.) (1982). *Proceedings of the workshop on computervision: Representation and control.* Silver Springs, MD: IEEE Computer Society Press.

Havens, W. S. (1978). A procedural model of recognition for machine perception. *Proceedings of the Second National Conference of the Canadian Society for Computational Studies of Intelligence,* 254–262.

Hewitt, C., Bishop, P., & Steiger, R. (1973). A universal modular *actor* formalism for artificial intelligence. *Proceedings of the Third International Joint Conference on Artificial Intelligence.* Hrechanyk, L. M., & Ballard, D. H. (1982). A connectionist model of form perception. *Proceedings of the workshop on computer vision: Representation and control.* Silver Springs, MD: IEEE Computer Society Press.

Kelley, M. D. (1971). Edge detection in pictures by computer using planning. In B. Meltzer & D. Michie (Eds.), *Machine intelligence* (Vol. 6), pp. 397–409. New York: American Elsevier.

Kuipers, B. J. (1975). A frame for frames: Representing knowledge for recognition. In D. G. Bobrow & A. Collins (Eds.), *Representation and understanding,* pp. 151–184. New York: Academic Press.

Lea, W. (1980). Speech recognition: Past, present, and future. In W. Lea (Ed.), *Trends in speech recognition,* pp. 39–89. Englewood Cliffs, NJ: Prentice-Hall.

Levine, M. D., & Shaheen, S. I. (1981). A modular computer vision system for picture segmentation and interpretation. *IEEE Transactions on Pattern Analysis and Machine Intelligence,* **PAMI-3,** 540–556.

Lowerre, B., & Reddy, R. (1980). The HARPY speech understanding system. In W. Lea (Ed.), *Trends in speech recognition,* pp. 340–360. Englewood Cliffs, NJ: Prentice-Hall.

Lozano-Perez, T. (1975). *Parsing intensity profiles* (AI Memo No. 329). Cambridge, MA: MIT AI Laboratory.

Mackworth, A. K. (1978). Vision research strategy: Black magic, metaphors, mechanisms, miniworlds and maps. In A. R. Hanson & E. M. Riseman (Eds.), *Computer vision systems,* pp. 53–59. New York: Academic Press.

Marr, D. (1976). Early processing of visual information. *Philosophical Transactions of the Royal Society of London (Series B),* **275,** 483–524.

Marr, D. (1978). Representing visual information. In A. R. Hanson & E. M. Riseman (Eds.), *Computer vision systems,* pp. 61–80. New York: Academic Press.

Minsky, M. A. (1975). A framework for representing knowledge. In P. H. Winston (Ed.), *The psychology of computer vision,* pp. 211–277. New York: McGraw-Hill.

Minsky, M., & Papert, S. (1970). *1968–1969 progress report* (AI Memo No. 200). Cambridge, MA: MIT AI Laboratory.

Minsky, M., & Papert, S. (1972). *Artificial intelligence progress report* (AI Memo No. 252), Cambridge, MA: MIT AI Laboratory.

Moses, J. (1967). *Symbolic integration* (Research Rep. No. MAC-TR-47). Cambridge, MA: MIT, Project MAC.

Mulder, J. A., & Mackworth, A. K. (1978). Using multi-level semantics to understand sketches of houses and other polyhedral objects. *Proceedings of the Second National Conference of the Canadian Society for Computational Studies of Intelligence,* 244–253.

Nusbaum, H. C. (1982). The Votrax Type-'N-Talk: Eyes vs. ears. *Popular Computing,* **1(12),** 14–15.

Reddy, D. R. (1978). Pragmatic aspects of machine vision. In A. R. Hanson & E. M. Riseman (Eds.), *Computer vision systems.* New York: Academic Press.

Reddy, D. R., Erman, L. D., Fennell, R. D., & Neely, R. B. (1976). The HEARSAY speech understanding system: An example of the recognition process. *IEEE Transactions on Computers,* **C-25,** 427–431.

Roberts, L. (1965). Machine perception of three-dimensional solids. In J. Tippett (Ed.), *Optical and electro-optical information processing,* pp. 159–197. Cambridge, MA: MIT Press.

Rosenfeld, A. (1981). Picture processing: 1980. *Computer Graphics and Image Processing,* **16,** 52–89.

Shirai, Y. (1975). Analyzing intensity arrays using knowledge about scenes. In P. H. Winston (Ed.), *The psychology of computer vision*, pp. 93–113. New York: McGraw-Hill.

Slagle, J. R. (1963). A heuristic program that solves symbolic integration programs in freshman calculus. In E. A. Feigenbaun, & J. Feldman (Eds.), *Computers and thought*, pp. 191–203. New York: McGraw-Hill.

Tenenbaum, J. M., & Barrow, H. G. (1976). IGS: A paradigm for integrating image segmentation and interpretation. In C. H. Chen (Ed.), *Pattern recognition and artificial intelligence*, pp. 472–507. New York: Academic Press.

Tsuji, S., & Nakano, H. (1981). Knowledge-based identification of artery branches in cineangiograms. *Proceedings of the Seventh International Joint Conference on Artificial Intelligence*, **2**, 710–715.

Waltz, D. (1975). Understanding line drawings of scenes with shadows. In P. H. Winston (Ed.), *The psychology of computer vision*, pp. 19–91. New York: McGraw-Hill.

Winston, P. H. (Ed.) (1975). *The psychology of computer vision*. New York: McGraw-Hill.

Woods, W. A. (1978). Theory formation and control in a speech understanding system with extrapolations toward vision. In A. R. Hanson & E. M. Riseman (Eds.), *Computer vision systems* pp. 379–390. New York: Academic Press.

Zucker, S. W. (1978). Low-level vision, consistency, and continuous relaxation. *Proceedings of the Second National Conference of the Canadian Society for the Computational Studies of Intelligence*, 107–116.

Zucker, S. W., Hummel, R., & Rosenfeld, A. (1975). *Applications of relaxation labelling, 1: Line and curve enhancement* (Tech. Rep. No. TR-419). Baltimore: University of Maryland, Computer Science Center.

Index